Drawn from the documentary history of emancipation that has been described as "this generation's most significant encounter with the American past," *Slaves No More* brings together three essays on the destruction of slavery and the redefinition of freedom in the midst of the nation's bloodiest conflict. Each of the essays addresses a central question in the study of the Civil War. How did slaves gain their freedom? What did freedom mean? How did wartime military service reshape the lives of black Americans? Emphasizing the active role of slaves and former slaves in remaking a war for the Union into a war for freedom, these essays demonstrate that emancipation transformed the lives of all Americans, white and black. American history would never be the same once there were slaves no more.

SLAVES NO MORE

SLAVES NO MORE

THREE ESSAYS ON EMANCIPATION
AND
THE CIVIL WAR

IRA BERLIN
BARBARA J. FIELDS
STEVEN F. MILLER
JOSEPH P. REIDY
LESLIE S. ROWLAND

CAMBRIDGE
UNIVERSITY PRESS

Published by the Press Syndicate of the University of Cambridge
The Pitt Building, Trumpington Street, Cambridge CB2 1RP
40 West 20th Street, New York, NY 10011-4211, USA
10 Stamford Road, Oakleigh, Melbourne 3166, Australia

© Cambridge University Press 1992

First published 1992
Reprinted 1993 (twice)

Printed in the United States of America

Library of Congress Cataloging-in-Publication Data is available.

A catalogue record for this book is available from the British Library,

ISBN 0-521-43102-6 hardback
ISBN 0-521-43692-3 paperback

For

Jeremiah G. Anderson
Osborn P. Anderson
John Brown
Oliver Brown
Owen Brown
Watson Brown
John E. Cook
John A. Copeland
Barclay Coppoc
Edwin Coppoc
Shields Green
Albert Hazlett
John H. Kagi
Lewis S. Leary
William H. Leeman
Francis J. Merriam
Dangerfield Newby
Aaron D. Stevens
Stewart Taylor
Dauphin Thompson
William Thompson
Charles P. Tidd

Who Risked All at Harper's Ferry
October 16, 1859

Contents

vii

Introduction

No event in American history matches the drama of emancipation. More than a century later, it continues to stir the deepest emotions. And properly so. Emancipation in the American South accompanied the military defeat of the world's most powerful slaveholding class. It freed a larger number of slaves than did the end of slavery in all other New World societies combined. Clothed in the rhetoric of biblical prophecy and national destiny and born of a bloody civil war, it accomplished a profound social revolution. That revolution destroyed forever a way of life based upon the ownership of human beings, restoring to the former slaves proprietorship of their own persons, liquidating without compensation private property valued at billions of dollars, and forcibly substituting the relations of free labor for those of slavery. In designating the former slaves as citizens, emancipation placed citizenship upon new ground, defined in the federal Constitution and removed beyond the jurisdiction of the states. By obliterating the sovereignty of master over slave, it handed a monopoly of sovereignty to the newly consolidated nation-state. The freeing of the slaves simultaneously overturned the old regime of the South and set the entire nation upon a new course.

With emancipation in the South, the United States enacted its part in a world-wide drama. Throughout the western world and beyond, the forces unleashed by the American and French revolutions and by the industrial revolution worked to undermine political regimes based upon hereditary privilege and economic systems based upon bound labor. Slavery had already succumbed in the Northern states and in the French and British Caribbean before the American Civil War, and it would shortly do so in its remaining strongholds in Spanish and Portuguese America. Almost simultaneously with the great struggle in the United States, the vestiges of serfdom in central and eastern Europe yielded to the pressure of the age. Only small pockets in Africa and Asia remained immune, and their immunity was temporary. The fateful lightning announced by the victorious Union army was soon to strike, if it had not already struck, wherever men and women remained in bonds of personal servitude.

For all systems of bondage, emancipation represented the acid test, the moment of truth. The upheaval of conventional expectations stripped away the patina of routine, exposing the cross purposes and warring intentions that had simmered – often unnoticed – beneath the surface of the old order. In throwing off habitual restraints, freedpeople redesigned their lives in ways that spoke eloquently of their hidden life in bondage, revealing clandestine institutions, long-cherished beliefs, and deeply held values. In confronting new restraints, they abandoned their usual caution in favor of direct speech and yet more direct action. Lords and serfs, masters and slaves had to survey the new social boundaries without the old etiquette of dominance and subordination as a guide. Their efforts to do so led to confrontations that could be awkward, painful, and frequently violent. The continued force of these encounters awakened men and women caught up in the drama to the realization that their actions no longer ratified old, established ways, but set radically new precedents for themselves and for future generations.

Moments of revolutionary transformation expose as do few human events the foundation upon which societies rest. Although those who enjoy political power and social authority speak their minds and indulge their inclinations freely and often, their subordinates generally cannot. Only in the upheaval of accustomed routine can the lower orders give voice to the assumptions that guide their world as it is and as they wish it to be. Some of them quickly grasp the essence of the new circumstance. Under the tutelage of unprecedented events, ordinary men and women become extraordinarily perceptive and articulate, seizing the moment to challenge the assumptions of the old regime and proclaim a new social order. Even then, few take the initiative. Some – perhaps most – simply try to maintain their balance, to reconstitute a routine, to maximize gains and minimize losses as events swirl around them. But inevitably they too become swept up in the revolutionary process. Barely conscious acts and unacknowledged motives carried over from the past take on a changed significance. Attempts to stand still or turn back only hasten the process forward. At revolutionary moments, all actions – those of the timid and reluctant as much as those of the bold and eager – expose to view the inner workings of society.

Because they allow for such full inspection, revolutionary transformations have long occupied scholars seeking to solve the mysteries of human society. Students of the American past have been drawn to the Civil War and Reconstruction for precisely this reason. Perhaps no period of American history has a fuller and more complex historiography, as scholars of all ideological persuasions have tried to comprehend the meaning of emancipation, for themselves and for posterity.

The Freedmen and Southern Society Project, a collaborative research enterprise at the University of Maryland, was established to write a documentary history of the transition from slavery to freedom in the American South. Drawing upon the unparalleled documentary holdings of the National Archives of the United States, the editors sought a fuller understanding of the process by which men and women moved from the utter dependence slaveholders demanded but never fully received, to the independence freedpeople desired but seldom attained. In the fall of 1976, the editors launched a systematic search of the archives. Over the course of the next three years, members of the project – including three of the present authors – selected and photocopied more than 40,000 items, representing perhaps 2 percent of the documents they examined. Subsequent research by graduate assistants added about 10,000 documents to the initial collection. Indexed and cross-referenced topically, chronologically, and geographically, this selection constitutes the project's documentary universe.

The Civil War brought ordinary Americans into contact with central-state authority as never before. During the conflict, both the Union and Confederate governments organized soldiers and laborers, mobilized material resources, fought battles, levied taxes, and confiscated property; the Union eventually emancipated slaves. After the war, federal agencies figured prominently in the reconstruction of the South's economy and society. The records created and collected by the Union and Confederate governments and now housed in the National Archives provide an unrivaled source for understanding the passage of black people from slavery to freedom. Such governmental units as the Colored Troops Division of the Adjutant General's Office; the American Freedmen's Inquiry Commission; the U.S. army at every level of command, from the headquarters in Washington to local army posts; army support organizations, including the Judge Advocate General's Office, the Provost Marshal General's Bureau, and the Quartermaster General's Office, and their subordinates in the field; the Civil War Special Agencies of the Treasury Department; individual regiments of U.S. Colored Troops; various branches of the Confederate government (whose records fell into Union hands at the conclusion of the war); the Southern Claims Commission; the Freedman's Bank; and, most important, the Bureau of Refugees, Freedmen, and Abandoned Lands all played a role in the coming of freedom.

The missions of these agencies placed them in close contact with a wide variety of men and women, and their bureaucratic structure provided a mechanism for the preservation of many documents by and about people generally dismissed as historically mute. Alongside official reports in the archival files, hundreds of letters and statements by former slaves give voice to people whose aspirations, beliefs, and behavior have gone largely unrecorded. Not only did extraordinary numbers of former slaves, many of them newly literate, put pen to paper in the early years of freedom, but hundreds of others, entirely illiterate, gave depositions to government officials, placed their marks on resolutions passed at mass meetings, testified before courts-martial and Freedmen's Bureau courts, and dictated letters to more literate black men and women and to white officials and teachers. The written record thus created constitutes an unparalleled outpouring from people caught up in the revolutionary process of emancipation. Many of these documents requested official action to redress wrongs committed by powerful former slaveholders who only reluctantly recognized ex-slaves as free, rarely as equal. Others, however, originated in relationships entirely outside the purview of either federal officials or former masters and employers. They include, for example, correspondence between black soldiers and their families and between kinfolk who had been separated during slavery. That such letters fell for various reasons into the bureaucratic net of government agencies (and thus were preserved along with official records) should not obscure their deeply personal origins.

These documents convey, perhaps as no historian can, the experiences of the liberated: the quiet personal satisfaction of meeting an old master on equal terms, as well as the outrage of ejection from a segregated streetcar; the elation of a fugitive enlisting in the Union army, and the humiliation of a laborer cheated out of hard-earned wages; the joy of a family reunion after years of forced separation, and the distress of having a child involuntarily apprenticed to a former owner; the hope that freedom would bring a new world, and the fear that, in so many ways, life would be much as before. Other documents offer insight into the diverse reactions of planters, Union officers, and Southern yeomen – men and women who faced emancipation with different interests and expectations. Taken together, the records now housed in the National Archives provide exceptionally full documentation of the destruction of a dependent social relationship, the release of a people from their dependent status, and the simultaneous transformation of an entire society. As far as is known, no comparable record exists for the liberation of any group of serfs or slaves or for the transformation of any people into wage-workers.

The mandate of the Freedmen and Southern Society Project is to make these documents accessible to all those interested in the history of emancipation. It is fulfilling its mission by publishing a multivolume edition entitled *Freedom: A Documentary History of Emancipation, 1861– 1867.* In constructing each volume, the editors must pick and choose from among millions of letters, reports, depositions, and statistical compilations, knowing that although the documents speak eloquently, they do so in many different voices and from many different vantage points. The task of selecting, transcribing, and annotating the archival record of emancipation is thus no different for the project's historians than for other scholars using the same records: to select those documents that best explain the transition from slavery to freedom. But even the most forthright document tells only part of the story, and for that reason, the editors introduce each volume of *Freedom* with an interpretive essay. Originally designed to provide historical context and to mediate between the documents and the secondary literature, the introductory essays have themselves become a history of emancipation during the Civil War. Like the volumes of which they are a part, the essays address a central question of the human experience: how men and women strive to enlarge their freedom and secure their independence from those who would dominate their lives.

The Freedmen and Southern Society Project now stands at its half-way point. During the past decade, four volumes of *Freedom* have reached print. *The Destruction of Slavery* explicates the process by which slavery collapsed under the pressure of federal arms and the slaves' determination to place their own liberty on the wartime agenda. In documenting the transformation of a war for the Union into a war against slavery, it shifts the focus from the halls of power in Washington and Richmond to the plantations, farms, and battlefields of the South and demonstrates how slaves accomplished their own liberation and shaped the destiny of the nation.

The Wartime Genesis of Free Labor: The Upper South and *The Wartime Genesis of Free Labor: The Lower South* consider the evolution of freedom in Union-occupied areas of the South. Describing the experiences of former slaves as military laborers, residents of government-sponsored "contraband camps," and wage-workers in both countryside and city, these volumes examine the freedpeople's struggle to attain economic independence in difficult wartime circumstances. They also recount the federal government's involvement in labor and relief programs on a scale unsurpassed until the New Deal and trace the interplay among the conflicting conceptions of freedom held by former slaves, former slave-holders, and Northern soldiers and civilians. In so doing, they touch upon a fundamental theme of the entire edition: how emancipation transformed the meaning of freedom not only for former slaves but for all Americans – black and white, Southern and Northern.

Finally, *The Black Military Experience* demonstrates how the enlistment and military service of almost 200,000 black soldiers and sailors — the vast majority of them former slaves — hastened the transformation of the Civil War into a war for universal liberty. A social history of Civil-War soldiering, the volume shows how the military experience reshaped the lives of black men, their families, and their communities, and also how it informed struggles against discrimination and for equality long after the war ended.

Although each volume of *Freedom* stands on its own, several themes unite the four published thus far. Foremost is the active role played by slaves and former slaves in destroying slavery and redefining freedom. *Freedom* thus broadens the terrain to include the emancipated as well as the emancipators, showing how the weak can lead the powerful and demonstrating the need for a democratic history — one in which all participants receive a full hearing.

Emphasizing the agency of slaves and former slaves does not simply alter the cast of characters in the drama of emancipation, displacing old villains and enthroning new heroes. Abraham Lincoln and the Radical Republicans do not play less significant parts once slaves gain an active role in their own liberation, but they do play different ones. Focusing on events beyond Washington and outside formally constituted political bodies does not excise politics from the study of the past. Rather, it reveals that social history is not history with the politics left out, but that all history is — and must be — political. The politics of emancipation in the countryside and towns of the South makes more comprehensible the politics of emancipation inside the capitol and the presidential mansion.

This book brings together the introductory essays from the first four volumes of *Freedom*. Each of the authors participated, as coeditor of one or more of those volumes, in writing the essays that appear here. We hope that this brief treatment will lead students, general readers, and scholars to the documents that have inspired our undertaking from the outset — not only the thousand-odd published to date in *Freedom*, but also the millions still awaiting examination in the vaults of the National Archives.

Introduction

The essays in this book do not differ markedly from their original form in the volumes of *Freedom*. We have resisted the temptation to overhaul them, confining ourselves to correcting errors, shifting misplaced emphases, rooting out infelicities, and imposing stylistic consistency on prose written over the span of a decade. The arguments are unchanged. The footnotes, however, have been substantially reworked. As initially published, the essays were accompanied by a large selection of the sources on which they rest; here they stand alone. We have therefore made fuller reference to the documents that shaped our interpretations. Moreover, an outpouring of scholarship on the Civil War and emancipation has appeared in recent years, and we have added relevant new publications to the notes.

From the start, the Freedmen and Southern Society Project has been a collaborative endeavor, based upon the understanding that no scholar could single-handedly master the records at the National Archives. As its work continued, the editors learned that collaborative work also had other advantages, as they taught and tested each other, broadening their collective understanding of the process by which slaves became free people and – more prosaically – sharing the drudgery that necessarily accompanies scholarly work.

The interpretations advanced in these essays owe much to colleagues who participated in the formal mutual criticism, informal brainstorming, and lunchtime chatter in which the project's work gets done. We wish especially to thank Thavolia Glymph, coeditor of *The Destruction of Slavery* and *The Wartime Genesis of Free Labor: The Lower South*, and Julie Saville, coeditor of *The Wartime Genesis of Free Labor: The Lower South*. Having left the project for academic appointments elsewhere, neither was on hand when these essays were written. However, both made valuable comments on one or more of them at some stage of development. Both also brought to the project a wealth of knowledge and a commitment to the highest intellectual standards that have immeasurably enriched our collective enterprise.

Others who have been associated with the project also deserve thanks. Steven Hahn and Wayne K. Durrill, who served stints as editors, and Michael K. Honey and Leslie Schwalm, one-year editing fellows, all advanced our collective work during their stays; Wayne Durrill commented on an early draft of "The Wartime Genesis of Free Labor," and Steven Hahn critiqued an advanced version of "The Destruction of Slavery." This book, like the volumes of *Freedom*, also owes much to the research assistance of Cindy S. Aron, Garrine P. Laney, and Gail M. Thomas, who were on hand during the lean and uncertain first years in the National Archives, and to Gregory LaMotta, whose archival detective skills served the project well during his long tenure as a graduate assistant. Special appreciation goes to Susan Bailey, Lorraine Lee, and Terrie Hruzd, successively the project's administrative assistant. Each somehow managed to keep pace with all the chores stacked upon her desk while still pursuing important work outside the office.

Over the course of the past sixteen years, the project has had numerous benefactors. The National Historical Publications and Records Commission and the University of Maryland underwrote its work at the beginning and have been generous with their material and moral support ever since. In subsequent years, the project has enjoyed long-term assistance from the National Endowment for the Humanities, as well as smaller grants from the Ford Foundation, the Rockefeller Foundation, the H. W. Wilson Foundation, Philip Morris Companies, Inc., and the Arco-Richfield Foundation.

Everyone who has worked for the Freedmen and Southern Society Project — and a great many others — learned from Sara Dunlap Jackson, who until her death in April 1991 served as its foremost mentor, booster, and friend. We miss her.

The Authors

IRA BERLIN teaches history at the University of Maryland. Founder of the Freedmen and Southern Society Project and its director from 1976 to 1991, he is coeditor of the first four volumes of *Freedom: A Documentary History of Emancipation*. He is also the author of *Slaves without Masters: The Free Negro in the Antebellum South* (1974) and editor of several other volumes on black life in the American South.

BARBARA J. FIELDS teaches history at Columbia University. A member of the Freedmen and Southern Society Project in 1981–82, she is coeditor of one of the first four volumes of *Freedom: A Documentary History of Emancipation*. She is also the author of *Slavery and Freedom on the Middle Ground: Maryland during the Nineteenth Century* (1985), and was a principal onscreen commentator in the PBS documentary, "The Civil War."

STEVEN F. MILLER is coeditor of the Freedmen and Southern Society Project and a research associate in the Department of History at the University of Maryland. A member of the project since 1984, he is coeditor of two of the first four volumes of *Freedom: A Documentary History of Emancipation*.

JOSEPH P. REIDY teaches history at Howard University. A member of the Freedmen and Southern Society Project from 1977 to 1984 and in 1989–90, he is coeditor of the first four volumes of *Freedom: A Documentary History of Emancipation*. He is also the author of *From Slavery to Agrarian Capitalism in Central Georgia, 1800–1880* (in press).

LESLIE S. ROWLAND teaches history at the University of Maryland and is director of the Freedmen and Southern Society Project. A member of the project since its founding in 1976, she is coeditor of the first four volumes of *Freedom: A Documentary History of Emancipation*.

Short Titles and Abbreviations

SHORT TITLES

Black Military Experience — *Freedom: A Documentary History of Emancipation, 1861–1867.* Series 2, *The Black Military Experience,* ed. Ira Berlin, Joseph P. Reidy, and Leslie S. Rowland (Cambridge, U.K., 1982).

Destruction of Slavery — *Freedom: A Documentary History of Emancipation, 1861–1867.* Series 1, volume 1, *The Destruction of Slavery,* ed. Ira Berlin, Barbara J. Fields, Thavolia Glymph, Joseph P. Reidy, and Leslie S. Rowland (Cambridge, U.K., 1985).

Official Records — U.S. War Department, *The War of the Rebellion: A Compilation of the Official Records of the Union and Confederate Armies,* 128 vols. (Washington, 1880–1901).

Statutes at Large — U.S., *Statutes at Large, Treaties, and Proclamations of the United States of America,* 17 vols. (Boston, 1850–73).

Wartime Genesis: Lower South — *Freedom: A Documentary History of Emancipation, 1861–1867.* Series 1, volume 3, *The Wartime Genesis of Free Labor: The Lower South,* ed. Ira Berlin, Thavolia Glymph, Steven F. Miller, Joseph P. Reidy, Leslie S. Rowland, and Julie Saville (Cambridge, U.K., 1990).

Wartime Genesis: Upper South — *Freedom: A Documentary History of Emancipation, 1861–1867.* Series 1, volume 2, *The Wartime Genesis of Free Labor: The Upper South,* ed. Ira Berlin, Steven F. Miller, Joseph P. Reidy, and Leslie S. Rowland (Cambridge, U.K., in press).

ABBREVIATIONS

NA	National Archives
RG	Record Group
ser.	series

I

The Destruction of Slavery
1861–1865

THE BEGINNING of the Civil War marked the beginning of the end of slavery in the American South.[1] At first, most white Americans denied what would eventually seem self-evident. With President Abraham Lincoln in the fore, federal authorities insisted that the nascent conflict must be a war to restore the national union, and nothing more. Confederate leaders displayed a fuller comprehension of the importance of slavery, which Vice-President Alexander Stephens called the cornerstone of the Southern nation.[2] But if Stephens and others grasped slavery's significance, they assumed that the Confederate

---

[1] This essay, like the others in this volume, is based primarily upon documents published in *Freedom: A Documentary History of Emancipation* and other documents from the National Archives of the United States. In addition, numerous published sources have been relied upon throughout. Most significant are U.S., War Department, *The War of the Rebellion: A Compilation of the Official Records of the Union and Confederate Armies*, 128 vols. (Washington, 1880–1901); and U.S., Navy Department, *Official Records of the Union and Confederate Navies in the War of the Rebellion*, 30 vols. (Washington, 1894–1922). A convenient compendium of the public record of the period is Edward McPherson, *The Political History of the United States of America during the Great Rebellion*, 2nd ed. (Washington, 1865). General secondary works on slavery and emancipation during the Civil War include Herbert Aptheker, *The Negro in the Civil War* (New York, 1938); W. E. B. Du Bois, *Black Reconstruction in America: An Essay toward a History of the Part Which Black Folk Played in the Attempt to Reconstruct Democracy in America, 1860–1880* (New York, 1935); Robert F. Durden, *The Gray and the Black: The Confederate Debate on Emancipation* (Baton Rouge, La., 1972); John Hope Franklin, *The Emancipation Proclamation* (Garden City, N.Y., 1963); Leon F. Litwack, *Been in the Storm So Long: The Aftermath of Slavery* (New York, 1979), chaps. 1–4; James M. McPherson, *The Struggle for Equality: Abolitionists and the Negro in the Civil War and Reconstruction* (Princeton, N.J., 1964), and *The Negro's Civil War: How American Negroes Felt and Acted during the War for the Union* (New York, 1965); Benjamin Quarles, *The Negro in the Civil War* (Boston, 1953), and *Lincoln and the Negro* (New York, 1962); James L. Roark, *Masters without Slaves: Southern Planters in the Civil War and Reconstruction* (New York, 1977), chaps. 1–3; Armstead L. Robinson, "Day of Jubilo: Civil War and the Demise of Slavery in the Mississippi Valley, 1861–1865" (Ph.D. diss., University of Rochester, 1976); Bell I. Wiley, *Southern Negroes, 1861–1865* (New Haven, Conn., 1938). Useful reference works are Mark M. Boatner III, *The Civil War Dictionary* (New York, 1959); Frederick H. Dyer, *A Compendium of the War of the Rebellion*, 3 vols. (Des Moines, Iowa, 1908); E. B. Long with Barbara Long, *The Civil War Day by Day: An Almanac, 1861–1865* (Garden City, N.Y., 1971); Raphael P. Thian, comp., *Notes Illustrating the Military Geography of the United States* (Washington, 1881); Ezra J. Warner, *Generals in Blue: Lives of the Union Commanders* (Baton Rouge, La., 1964), and *Generals in Gray: Lives of the Confederate Commanders* (Baton Rouge, La., 1959).

[2] Henry Cleveland, *Alexander H. Stephens, in Public and Private; With Letters and Speeches* (Philadelphia, 1866), pp. 721–23.

struggle for independence would require no change in the nature of the institution. A Southern victory would transform the political status, not the social life, of the slave states; black people would remain in their familiar place. Despite a vigorous dissent from Northern abolitionists, most white people – North and South – saw no reason to involve slaves in their civil war.

Slaves had a different understanding of the sectional struggle. Unmoved by the public pronouncements and official policies of the federal government, they recognized their centrality to the dispute and knew that their future depended upon its outcome. With divisions among white Americans erupting into open warfare, slaves watched and waited, alert for ways to turn the military conflict to their own advantage, stubbornly refusing to leave its outcome to the two belligerents. Lacking political standing or public voice, forbidden access to the weapons of war, slaves nonetheless acted resolutely to place their freedom – and that of their posterity – on the wartime agenda. Steadily, as opportunities arose, they demonstrated their readiness to take risks for freedom and to put their loyalty, their labor, and their lives in the service of the federal government. In so doing, they gradually rendered untenable every Union policy short of universal emancipation and forced the Confederate government to adopt measures that severely compromised the sovereignty of the master. On both sides of the line of battle, Americans came to know that a war for the Union must be a war for freedom.

The change did not come easily or at once. At first, Northern political and military leaders freed slaves only hesitantly, under the pressure of military necessity. But, as the war dragged on, their reluctance gave way to an increased willingness and eventually to a firm determination to extirpate chattel bondage. The Emancipation Proclamation of January 1, 1863, and the enlistment of black soldiers into Union ranks in the following months signaled the adoption of emancipation as a fundamental Northern war aim, although that commitment availed little until vindicated by military victory. Even after the surrender of the Confederacy, slavery survived in two border states until the Thirteenth Amendment became part of the United States Constitution in December 1865.

The Destruction of Slavery

Whereas Union policy shifted in favor of emancipation, Confederate leaders remained determined to perpetuate slavery. But the cornerstone of Southern nationality proved to be its weakest point. Slaves resisted attempts to mobilize them on behalf of the slaveholders' republic. Their sullen and sometimes violent opposition to the Confederate regime magnified divisions within Southern society, gnawing at the Confederacy from within. In trying to sustain slavery while fending off the Union army, Confederate leaders unwittingly compromised their own national aspirations and undermined the institution upon which Southern nationality was founded. In the end, the victors celebrated slavery's demise and claimed the title of emancipator. The vanquished understood full well how slavery had helped to seal their doom.[3]

The war provided the occasion for slaves to seize freedom, but three interrelated circumstances determined what opportunities lay open to them and influenced the form that the struggle for liberty assumed: first, the character of slave society; second, the course of the war itself; and third, the policies of the Union and Confederate governments. Although none of these operated independently of the others, each had its own dynamic. All three were shaped by the particularities of Southern geography and the chronology of the war. Together, they made the destruction of slavery a varying, uneven, and frequently tenuous process, whose complex history has been obscured by the apparent certitude and finality of the great documents that announced the end of chattel bondage. Once the evolution of emancipation replaces the absolutism of the Emancipation Proclamation and the Thirteenth Amendment as the focus of study, the story of slavery's demise shifts from the presidential mansion and the halls of Congress to the farms and plantations that became wartime battlefields. And slaves — whose persistence forced federal soldiers, Union and Confederate pol-

---

[3] On slavery and the collapse of the Confederacy, see Robinson, "Day of Jubilo," especially chap. 8; Charles H. Wesley, *The Collapse of the Confederacy* (Washington, 1937); Paul D. Escott, *After Secession: Jefferson Davis and the Failure of Confederate Nationalism* (Baton Rouge, La., 1978), especially chap. 8; Wiley, *Southern Negroes*, pt. 1.

icy makers, and even their own masters onto terrain they never intended to occupy – become the prime movers in securing their own liberty.

On the eve of the Civil War, the South was a deeply divided society. Although slavery was central to the social order, most Southerners were white and owned no slaves. Apart from their common race and their nonslaveholding status, they lived in widely varying circumstances. A majority of this white majority were farmers, although some earned their livelihood as artisans and small proprietors and many – without property or skill – worked for wages. By residence, by nationality and religion, by education and wealth, by work routine and experience, they differed from each other. A shared desire to live and work on their own drew them together, and most sought an independent social standing by separating themselves ideologically and geographically from the slaveholders' world.[4] A minority, however, struggled to enter the ranks of the masters; aspiration, if not wealth and status, aligned these men and women with the slaveholders. At the margins, some people slid in and out of slave ownership. But even among slaveholders of long standing, the mass stood apart from the grandees – those planters who owned large numbers of slaves, produced staple crops for an international market, and dominated Southern politics and society. Although the great planters differed among themselves, their common concern for their own dominance engendered a strong sense of unity; and their

[4] Frank L. Owsley, *Plain Folk of the Old South* (Baton Rouge, La., 1949); Elizabeth Fox-Genovese and Eugene D. Genovese, *Fruits of Merchant Capital: Slavery and Bourgeois Property in the Rise and Expansion of Capitalism* (New York, 1983), chap. 9; Steven Hahn, *The Roots of Southern Populism: Yeoman Farmers and the Transformation of the Georgia Upcountry, 1850–1890* (New York, 1983), chaps. 1–3; Lacy K. Ford, Jr., *Origins of Southern Radicalism: The South Carolina Upcountry, 1800–1860* (New York, 1988); Harry L. Watson, "Conflict and Collaboration: Yeomen, Slaveholders, and Politics in the Antebellum South," *Social History* 10 (Oct. 1985): 273–98; Ira Berlin and Herbert G. Gutman, "Natives and Immigrants, Free Men and Slaves: Urban Workingmen in the Antebellum American South," *American Historical Review* 88 (Dec. 1983): 1175–1200.

political, economic, and social power extended that unity over the South as a whole.[5]

The lives of black Southerners were no more at one than those of white Southerners. Life in bondage assumed distinctive forms as a result of the pattern of the slave trade, the demographic balance of slave and free, the size of slaveholdings, and the labor requirements of particular crops, among other circumstances. Many of the nearly four million slaves resided on large plantations among a black majority and answered only to black drivers or white overseers. Those on the largest estates hardly knew their owners. Other slaves lived on small farmsteads, worked alongside their owners, and ate from the same pot, if rarely at the same table. Within the bounds of a single plantation or farm, a handful of slaves occupied special status as drivers, artisans, or house servants and were able to use their positions to gain a variety of prerogatives and a measure of independence; the vast majority never escaped the drudgery of agricultural labor. Differences could also be found among the mass of field hands. Some worked in gangs, some by the task, and others by a combination of the two. Work patterns shaped black life in slavery as they would in freedom.[6]

Some black Southerners – a quarter of a million by 1860 – had already achieved free status. Although they labored under constraints that deprived them of citizenship and severely circumscribed their

[5] Eugene D. Genovese, *The Political Economy of Slavery: Studies in the Economy and Society of the Slave South* (New York, 1965), and *The World the Slaveholders Made: Two Essays in Interpretation* (New York, 1969); Fox-Genovese and Genovese, *Fruits of Merchant Capital*, chaps. 1–2; James Oakes, *The Ruling Race: A History of American Slaveholders* (New York, 1982); Michael P. Johnson, *Toward a Patriarchal Republic: The Secession of Georgia* (Baton Rouge, La., 1977); Elizabeth Fox-Genovese, *Within the Plantation Household: Black and White Women of the Old South* (Chapel Hill, N.C., 1988).

[6] Eugene D. Genovese, *Roll, Jordan, Roll: The World the Slaves Made* (New York, 1974); John W. Blassingame, *The Slave Community: Plantation Life in the Antebellum South*, rev. ed. (New York, 1979); Herbert G. Gutman, *The Black Family in Slavery and Freedom, 1750–1925* (New York, 1976); Nathan I. Huggins, *Black Odyssey: The Afro-American Ordeal in Slavery* (New York, 1977); Fox-Genovese, *Within the Plantation Household*. The spatial diversity and temporal development of slavery in the United States are captured in Willie Lee Rose, ed., *A Documentary History of Slavery in North America* (New York, 1976).

liberty, free-black men and women collected their own wages, governed their own family life, and created their own institutions. Just as they stood apart from slaves, free blacks also differed among themselves. Most lived in abject poverty, but some of them climbed off the floor of Southern society, gained an education, and accumulated modest wealth. A handful became slaveholders themselves.[7] These diverse experiences guaranteed that wartime developments would affect different groups of black people differently.

In the various theaters of the war, events seldom followed the same course. Military developments multiplied the channels through which slaves might escape bondage.[8] The prospects for freedom emerged in different ways when a sudden Union invasion forced slaveholders to abandon their slaves, when continual skirmishing gave slaves opportunities to flee to the Union army, when a slowly developing line of battle spurred masters to remove their slaves to the interior, and when the confusion attending removal allowed slaves to flee in the opposite direction from their owners. While some slaves remained on their native ground when their masters turned fugitive, others left family and friends to become fugitives themselves. The establishment of secure federal enclaves on the fringes of the Confederacy created havens from which successful runaways might return to their former homes to guide enslaved loved ones out of slavery. Many such fugitives joined federal forces as guides, laborers, and eventually soldiers, helping to expand the Union's domain. In other parts of the Confederacy, contested territory and shifting military fortunes made escape more uncertain and precarious. Fugitive slaves in these areas followed Union soldiers and lived off the land or the meager charity of Northern philanthropists and Union authorities. Eventually, however, the march of federal armies announced the end of slavery throughout the war zone.

---

[7] Ira Berlin, *Slaves without Masters: The Free Negro in the Antebellum South* (New York, 1974).

[8] For the pattern of military developments in different regions, see Shelby Foote, *The Civil War: A Narrative*, 3 vols. (New York, 1958–74); Herman Hattaway and Archer Jones, *How the North Won: A Military History of the Civil War* (Urbana, Ill., 1983); James M. McPherson, *Battle Cry of Freedom: The Civil War Era* (New York, 1988).

Slaves distant from the conflict, with little chance of escape, did not simply wait for freedom to come to them. As news of the war spread – often by recaptured runaways, by slaves impressed for Confederate military labor, or by slaves removed to the interior from areas threatened by Union advances – resistance to slavery stiffened. Confederate slaveholders far from the fighting found that their most trusted servants had turned against them, requiring them to concede new privileges and redefining the relationship between master and slave. The same was true in the border states, whose loyalty to the Union exempted them from military emancipation measures. There, too, slaves seized upon opportunities offered by the war to free themselves, forcing their masters into coercive rearguard actions that steadily undermined their standing in the Union and ultimately required them to accept emancipation.[9] Throughout the South, the character of the war helped determine who would be free, how they would become free, and what freedom would mean.

Amid the diverse responses of slaves to wartime opportunities, both Union and Confederate leaders debated the employment of black men and women as military laborers, the recruitment of black men as soldiers, and, in the Union's case, their transformation from slaves into citizens. Decisions in Washington and Richmond, as well as on the field of battle, rested only partly on military exigencies. Political leaders, North and South, formulated policy in response to the demands of diverse constituencies, as well as considerations of world opinion. Merchants and manufacturers in the North and slaveholding planters in the South stood atop their respective societies, but other white men – including farmers, artisans, and unskilled laborers – exercised significant political power in these constitutional democracies and filled the ranks of both armies. Abolitionists in the North and

[9] On the border states, see *Destruction of Slavery*, chaps. 6–8; Barbara Jeanne Fields, *Slavery and Freedom on the Middle Ground: Maryland during the Nineteenth Century* (New Haven, Conn., 1985); Victor B. Howard, *Black Liberation in Kentucky: Emancipation and Freedom, 1862–1884* (Lexington, Ky., 1983); William E. Parrish, *Turbulent Partnership: Missouri and the Union, 1861–1865* (Columbia, Mo., 1963); Charles L. Wagandt, *The Mighty Revolution: Negro Emancipation in Maryland, 1862–1864* (Baltimore, 1964).

proslavery apologists in the South – propelled by religious zeal and moral righteousness – determined to remake their respective societies. They lobbied those in power and sometimes moved into positions of authority themselves. A complex internal politics developed within both the Union and the Confederate chains of command, creating shifting alliances among state and national officials, members of the executive and legislative branches of government, and civilian authorities and military commanders. The demands of office, the needs of particular constituents, notions of the general good, and the prejudices and ambitions of individuals also helped determine the course of slavery's demise.[10]

Slavery in the American South rested upon an unequal and uneasy balance of power between master and slave. In principle, the slaveholder's authority went almost unchallenged; in practice, it was limited by a variety of constraints. Refusing to be reduced to a mere extension of their owners' will, slaves did not willingly defer or freely relinquish their labor. Although slaveholders rarely hesitated to apply force in exacting deference and extorting labor, they found it both easier and more profitable to achieve these ends by conceding to the slaves some control over their own daily lives. Such hard-won concessions helped mute the conflict inherent in slavery and permitted masters to maintain their dominant place in Southern society.

[10] On the Union, see Herman Belz, *Reconstructing the Union: Theory and Policy during the Civil War* (Ithaca, N.Y., 1969); Leonard P. Curry, *Blueprint for Modern America: Nonmilitary Legislation of the First Civil War Congress* (Nashville, 1968); David Montgomery, *Beyond Equality: Labor and the Radical Republicans, 1862–1872* (New York, 1967); Allan Nevins, *The War for the Union*, 4 vols. (New York, 1959–71); Phillip Shaw Paludan, *"A People's Contest": The Union and Civil War, 1861–1865* (New York, 1988). On the Confederacy, see Curtis A. Amlund, *Federalism in the Southern Confederacy* (Washington, 1966); Thomas L. Connelly and Archer Jones, *The Politics of Command: Factions and Ideas in Confederate Strategy* (Baton Rouge, La., 1973); Escott, *After Secession*; Frank L. Owsley, *State Rights in the Confederacy* (Chicago, 1925); May S. Ringold, *The Role of the State Legislatures in the Confederacy* (Athens, Ga., 1966); Emory M. Thomas, *The Confederate Nation, 1861–1865* (New York, 1979). For a comparative view, see Richard Franklin Bensel, *Yankee Leviathan: The Origins of Central State Authority in America, 1859–1877* (Cambridge, U.K., 1990), chap. 3.

Slaves also gained from these concessions. Within the tight social space they wrested from their owners, slave men and women created a distinctive culture and a variety of institutions of their own. Slaveholders continually challenged this limited independence, and slaves maintained it only by constant struggle, often at great cost and sometimes not at all. But whatever the slaves' success in maintaining or expanding their independent realm, it stopped far short of freedom. Ultimately, they accepted their status only because of the superior power of their owners. Despite its seeming flexibility, slavery was a brittle institution. Any change threatened it.[11]

Even before sectional discord erupted into war, the debate over slavery was disturbing the delicate balance between master and slave. Slaveholders had long feared that abolitionists or their emissaries would stir bloody insurrection by awakening the slaves to the possibility of liberty. Although a few such emissaries carried the abolitionist message directly to the plantation gate, most slaves learned about the deepening sectional dispute from their owners' denunciation of the North and of the Republican party and its champions, the most threatening of whom was Abraham Lincoln. Indeed, the slaveholders' indiscriminate condemnations exaggerated the antislavery commitment of white Northerners, "Black Republicans," and Lincoln himself. Masters with no doubts about the abolitionist intentions of the North inadvertently persuaded their slaves of the ascendancy and pervasiveness of antislavery sentiment in the free states. The general politicization of Southern society thus reached deep into the slave community, imparting momentous significance to Lincoln's election, Southern secession, and military mobilization.

Yet the slaves did not immediately accept their owners' assumptions about the intentions of the North. Suspicious of all white people, many slaves doubted that any of them — of whatever provenance — would act in their behalf. Slaveholders fueled this well-founded distrust. Their

[11] Genovese, *Roll, Jordan, Roll*; Blassingame, *Slave Community*; Gutman, *Black Family*; Albert J. Raboteau, *Slave Religion: The "Invisible Institution" in the Antebellum South* (New York, 1978); Thomas L. Webber, *Deep like the Rivers: Education in the Slave Quarter Community, 1831–1865* (New York, 1978).

loud pronouncements that the Yankee devils – horned and tailed – would sell slaves to Cuba, sundering families and friendships, had a sobering effect in the quarters.[12] The slaves debated among themselves the meaning of the onrushing conflict, weighing their masters' claim that the Yankees would reopen the international slave trade against reports that they would abolish slavery. Neither position won immediate or universal assent, but even before the first shots at Fort Sumter, some slaves had resolved the question and acted upon their convictions. In March 1861, for instance, eight runaways presented themselves at Fort Pickens, a Union garrison in Florida, "entertaining the idea" – in the words of the fort's commander – that federal troops "were placed here to protect them and grant them their freedom."[13]

Generally slaves were more circumspect, fearing that any change might be for the worse. Once the fighting began, some of these cautious men and women openly sided with their owners, urging them to whip the Yankees and offering to aid them in doing so. Perhaps they hoped that loyalty would earn them new privileges or feared that disloyalty would bring harsh retribution, especially if the Confederacy triumphed. A few black men, free as well as slave, succumbed to the martial fervor. A chance to escape the stultifying plantation routine and see something of the world may well have animated those who volunteered to accompany their masters into battle as personal servants. Some free blacks, desperate for any opportunity to steady their precarious position in Southern society, offered to take up arms for the Confederacy. In Louisiana and a few other places, free men of color were mustered into Native Guard units.[14]

---

[12] On the slaves' interpretation of the politics of secession and the outbreak of war, see, for example, *Destruction of Slavery*, docs. 81, 318A, 330–31; *Wartime Genesis: Upper South*, docs. 96, 118; *Black Military Experience*, docs. 113–14. On threats by slave owners regarding the Yankees' intentions, see *Destruction of Slavery*, doc. 81; *Wartime Genesis: Lower South*, doc. 33; *Black Military Experience*, doc. 1.

[13] *Official Records*, ser. 2, vol. 1, p. 750. "I did what I could to teach them the contrary," added the commander, who drove the lesson home by delivering the fugitives to the city marshal of Pensacola "to be returned to their owners."

[14] On the Native Guards, see *Black Military Experience*, docs. 11, 127; Mary F. Berry, "Negro Troops in Blue and Gray: The Louisiana Native Guards, 1861–1863," *Louisiana History* 8 (Spring 1967): 165–90; Manoj K. Joshi and Joseph P. Reidy,

But most black people, reasoning that the enemy of their enemy must be their friend, quietly waited for events to turn in their favor. Anxious observers throughout the South described the slaves' unprecedented sense of anticipation that a Union victory would end slavery; an Alabama farmer characterized them as "very Hiley Hope up that they will soon Be free."[15] Whatever their assessment of the meaning of the war, slaves generally kept their own counsel, in accordance with time-honored practice. Their stolid silence and manifest preoccupation with the extraordinary events that surrounded them worried their owners as much as any formal declaration.

Fears real and imagined induced many slaveholders to slap new restrictions on their slaves, violating the longstanding – if silent – compromises upon which slavery rested. With agricultural productivity increasing in importance, masters pressed slaves hard, thereby imposing a more exacting work routine. With fear of enemy infiltration escalating, masters restricted travel, thereby denying slaves the chance to visit families and friends. With the possibility of insurrection growing, masters enacted new strictures and enforced old ones, thereby heightening the standards of discipline. Edgy slaveholders answered with the lash violations of plantation etiquette that might once have been overlooked. The imposition of such seemingly arbitrary changes evoked angry and sometimes violent responses from men and women unwilling to bear additional burdens – especially when their expectations ran in the other direction. Exasperated slaves struck out at their masters, ran away, or turned increasingly sullen. Although most slaves continued to mask their true feelings, the new repression revealed, even to the most cautious, the folly of expecting that loyalty to the old regime would be rewarded. Changes in plantation life magnified the possibilities of the moment.

Those possibilities multiplied as the Confederacy mobilized for war. Long accustomed to political leadership and proud of their military

" 'To Come Forward and Aid in Putting Down This Unholy Rebellion': The Officers of Louisiana's Free Black Native Guard during the Civil War Era," *Southern Studies* 21 (Fall 1982): 326–42.

[15] *Black Military Experience*, docs. 113–14.

prowess, slaveholders great and small placed their estates in the hands of relatives, overseers, or agents and marched off to confront the Northern enemy. On some estates, the master's absence and the slaves' familiarity with plantation routine allowed the slaves greater control over their daily lives. Elsewhere, supervision by an overseer meant hard driving and arbitrary punishment, without the recourse of an appeal to the master. But as overseers and younger sons followed the master into the army, leaving women and old men in charge, the balance of power gradually shifted, undermining slavery on farms and plantations far from the line of battle.[16]

Not all slaves remained at home when their masters marched off to war. In preparing to meet the enemy, slaveholders-turned-warriors almost always took personal manservants with them to tidy their camp and provide for their toilet. Many of these trusted body servants would have an opportunity to trade their owners' faith for their own freedom, leaving their masters to cook and care for themselves.[17]

Personal servants were only the first slaves directly affected by Confederate mobilization. The defense of the Confederacy demanded thousands, ultimately tens of thousands, of military laborers to wield picks and shovels. Countless others labored as teamsters, stable hands, and boatmen; butchers, bakers, and cooks; nurses, orderlies, and laundresses; and blacksmiths, coopers, and wagon makers. Slaves had long filled these roles and, in many places, no other labor force existed. Slaveholders knew this and at first did not have to be asked to volunteer their slaves to the Southern cause. Carried forward by a wave of martial enthusiasm and the belief that their contributions would aid the South in smiting the Yankee invaders, the most patriotic masters gladly sent

[16] On changes in plantation life and slave discipline early in the war, see Robinson, "Day of Jubilo," chaps. 1–2; Clarence L. Mohr, *On the Threshold of Freedom: Masters and Slaves in Civil War Georgia* (Athens, Ga., 1986), chap. 2.

[17] For a body servant from Georgia who, upon returning home from the Virginia battlefront, used the knowledge he had gained of Union policy to encourage fellow slaves to escape to Yankee forces on the coast, see *Destruction of Slavery*, doc. 37. For body servants captured with Confederate troops during the Confederate invasion of Kentucky in 1862, see *Destruction of Slavery*, doc. 210.

their slaves to work on Confederate defenses. Some even offered to lead them in battle against the Union army.[18]

But the dislocations that accompanied the employment of slaves in Confederate service eroded the masters' patriotism. Before long, slaveholders began to remove their slaves beyond the reach of either Yankee invaders or Confederate impressment agents. Political uncertainty, particularly in the border states, also caused slave owners to transfer, or (as the process became known) "refugee," their slaves to the Confederate interior. Slaveholders along the exposed periphery of the South soon joined those in the border states in refugeeing the slaves most likely to bolt for the Union lines. Usually they moved suspect slaves to their own or relatives' estates farther from the military action. When this was not possible, they often hired out the slaves or — as a last resort — sold them for whatever they would bring.[19]

Slaves hated these frightening removals and the resulting separation from family and friends. Many of them fled at the first hint of transfer. Escape itself was difficult enough, even in the confusion of wartime mobilization. But translating escape into freedom was nearly impossible in the absence of a safe harbor. Many slaves hoped that the arrival of the Union army would change that.

In April 1861, within days of Lincoln's call for volunteers to protect the nation's capital and put down the rebellion, the first Northern soldiers arrived in Washington. During the succeeding months, their numbers increased manyfold. As they took up positions around Washington and in the border states, they encountered slaves set in motion by the new disciplinary measures, by the attempts to conscript them into Confederate labor gangs or to refugee them to the interior, and — most importantly — by the desire to be free.

Before long, fugitive slaves began to test their owners' assertions about Yankee abolitionism. Those who ventured into Union army lines

---

[18] See, for example, *Destruction of Slavery*, doc. 257; *Black Military Experience*, docs. 114–15.

[19] For examples of refugeeing early in the war, see *Destruction of Slavery*, docs. 197, 259.

early in the war were mostly young men. Camps composed of hundreds of soldiers could be forbidding and dangerous places for women and children, and keeping up with an army on the march was nearly impossible for all but young and healthy adults. Fugitive-slave men also outnumbered women and children because men generally had greater opportunities to leave the home farm or plantation. Slave artisans, wagoners, and boatmen often had permission to move about in the course of their work, and sometimes to seek employment on their own; nearly all of them were men. Moreover, where slave hiring was common – as it was throughout the Upper South – seasonal agricultural labor kept hired men on the move between owner and employer.

Family arrangements also contributed to the greater mobility of slave men. Because small slaveholdings predominated in the Upper South, members of slave families often had different owners and lived on different farms. Slaveholders customarily permitted men with "broad wives" to visit the farm of their wife's owner, and many a slave man resided away from his master's place on a regular basis, journeying to his wife's home at the end of each day's work. Routinely visible on the public roads in pursuit of such errands and frequently brandishing written passes, slave men might turn their steps in the direction of a federal camp without arousing suspicion. No doubt the unmarried and childless found it easiest to leave home. But since children usually shared their mother's residence, even fathers could depart without completely disrupting day-to-day family life. And those slave men who had been mobilized for labor on Confederate defenses and were already separated from home could head in one direction as easily as another.

Whatever their opportunities for flight, these first fugitives took a considerable chance. They understood on good authority that runaway slaves risked severe punishment, even death, and they had no certain knowledge of the truth of their masters' allegations about Northern intentions. Indeed, fugitive slaves found that few Northern soldiers measured up to their owners' worst fears. In the early months of the war, federal commanders hewed close to the Lincoln administration's policy of noninterference with slavery. Eager to reassure wavering slaveholders in the border states and encourage unionism in the Confederacy,

Union officers reiterated their determination not to tamper with slavery. Some stumbled over themselves in declaring their readiness to protect slaveholders from their slaves. Benjamin F. Butler, a political general sensitive to the concerns of loyal owners, had no sooner arrived in Maryland in April 1861 than he ostentatiously offered to help suppress a rumored servile rebellion. General William S. Harney, commander of the Department of the West, applauded Butler's offer and gave Missouri slaveholders full assurances of protection for their property. Similar promises not to interfere with slavery and to crush any attempt at slave insurrection were promulgated in May by General Robert Patterson as his forces moved upon Harper's Ferry, and by General George B. McClellan as troops under his command entered western Virginia.[20]

During the summer of 1861, such sentiment received confirmation from federal authority at the highest level. In an Independence Day oration, President Lincoln pointedly omitted any mention of slavery in his discussion of Northern war aims and assured the South that he had not altered his views on the rights of the states within the federal government.[21] Congress added its imprimatur by adopting a resolution, introduced by Kentucky's John J. Crittenden, asserting that the North fought only to preserve the Union and posed no threat to Southern institutions.[22] The President's words and the Congress's resolves reinforced the determination of federal field commanders to honor the claims of slaveholders. They also seemed to unleash racial animosities rampant throughout American society. Instructed to expel fugitive slaves, some Northern soldiers did so with enthusiasm, turning their overwhelming power on the refugees from slavery.[23]

---

[20] *Official Records*, ser. 1, vol. 2, pp. 593, 661–62, and ser. 2, vol. 1, p. 753; *Destruction of Slavery*, doc. 153.

[21] Abraham Lincoln, *Collected Works*, ed. Roy P. Basler, Marion D. Pratt, and Lloyd A. Dunlap, 9 vols. (New Brunswick, N.J., 1953–55), vol. 4, pp. 421–41.

[22] McPherson, *Political History*, p. 286. Following approval of Crittenden's resolution in the House of Representatives, Andrew Johnson of Tennessee secured its passage in the Senate.

[23] For examples of the expulsion of fugitive slaves from Union camps, often into the custody of their owners, see *Destruction of Slavery*, docs. 81, 131A, 153, 201.

Not all Union soldiers shared the convictions of those at the top of the chain of command. Although many – perhaps most – held black people in contempt, some were fierce opponents of slavery and itched for a chance to put their principles into practice. The arrival of fugitive slaves at Union camps – breathless, clothed in tatters, bearing the marks of abuse – gave these antislavery soldiers the opportunity they sought. They offered the fugitives food and protection and permitted them to share their bivouac or accompany them on the march. Such encounters with runaway slaves intent upon freedom, and their often terrifying aftermath – when slaveholders and their agents dragged frightened men and women back into bondage – moved many soldiers who had previously cared nothing about slavery. What they saw sickened them and sometimes drew them into the antislavery fold. Indeed, as slaves continued to flee to the army camps despite the risk of recapture and punishment, even the most hard-hearted soldiers found it difficult to remain oblivious to the unfolding drama, particularly when the fugitives offered to relieve them of the more onerous aspects of camp life in exchange for a few morsels of food. Many slaves won the protection of Union soldiers by providing bits of useful military information or news of local secessionist activities. In this manner, increasing numbers of black men and women gained residence in and near federal camps as guides, cooks, servants, hostlers, and laundresses.[24]

The protection and employment offered fugitive slaves by individual Northern soldiers, often against the wishes of their superiors, created numerous conflicts between masters and the Union army. Slaveholders, many of them flaunting unionist credentials, demanded that Northern troops return fugitives who had taken refuge within their encampments. When regimental officers would not or could not comply, masters objected loudly and blustered about connections that reached to the highest levels in Washington. Generally the bluster was just that. But often enough, the officers soon felt the weight of high authority, as cabinet members and other officials took time from the business

---

[24] See, among many examples, *Destruction of Slavery*, docs. 46, 51, 124A-C, 130, 134–35, 156, 158, 165, 197.

of war to respond to the complaints of slaveholders and their representatives. Federal authorities solemnly reiterated their respect for slavery and curtly ordered field officers to cooperate with slaveholders and to discipline soldiers who assisted runaways. However, demeaning field commanders before the local citizenry and embarrassing them before their men hardly disposed them to obey with much enthusiasm. Even unionist masters found that they paid a price for their appeals to higher authority. Both regimental officers and soldiers grew contemptuous of slaveholders who seemed more concerned with recapturing slaves than with maintaining the Union.[25]

Confrontations between slaveholders and soldiers multiplied as the number of Union troops in the slave states increased. In late May 1861, when Virginia voters ratified secession, federal forces crossed the Potomac into the northern part of the state, and disputes between masters and military officers became endemic. The conflicts soon made their way into the press, rousing the ire of abolitionists who were outraged by the use of federal soldiers as slave catchers. In July, antislavery congressmen pushed a resolution through the House of Representatives declaring it "no part of the duty of the soldiers of the United States to capture and return fugitive slaves."[26] Although the resolution had no binding effect, it bolstered antislavery sentiment within the Northern army.

The rumblings of congressional radicals were only one indication of the Lincoln administration's difficulty in sustaining a consistent policy regarding slavery. Orders to return fugitive slaves to their owners — designed to preserve the loyalty of the border states and encourage unionism in the Confederacy — lost their rationale once Northern soldiers encountered slaves whose owners were patently disloyal. The change first became apparent under the aegis of General Butler, who in May 1861 took command at Fortress Monroe, in tidewater Virginia.

Antebellum agricultural developments in eastern Virginia had set the stage for wartime events by transforming slaves into a mobile lot.

[25] See, for example, *Destruction of Slavery*, docs. 46, 51, 124A-C, 129–30, 134–35, 154, 158, 163, 165, 199.
[26] *Official Records*, ser. 2, vol. 1, p. 759.

The decline of tobacco, the concomitant expansion of mixed farming — in which tobacco shared the fields with grains, forage crops, and cattle — and the beginning of truck farming for urban markets had shrunk the size of the region's plantations. The new agricultural regimen depended upon hiring slaves to satisfy seasonal labor demands. As a result, slaves encountered a variety of masters and employers, worked alongside slaves from other farms and black people who were free, and acquired a familiarity with nearby roads and waterways. Some slaves, permitted to hire their own time, succeeded in buying their way out of bondage, adding to the already substantial free-black population. Free blacks lived scattered among the plantations on hardscrabble farms, scratching the soil, fishing and oystering, and hiring themselves to planters for short stints. Shared labor along with ties of kinship and friendship knit free blacks and slaves into a single community.[27]

The pattern of slavery in tidewater Virginia enabled some slaves to turn wartime mobilization to their own advantage. The local Confederate commander unwittingly opened the door by impressing nearly all able-bodied black men, slave and free, to construct fortifications. Slaveholders objected to this dragnet impressment nearly as much as did their slaves and by the summer of 1861 had begun to refugee them from the tidewater.[28] Pulled in two directions and unwilling to go in either, many of the slaves struck out on their own, employing their knowledge of the region's geography to guide them to the federal outpost at Fortress Monroe.

General Butler, who only weeks earlier had volunteered to protect Maryland masters against their slaves, now reversed himself. Realizing that they would be used against the Union if not employed for it, he

---

[27] On slave and free-black life in tidewater Virginia, see Willard B. Gatewood, Jr., ed., *Free Man of Color: The Autobiography of Willis Augustus Hodges* (Knoxville, Tenn., 1982); Luther Porter Jackson, *Free Negro Labor and Property Holding in Virginia, 1830–1860* (Washington, 1942); Edna Greene Medford, "The Transition from Slavery to Freedom in a Diversified Economy: Virginia's Lower Peninsula, 1860–1900" (Ph.D. diss., University of Maryland, 1987), chap. 1. See also *Wartime Genesis: Upper South*, doc. 10. On wartime emancipation in tidewater Virginia, see *Destruction of Slavery*, chap. 1; *Wartime Genesis: Upper South*, chap. 1.

[28] *Destruction of Slavery*, docs. 260A-H, 295.

accepted runaway slaves and put the able-bodied men to work on federal fortifications. In carefully drawn letters to General-in-Chief Winfield Scott and Secretary of War Simon Cameron, Butler detailed a policy that he clearly viewed as simple necessity but feared might be interpreted as a radical departure. He had seized the slaves, he argued, just as he seized other contraband of war and would return them, along with compensation for their use, if their owners took an oath of loyalty. Scott and Cameron, weary of conciliating secessionists, required little convincing. They promptly endorsed Butler's policy, and Cameron ordered him not to surrender fugitives to their "alleged masters."[29] Butler's designation of fugitive slaves as "contrabands" captured the Northern imagination, and slaves throughout tidewater Virginia – women and children, as well as men – began fleeing to Fortress Monroe, where they exchanged the status of slave for that of contraband.

Butler's policy also found support in Congress during the summer of 1861. Defeat at Bull Run in July dashed expectations of quick victory over the Confederacy, and the Northern public grew less reluctant to punish traitors. Early in August, just before adjourning its special session, Congress passed and Lincoln signed the First Confiscation Act. Scrupulously following the standard usages of war, the act sought to weaken the Confederate military effort by making all property used in support of the rebellion "subject of prize and capture wherever found." Its provisions specifically included slaves who had been "employed in or upon any fort, navy yard, dock, armory, ship, entrenchment, or in any military or naval service." Although the act did not explicitly declare such slaves free, it nullified all claims by the masters to their labor.[30]

Despite the absence of an unequivocal declaration of freedom, the First Confiscation Act provided the bedrock for future development of federal policy regarding fugitive slaves. Secretary of War Cameron understood the significance of the new departure and pressed upon Butler an expansive reading of the legislation. Although he accepted the necessity of enforcing all federal laws (including the fugitive slave

---

[29] *Destruction of Slavery*, docs. 1A-B.
[30] *Statutes at Large*, vol. 12, p. 319. For a contemporary legal interpretation of the act's intent and meaning, see *Destruction of Slavery*, doc. 162.

law) "within States and Territories in which the authority of the Union is fully acknowledged," Cameron admitted no such necessity in insurrectionary states, which, by their treason, had forfeited federal protection. There, according to the confiscation act, the Union could freely accept the services of slaves previously employed on behalf of the Confederacy. Furthermore, Cameron argued, the "substantial rights" of unionist slaveholders in the seceded states would also be served by receiving their fugitive slaves into federal lines, holding out the possibility of compensation to such slaveholders at some future date. Although he explicitly prohibited Butler from interfering with the "servants of peaceful citizens, in house or field," Cameron's instructions worked to the advantage of slaves who came into Union lines, whatever the politics of their owners. With Cameron's blessing, Butler treated all incoming slaves as "if not free born, yet free, manumitted, sent forth from the hand that held them, never to be reclaimed." Butler's successors at Fortress Monroe did the same.[31]

As Cameron and Butler inched beyond the confiscation act, General John C. Frémont leaped. Appointed commander of the Western Department in July 1861, the former Republican presidential candidate arrived in St. Louis determined to give practical application to his antislavery principles. At the end of August, citing civil violence and rampant disloyalty, Frémont proclaimed martial law in Missouri and declared free the slaves of all rebel masters in the state. Local opponents of slavery rallied to Frémont's side, as did abolitionists in the free states. But unlike Butler's stance in secessionist Virginia, which received wide acclaim, Frémont's proclamation in loyal Missouri met strong opposition. Slaveholding unionists in Missouri and in the other border states lambasted the proclamation, objecting that it would drive masters of wavering loyalty into the waiting arms of the Confederacy. Northern conservatives warned that the allegiance of Kentucky – still hovering in precarious neutrality as Confederate soldiers assembled along its southern border – was hanging in the balance. Convinced of the wisdom of such arguments, Lincoln advised Frémont to modify his

---

[31] *Destruction of Slavery*, doc. 1C; *Official Records*, ser. 2, vol. 1, pp. 770–71.

proclamation to conform with the far more limited confiscation act, lest the general's action "ruin our rather fair prospect for Kentucky." When Frémont refused, Lincoln ordered him to make the required change, and Frémont complied. That done, the specter of wholesale military emancipation disappeared.[32]

As summer turned into fall and fall into winter, the confiscation act alone dictated the terms by which slaves might legally exit slavery. In most places, it provided but slight access to freedom, assuring slaveholders the return of any fugitive who had not been directly engaged in labor for the Confederacy. After federal troops moved into Kentucky in September 1861, for example, Union generals in the state – including Ulysses S. Grant and William T. Sherman – presumed it their duty to return runaway slaves to their owners. Their conviction was shared by General John A. Dix in Maryland and by General McClellan, now commanding in northern Virginia and the District of Columbia.[33]

The slaves were not deterred. They searched the seams of federal policy looking for ways to expand the fissures opened at Fortress Monroe and enlarged by the confiscation act. In every theater of operation, fugitive slaves moved toward Union army camps. Although single men continued to predominate, groups including women and children also began to appear. Intimidated by the mass of armed white men and discouraged by reports of rough treatment, many runaways kept a healthy distance, trailing moving columns or camping outside federal bivouacs – just far enough to avoid expulsion by Union commanders, just close enough to discourage Confederate soldiers and slave catchers. Other fugitive slaves marched boldly into Union camps and tried to barter for protection. Some offered useful information – the length and direction of navigable rivers and roads, the movement of Confederate troops, the layout of fortifications and positions of artillery. Others contributed the bounty of their masters' larders or their own. Most declared their willingness to labor at anything from constructing defenses to cleaning a soldier's tent. Many fugitives were seized and returned to their owners, or simply sent

---

[32] *Destruction of Slavery*, doc. 155.
[33] *Destruction of Slavery*, docs. 46–47, 197, 199; *Official Records*, ser. 2, vol. 1, pp. 763, 765.

away to fend for themselves. But some Yankee soldiers always seemed to be willing, for whatever reason, to shelter runaways, and a few actively encouraged slave flight.[34]

The slaves' persistence complicated what at first seemed a simple matter of enforcing the fugitive-slave law. When slaveholders pursued runaways to a Union camp, military officers became embroiled in disagreeable contests whose resolution required considerable time and skill, especially when slaveholders claimed to be loyal and slaves professed to have labored in Confederate service. Masters demanded rendition and slaves begged for protection; Union officers sought a way out of the imbroglio.

Struggling to escape the cross fire of master and slave — to be neither slave stealer nor slave catcher, in the idiom of the day — federal commanders throughout the border states attempted to exclude fugitive slaves from army camps and posts. In the fall of 1861, General Henry W. Halleck, commanding in Missouri and western Kentucky, General Don Carlos Buell in central Kentucky, and General Dix in Maryland all issued orders barring slaves from army lines. All three acted with the encouragement and approval of General McClellan, newly elevated to command as general-in-chief of the Union armies.[35] The architects of exclusion hoped that denying fugitives access to army camps would also make the larger problem of slavery disappear. They expected that, by reducing contact between Union soldiers and both slaves and slaveholders, exclusion would dissipate the growing revulsion in the ranks against returning fugitives to their owners. Without questioning the particular political and military circumstances that made exclusion practicable in the border states, Union military authorities assumed that they had discovered a policy of universal genius, appropriate wherever federal troops encoun-

---

[34] On fugitive slaves as guides and sources of information, see, for example, *Destruction of Slavery*, docs. 2, 28, 53, 99–100, 104–5, 164, 215, 218; *Wartime Genesis: Upper South*, doc. 7; *Black Military Experience*, doc. 207. On their express willingness to work for the Union, see *Destruction of Slavery*, docs. 26B, 81; *Wartime Genesis: Upper South*, doc. 7; *Black Military Experience*, doc. 9.

[35] *Destruction of Slavery*, docs. 129, 157; *Official Records*, ser. 2, vol. 1, pp. 764–66, 775–77. On the enforcement of exclusion orders by subordinate officers, see *Destruction of Slavery*, docs. 160A-C, 163, 165.

tered slaves. Little did they anticipate the problems that awaited their armies as they advanced into Confederate territory, where the slaveholders were avowed enemies – not wavering friends – and large numbers of slaves had been employed in the Confederate war effort.

Such problems were not long in coming. Through the summer and fall of 1861, as Union officials pondered what to do with slaves, the Confederates were acting with dispatch. They mobilized slave laborers to construct Southern defenses on the Atlantic and Gulf coasts and at strategic points along inland waterways and railroads. When Union troops tested Confederate lines, they encountered slave-built fortifications and often the slaves themselves. In such circumstances, the confiscation act became a veritable emancipation proclamation.

Yet, the First Confiscation Act remained a narrow instrument of liberation. The farther south federal forces advanced, the more apparent became its limitations. In November 1861, when Union sailors and soldiers invaded the South Carolina Sea Islands around Port Royal, the inadequacy of the act became transparent. General Thomas W. Sherman and Flag Officer Samuel Du Pont, joint commanders of the expedition, had been furnished copies of Secretary of War Cameron's instructions to General Butler regarding fugitive slaves. Although the War Department explicitly warned Sherman and Du Pont against interfering with the "[s]ocial systems or local institutions" of the islands, it encouraged them to employ captured or fugitive slaves at military labor, much as Butler had done at Fortress Monroe.[36] But the federal forces who stormed ashore at Port Royal, bearing assurances that slave property would be respected, found few slaveholders to assure. The resident planters – many of them leaders of the movement for Southern independence – had fled at the sight of the Union gunboats. Most of the slaves remained behind, having thwarted their owners' frantic attempt to evacuate them to the mainland, some by openly resisting, others by simply escaping in the confusion of the moment. Once their owners had gone, the slaves returned to their homes and celebrated their new freedom – sometimes taking the opportunity to even old

---

[36] *Destruction of Slavery*, doc. 18.

scores with their fugitive owners by helping themselves to the carpets, furniture, and other amenities of the big house. In the months and years to come, they were joined on the Union-occupied Sea Islands by hundreds of slaves from the mainland.

What the slaves took for granted, neither Sherman nor Du Pont would immediately concede. Although the masters' flight rendered the Port Royal slaves de facto freedpeople, their legal status remained moot, unaffected by the First Confiscation Act since few, if any, had been employed in Confederate service. Sherman and Du Pont put some of them to work for the army and navy, but most remained on the plantations and set about reconstructing their lives, now independent of their former owners.[37]

The nature of slavery shaped the struggle for freedom in the Union-occupied Sea Islands much as it did in tidewater Virginia. Under the old regime, the slaves – who composed an overwhelming majority of the population – had enjoyed considerable control over their own lives. Many of them had access to gardens or provision grounds, which they cultivated on their own account after finishing each day's plantation task. The produce they raised allowed them to participate in the region's local economy and to accumulate property – including barnyard fowl, hogs, and small boats – of modest worth. With the flight of their owners, Port Royal slaves turned their backs on cotton, the plantation staple, and devoted their full attention to the provision grounds. Federal officials made no declaration of emancipation, but the actions of the slaves and the flight of their owners made such a pronouncement unnecessary.[38]

---

[37] *Destruction of Slavery*, docs. 20–21; *Wartime Genesis: Lower South*, docs. 1, 4, 6, 8. On wartime emancipation in the Sea Islands and elsewhere along the coast of South Carolina, Georgia, and Florida, see *Destruction of Slavery*, chap. 2; *Wartime Genesis: Lower South*, chap. 1; Willie Lee Rose, *Rehearsal for Reconstruction: The Port Royal Experiment* (Indianapolis, Ind., 1964).

[38] On the task system and slave-owned property in lowcountry South Carolina and Georgia, see Philip D. Morgan, "Work and Culture: The Task System and the World of Lowcountry Blacks, 1700 to 1880," *William and Mary Quarterly* 3rd ser., 39 (Oct. 1982): 563–99, and "The Ownership of Property by Slaves in the Mid-Nineteenth-Century Low Country," *Journal of Southern History* 49 (Aug. 1983): 399–420. See also *Destruction of Slavery*, docs. 32–33, 36–38, 330; *Wartime Genesis: Lower South*, doc. 8.

Still, the absence of a legal foundation for their liberty left black people in the Sea Islands in a precarious position. The consequences of such insecurity would become evident as Union forces extended their control to other parts of the South Atlantic coast. In coastal Florida, for example, many slaveholders declared themselves loyal to the federal government. Eager to cultivate indigenous unionism, Northern officers honored the masters' claims by paying them when the army employed their slaves and by helping them recapture runaways.[39]

Events in lowcountry Florida and South Carolina paralleled developments in the Upper South. Everywhere, federal policy regarding fugitive slaves moved in two directions: rendition or exclusion where masters remained loyal to the Union; acceptance and employment where slaveholders stood with the Confederacy. When the loyalty of slaveholders was in doubt, the two tendencies mixed in complex ways. Officers and soldiers of abolitionist bent protected fugitive slaves from their owners; those who believed that respecting slavery would speed restoration of the Union returned fugitives or excluded them from army lines. But slaves, refusing to relinquish their view of the Union army as a refuge from slavery, would not permit exclusion to settle the question. Although national law and military policy provided only a small opening by which slaves might gain liberty, they struggled to enlarge it. Their determination awakened field officers to the possibility of employing black men in behalf of the Union, a possibility that seemed increasingly reasonable, if not essential, in the face of the slave-built breastworks and slave-supplied armies of the Confederacy.

By year's end, what had begun to appear as common sense to officers and soldiers in the field seemed even more compelling to Secretary of War Cameron in Washington. In November 1861, Cameron publicly endorsed a proposal to arm slaves to fight for the Union and freedom. He elaborated the idea in his annual report, which he forwarded to the press before it had received Lincoln's endorsement. Condemning as "madness" the practice of leaving the enemy "in peaceful and secure possession of slave property," Cameron proposed that the North free all

---

[39] *Destruction of Slavery*, docs. 22, 26B.

slaves owned by rebels, employ them in the Union war effort, and arm those capable of military service against their masters. His call for emancipation and the enlistment of black soldiers outraged border-state loyalists and Northern conservatives. It also displeased the President, who required Cameron to expunge the offending passage – to the relief of unionist slaveholders and the consternation of the growing antislavery constituency in and out of the army.[40] By the end of January 1862, Cameron had been banished to an ambassadorship in Russia, and the more circumspect Edwin M. Stanton sat as Secretary of War.

Lincoln's suppression of Cameron's recommendation belied the progress of antislavery sentiment in the North. When Congress reconvened in December 1861, its proceedings reflected growing impatience with a policy that protected the property of unrepentant rebels. Northern constituents flooded congressional mailboxes with antislavery petitions and demands for stern punishment of secessionists.[41] Radical congressmen filled the legislative hoppers with measures that urged the confiscation of rebel property, including slaves. Such proposals sat well with those Northerners who had achieved political maturity in the abolitionist movement and who traced the Union's military failures directly to

[40] For Cameron's public endorsement of arming black men and both the original and modified versions of his annual report, see McPherson, *Political History*, pp. 249, 416. For a favorable reaction to Cameron's original report by one Northerner, see *Destruction of Slavery*, doc. 81.

[41] See, for example, *Destruction of Slavery*, doc. 50; H. P. McChurkin et al. to the Congress of the United States, Dec. 1861, 37A-G21.4, Senate Committee on Emancipation, Petitions & Memorials Tabled, ser. 468, 37th Congress, Records of the U.S. Senate, RG 46, NA [E-47]; Calvin Gray et al. to the Congress of the United States, 10 Dec. 1861, 37A-G7.2, House Committee on the Judiciary, Petitions & Memorials, ser. 467, 37th Congress, Records of the U.S. House of Representatives, RG 233, NA [D-58]; R. F. Fenton to the Congress of the United States, [Feb. 1862], 37A-G7.13, Senate Committee on the Judiciary, Petitions & Memorials, ser. 582, 37th Congress, Records of the U.S. Senate, RG 46, NA [E-19]. (A bracketed number at the end of a citation is the document's control number in the files of the Freedmen and Southern Society Project.) The fact that many petitions arrived in multiple copies on printed forms is indicative of their general and systematic circulation. For a sample of wartime petitions pertaining to emancipation and a discussion of their importance, see Ira Berlin, Wayne K. Durrill, Steven F. Miller, Leslie S. Rowland, and Leslie Schwalm, " 'To Canvass the Nation': The War for Union Becomes a War for Freedom," *Prologue* 20 (Winter 1988): 227–47.

the policy of waging war on the narrowest moral and political grounds. But, in many instances, disenchantment with the course of the war also propelled Northerners of a conservative stripe beyond the bounds of punishing Confederate slaveholders, to a more generalized recognition of slavery as the root cause of secession. An attempt to reaffirm the Crittenden resolution, passed so easily the previous summer, met decisive defeat in the House of Representatives. Instead, the House adopted a resolution calling for emancipation of the slaves of disloyal masters in all military jurisdictions – endorsing, in effect, Frémont's proclamation of the previous August – and defeated by only a narrow margin a resolution censuring General Halleck's order to exclude slaves from army lines.[42]

Apparently unmoved by the flurry of congressional activity, Lincoln never seemed more out of touch with Northern opinion. But behind the scenes, he was considering various plans for gradual emancipation and compensation to slaveholders – perhaps in the hope of fending off more drastic antislavery measures, certainly with an eye to the special difficulty of slavery in the loyal border states. He began by suggesting that the federal government help Delaware initiate gradual, compensated emancipation. A blow at slavery in Delaware – where fewer than 1,800 black people remained in bondage – would hardly shake the institution, but Lincoln's proposal did reveal that his position was shifting under the weight of events. Although the Delaware legislature rejected the idea of emancipation in any form, Lincoln persevered. In the following months, he reiterated his support for gradual, compensated emancipation on several occasions, and in April 1862, at his behest, Congress resolved to provide financial assistance to any state that enacted such a measure.[43] Antislavery Northerners, black and white, denounced the resolution as evidence of the President's antiquated preoccupation with the rights of loyal masters. Abolitionists argued that justice would be better served by compensating slaves for their long years in bondage

[42] McPherson, *Political History*, pp. 253–54, 286–87; Nevins, *War for the Union*, p. 402.
[43] Lincoln, *Collected Works*, vol. 5, pp. 29–31, 144–46; *Statutes at Large*, vol. 12, p. 617; Henry Wilson, *History of the Antislavery Measures of the Thirty-Seventh and Thirty-Eighth United-States Congresses, 1861–64* (Boston, 1864), chap. 4.

than by indemnifying slaveholders for their grudging loyalty to the Union. Yet, those same loyal owners discerned the frightening implications of Lincoln's proposal and rejected it out of hand. They understood that Lincoln was edging toward emancipation.

Whereas Lincoln followed Northern opinion on the question of slavery, others led it. Radical Republicans pressed for a bolder assault. In March 1862, Congress enacted an additional article of war that prohibited the employment of Union soldiers in returning fugitive slaves to their masters. The new article went beyond the simple expression of opinion offered in the House resolution of the previous summer, for it provided antislavery soldiers with legal grounds to resist the orders of proslavery superiors.[44] Having bolstered the position of their comrades in the army, congressional radicals turned their attention directly to slavery. No target seemed more inviting than the 3,000 slaves in the District of Columbia, where the presence of slavery had long been a source of embarrassment to abolitionists and where federal authority over slavery was certain. Early in the session, Senator Henry Wilson, a Massachusetts Republican, introduced legislation to abolish slavery in the District. Although the measure provided for immediate rather than gradual emancipation, it borrowed in other respects from Lincoln's position, authorizing compensation to slaveholders and urging colonization of the freed slaves outside the limits of the United States. Its passage in April 1862 constituted the first time that the federal government had directly legislated the emancipation of any slave. To be sure, the compensation of slaveholders accorded slavery a legitimacy that abolitionists were loath to concede. Nonetheless, abolition in the national capital put slaveholders in the Union's own slave states on the defensive, and marked a significant step toward placing the federal government on the side of freedom.[45]

---

[44] *Statutes at Large*, vol. 12, p. 354. For instances of the use of the additional article of war by antislavery commanders and soldiers, see *Destruction of Slavery*, docs. 63, 178, 201.

[45] *Statutes at Large*, vol. 12, pp. 376–78; Wilson, *History of Antislavery Measures*, chap. 3. On wartime emancipation in the District of Columbia and vicinity, see *Destruction of Slavery*, chap. 3; *Wartime Genesis: Upper South*, chap. 2.

As the groundswell of antislavery sentiment in the North began to register in the halls of Congress, the military offensives of early 1862 dramatized the need for a more forthright commitment to emancipation. Shortly after the new year, the Northern armies advanced on several fronts. Moving deep into enemy territory, they encountered larger and larger numbers of slaves, some of whom had been in Confederate employ. In such circumstances, most field officers quickly applied the provisions of the First Confiscation Act and put black men (and some black women) to work on the Union side of the line of battle. As they did, federal forces became increasingly dependent on black military laborers.[46]

The army's growing appetite for laborers deepened its complicity in the slaves' struggle for freedom. Fugitive slaves encouraged this complicity by volunteering important military intelligence and by applying their skill and muscle in the Union cause. Standard usages of war authorized protection in exchange for such assistance, and few officers were so lacking in gratitude as to withhold it. But in so doing, they acted against the explicit instructions of their superiors, who had ordered the exclusion and expulsion of fugitive slaves from army lines. Conflicts multiplied within the ranks, sometimes ending in the resignation, court-martial, and even dismissal of officers determined to shield fugitives from recapture.[47] Nevertheless, as the Union army advanced, the utility of black labor — if not the morality of protecting runaway slaves — wore upon the policy of exclusion. Whatever its advantages in the border states, it became increasingly inadequate as the Union army occupied portions of the Confederacy. Federal commanders had believed exclusion to be a panacea for their problems with slavery. It proved to be no solution at all.

General-in-Chief McClellan, whose determination to preserve the war from abolitionist taint had been established in the first months of fighting, directed the Union offensives in the east. Early in 1862, he ordered a joint naval and army expedition to establish a third Union

[46] See, for example, *Wartime Genesis: Upper South*, doc. 7; *Wartime Genesis: Lower South*, docs. 63, 147.

[47] See, for example, *Destruction of Slavery*, docs. 63, 85, 87, 166, 200–204.

beachhead on the Atlantic coast by invading tidewater North Carolina. In accordance with instructions from McClellan, General Ambrose E. Burnside promised to respect slavery as his soldiers smashed Confederate coastal defenses and occupied strategic positions.[48] But slaveholders in tidewater North Carolina, some of whom had already lost slaves to the Union outpost at Fortress Monroe, did not wait to test Burnside's guarantees; they fled before the Northern advance. Federal officers recognized that those who remained did so only from lack of choice. Meanwhile, slaves – moving east as their owners migrated west – flooded into Union lines. As in tidewater Virginia, small farms and extensive slave hiring had familiarized slaves with the geography of the region and given them considerable knowledge of Confederate movements. They volunteered this information and their own labor to Burnside's short-handed command. Their presence in large numbers promised to make a mockery of any attempt at exclusion, and Burnside did not even try. Instead, he employed the fugitives as Butler had at Fortress Monroe, paying them for their labor and elevating them to the status of contrabands.[49]

General McClellan, by contrast, strove to preserve his reputation as the slaveholders' friend. In March 1862, he was relieved as general-in-chief to take personal command of the massive Army of the Potomac for a campaign in tidewater Virginia. Through the spring and into the summer, McClellan inched cautiously up the peninsula formed by the York and James rivers, waging several costly battles before succumbing to the paralyzing conviction that a superior Southern army threatened to overwhelm him. Confederate forces in fact never equaled the number of Union soldiers, but McClellan's prophecy proved correct, in that the rebel army under General Robert E. Lee rallied to halt the Northern advance. Meanwhile, the turmoil created by the tramping armies allowed large numbers of slaves to escape, including many who had been

---

[48] *Official Records*, ser. 1, vol. 9, pp. 363–64.
[49] *Destruction of Slavery*, doc. 6; *Wartime Genesis: Upper South*, docs. 6–7. On wartime emancipation in tidewater North Carolina, see *Destruction of Slavery*, chap. 1; *Wartime Genesis: Upper South*, chap. 1.

brought into the area to construct Confederate defenses. Even after fighting his way through a network of slave-built fortifications, McClellan's opinions about slavery remained unchanged. In a letter to President Lincoln, written on the eve of Union withdrawal from the peninsula, McClellan reiterated his belief that "[n]either confiscation of property, political executions of persons, territorial organization of States, or forcible abolition of slavery, should be contemplated for a moment."[50] But slaves in tidewater Virginia attached little importance to McClellan's opinions, preferring instead the precedent established earlier in the war at Fortress Monroe. They simply bypassed McClellan and his subordinates and took refuge at the federal fortress at the tip of the peninsula.

The war followed a different course in the western theater. In the east, both Burnside and McClellan operated within narrow geographical bounds. In the west, the Union offensive stretched from the Ohio River deep into the Mississippi Valley. Slavery also differed markedly in the valley. Cotton was the great staple crop and plantations were large, with slaveholdings sometimes extending into the hundreds on the rich bottom lands. Slaves generally worked in gangs and often lived their entire lives within the confines of a single estate. Yet, if large units and the absence of extensive hiring deprived most slaves of knowledge of the region's geography, the community that developed within the slave quarters and the network of communication that radiated outward from each plantation allowed them to mobilize quickly to take advantage of opportunities presented by the war. However, not all slaves in the Mississippi Valley resided on plantations. Some dwelled on small farms in the interstices between the great river estates. In the region's upcountry districts, small holdings predominated and slavery exhibited many of the features prevalent in tidewater Virginia and North Carolina. Throughout the Mississippi Valley, slaves quickly became aware of the federal military presence and pushed their way toward Union lines. Wherever Union

---

[50] McPherson, *Political History*, pp. 385–86.

soldiers entered the Confederacy, the policy of exclusion fell into disrepair.[51]

West of the Mississippi River, military events transformed federal forces into an army of emancipation. In February 1862, General Samuel R. Curtis and his Army of the Southwest advanced upon the Confederate troops who had wintered in southwest Missouri. When they retreated into Arkansas, Curtis followed, winning an important victory at Pea Ridge in early March. He then embarked on a grueling trek across the state, emerging at Helena, on the banks of the Mississippi, in July. All along his route, Curtis encountered obstacles constructed by impressed slaves — many of whom escaped in the tumult that accompanied the arrival of Union soldiers. By the time he reached Helena, a considerable number of fugitive slaves were following in his train. A three-term Iowa congressman with solid antislavery credentials, Curtis refused to permit these slaves to be recaptured by their owners and redeployed against his army. Instead, he issued certificates of freedom on the basis of the First Confiscation Act, making the Union-controlled portion of Arkansas a haven for fugitive slaves.[52]

East of the Mississippi River, the transformation of federal policy proceeded at a much slower pace. In February 1862, Union troops from General Halleck's Department of the Missouri (soon expanded and renamed Department of the Mississippi) entered Tennessee. General Ulysses S. Grant advanced up the Cumberland and Tennessee rivers to capture Fort Henry and Fort Donelson, shattering the Confederate line of defense that protected Tennessee and the states farther south. Meanwhile, General John Pope traced the Mississippi, opening the way for federal occupation of Memphis in June. In late February, as his subordi-

---

[51] On slavery in the Mississippi Valley, see Charles S. Sydnor, *Slavery in Mississippi* (New York, 1933); Chase C. Mooney, *Slavery in Tennessee* (Bloomington, Ind., 1957); Orville W. Taylor, *Negro Slavery in Arkansas* (Durham, N.C., 1958); Joe Gray Taylor, *Negro Slavery in Louisiana* (Baton Rouge, La., 1963). See also *Wartime Genesis: Lower South*, docs. 182–84; *Wartime Genesis: Upper South*, docs. 89, 113. On wartime emancipation in the Mississippi Valley, see *Destruction of Slavery*, chap. 5; *Wartime Genesis: Lower South*, chap. 3; *Wartime Genesis: Upper South*, chap. 3.

[52] *Destruction of Slavery*, doc. 95; *Wartime Genesis: Lower South*, doc. 151. For a description of the results of Curtis's policy by a Confederate general who owned a plantation near Helena, see *Destruction of Slavery*, doc. 92.

nates launched the offensive into the Confederacy, Halleck preached anew the doctrine of noninterference with slavery. "Let us show to our fellow-citizens . . . that we come merely to crush out rebellion . . . [and] that they shall enjoy . . . the same protection of life and property as in former days." Admonishing his troops that "[i]t does not belong to the military to decide upon the relation of master and slave," Halleck ordered that no slaves be admitted into Union lines. As though to leave no doubt about his firmness on the subject, he required that the order be read to every regiment and commanded all officers to enforce it strictly.[53]

Most of Halleck's subordinates executed his exclusion policy scrupulously, a comparatively easy task while they were on the move in areas with few slaves. But as Union forces overran Confederate positions, they inevitably captured slave laborers subject to the provisions of the First Confiscation Act and put them to work for the Union. The captives thereafter labored with the same tools, often in the same ditch, but now as free men protected by federal arms.[54]

Simultaneously with the movement of Northern forces into west Tennessee, General Don Carlos Buell's Army of the Ohio advanced into middle Tennessee, occupying Nashville as its new base of operations. Many middle Tennessee slaveholders professed loyalty to the Union, a circumstance that gave Buell added reason to stand by his order to exclude slaves from army lines and, when exclusion failed, to return them to their owners.[55] Conservative Buell remained convinced that respect for slavery on the part of the Union army would disabuse Confederates of mistaken notions about the antislavery intentions of the North, wean them from secession, and foster Southern unionism. Nevertheless, slaves fled to Buell's lines and sought admission. Sympathetic officers and men obliged. Indeed, when one division of the Army of the Ohio

[53] *Official Records*, ser. 1, vol. 8, pp. 563–65. For an order by Grant reiterating Halleck's exclusion policy, see *Official Records*, ser. 1, vol. 7, p. 668. On the enforcement of Halleck's policy by other subordinate officers, see *Destruction of Slavery*, docs. 82, 88, 199.

[54] See, for example, *Destruction of Slavery*, doc. 82.

[55] *Official Records*, ser. 1, vol. 7, pp. 669–70. On the enforcement of Buell's policy by his subordinates, see *Destruction of Slavery*, docs. 83, 85.

pressed into northern Alabama, some of its officers, deeming the slaves "our only friends," promised to protect fugitives who provided military information.[56] These officers did so in direct violation of Buell's orders, and he did his best to force them into line or drum them out of his command. More fully than any other general in the western theater, Buell was determined to protect slave property. But changes in federal policy undercut his commitment to the rights of slaveholders. Much to Buell's dismay, the new article of war in particular gave antislavery officers and soldiers greater latitude to act upon their principles.[57]

The policy of exclusion frayed as Northern armies took control of larger expanses of Confederate territory. It came completely undone when they reached the plantation South. There, slaves, women and children as well as men, entered Union lines in such numbers that it was nearly impossible to keep them out. Whatever the fugitive-slave policies undertaken – from rendition to unauthorized declarations of freedom – exclusion did not merit so much as a trial. Instead, Union commanders openly debated the question of universal emancipation.

The debate flared first in southern Louisiana, where General John W. Phelps squared off against the ubiquitous General Butler, under whose command federal forces captured New Orleans in April 1862. Phelps, a Vermont free-soiler who represented the growing commitment to emancipation within the Union army, believed the federal government should abolish slavery as the French had destroyed the *ancien régime*. When his troops occupied Ship Island, Mississippi, in December 1861, Phelps prepared to launch a war against slavery.[58] But before he could act, he became a post commander within Butler's Department of the Gulf.

Unlike Phelps, Butler was no abolitionist. Finding that a good many southern Louisiana slaveholders professed loyalty to the Union, Butler took them at their word and instructed his troops to assist in maintaining plantation discipline and to return runaway slaves to loyal owners. His orders appeared to violate the additional article of war recently

[56] *Destruction of Slavery*, doc. 86n.   [57] *Destruction of Slavery*, docs. 89, 91A-B.
[58] *Destruction of Slavery*, doc. 58.

adopted by Congress, but federal authorities neither reprimanded him nor instructed him to do otherwise. The general who had earlier stolen a march by transforming the slaves of disloyal owners into contrabands, now reversed the process for those who fled from loyal owners. Unionism in Louisiana would be built with the support of whites, not blacks; slaveholders, not slaves. For the time being, Butler simply ignored the large number of prosperous, cosmopolitan free people of color, most of whom resided in New Orleans. Nevertheless, free men of color who had previously been mustered into Confederate Native Guard units now proclaimed their loyalty to the Union and declared their readiness to fight for the federal cause.[59]

Many slave owners, particularly those of Whig pedigree, found Butler's program attractive. Yet Union policy – some of it Butler's own doing – had proceeded too far toward emancipation to reassure all slaveholders in southern Louisiana. Upon federal invasion, many fled the region. Fugitive masters attempted to take their slaves with them to the interior, but – as in the South Carolina Sea Islands – plantation hands resisted the passage.

Again, black people drew upon their experience as slaves in struggling for freedom. Slavery in southern Louisiana – with its large waterfront estates; its dependence upon skilled workers, especially in sugar processing; and its connections with the great metropolis of New Orleans – provided slaves with the means to resist their masters.[60] Familiar with the dense network of forests and swamps that surrounded almost every plantation, slaves took to the woods to wait out their owners' evacuation. Many of them subsequently headed for New Orleans or the Union camps on its outskirts. Some occupied abandoned estates in the midst of functioning slave plantations. Sometimes under the direction of an old driver, sometimes as groups of independent

[59] *Destruction of Slavery*, doc. 61. On the Native Guard units, see the sources cited above, in note 14.

[60] On slavery in southern Louisiana, see J. Carlyle Sitterson, *Sugar Country: The Cane Sugar Industry in the South, 1753–1950* (Lexington, Ky., 1953), chaps. 2–9; Taylor, *Negro Slavery in Louisiana*; Roderick A. McDonald, *"Goods and Chattels": The Economy and Material Culture of Slaves on Sugar Plantations in Jamaica and Louisiana* (Baton Rouge, La., in press). See also *Wartime Genesis: Lower South*, docs. 104, 111.

households, they began to sow subsistence crops while weeds choked the fields of sugar cane and cotton. These settlements of runaways soon attracted other fugitives, and they also affected slaves who remained at home, many of whom now refused to work under the old terms. Confronting their masters directly, they demanded an end to gang labor, the removal of overseers, and the payment of wages. Despite Butler's efforts to sustain unionist masters, the slave regime in southern Louisiana had been shaken beyond repair. Black people made it known that they would never again accept the old order.[61]

Stationed above New Orleans at Camp Parapet, General Phelps aided their cause. He broadcast his willingness to shelter fugitives, and, before long, slaves from miles around packed their few belongings and headed for his camp. When they appeared in rags, beaten and bloody, the enraged general ordered retributive raids, liberating other slaves and dramatically demonstrating the diminished authority of the planter class.[62]

Although not opposed to freeing the slaves of outright rebels, Butler demanded that his subordinates distinguish the slaves of the loyal from those of the disloyal. Phelps knew no such distinction. The two generals warred openly, and each appealed to higher authority in Washington. Butler expected a restatement of the prevailing policy of honoring the claims of loyal owners; Phelps sought a new commitment to universal emancipation. But Secretary of War Stanton sidestepped their dispute, and it continued into the heat of the Louisiana summer. Meanwhile, slaves expanded their liberty inside and outside the old system; slavery languished, even if freedom had not yet arrived.[63]

While Butler and Phelps dueled, General David Hunter, fresh from the Kansas border wars, took command of the South Carolina Sea

---

[61] On patterns of flight, see *Destruction of Slavery*, doc. 64. On the occupation of abandoned plantations, see *Wartime Genesis: Lower South*, doc. 79. On slaves' direct resistance to owners and overseers, see *Destruction of Slavery*, docs. 62, 66B, 68–69; *Wartime Genesis: Lower South*, docs. 69, 79. On wartime emancipation in southern Louisiana more generally, see *Destruction of Slavery*, chap. 4; *Wartime Genesis: Lower South*, chap. 2.

[62] For a description of one raid, see *Destruction of Slavery*, doc. 62.

[63] *Destruction of Slavery*, docs. 59–63; *Black Military Experience*, docs. 9–10.

Islands determined to become the great emancipator. He immediately set to work making Port Royal the base for a grand assault against the Confederacy. In April 1862, he sought War Department permission to enlist black men into the Union army, in part to reinforce his short-handed command and in part to strike a blow at slavery. When the department ignored his request, Hunter began recruiting anyway – often dragooning men at work on the islands' plantations into military service. In May, he proclaimed martial law throughout South Carolina, Georgia, and Florida, even though he controlled only a few coastal outposts. Then, pronouncing slavery incompatible with martial law, he declared that the slaves in those states were free.[64]

Although they disliked Hunter's recruitment methods, black people at Port Royal welcomed his audacious initiatives on behalf of freedom. President Lincoln was considerably less impressed, and he promptly reversed them. In acting against slavery, Hunter had moved far beyond the First Confiscation Act, much as Frémont had done the previous August. Northern opposition to slavery had increased during the intervening months, but Hunter's proclamation still challenged the Lincoln administration. The Secretary of War and the President reined the general. Stanton refused to sanction or provision Hunter's black regiment, which, as a result, eventually had to be disbanded. Ten days after Hunter abolished slavery in the Department of the South, Lincoln nullified Hunter's proclamation, reasserting his own authority over the disposition of slavery and restating his commitment to gradual, compensated emancipation.[65]

Although he felt compelled to repudiate Hunter's bold stroke, Lincoln understood that the war was fast eroding his own policy of noninterference with slavery, along with its corollaries – rendition and exclusion. Indicative of the growing strength of antislavery sentiment in the North, Congress prohibited slavery in the territories in June 1862, and soon thereafter took the first steps toward severing West Virginia from

---

[64] On Hunter's recruitment and its effects, see *Black Military Experience*, pp. 37–39, and docs. 1–4; *Destruction of Slavery*, docs. 20–21. For his emancipation edict, see *Wartime Genesis: Lower South*, doc. 24.

[65] *Destruction of Slavery*, doc. 24; *Black Military Experience*, pp. 38–39.

Virginia, which paved the way for its admission to the Union as a free state.[66] In a meeting with border-state congressmen in mid-July, Lincoln himself pointedly called attention to the changing circumstances. Warning them that time was running out for slavery, he predicted its inevitable dissolution in their own states "by mere friction and abrasion — by the mere incidents of the war." Lincoln also served notice that he could not continue to contravene the antislavery constituents whom he had offended by abrogating Hunter's proclamation. Once more, he urged that the border states adopt a gradualist plan of compensated emancipation.[67] Events were bypassing border-state slaveholders, but Lincoln would not remain behind.

A few days after the border-state meeting, as though to confirm Lincoln's warning, Congress expanded the legal basis for the extinction of slavery. The Second Confiscation Act, approved on July 17, declared slaves owned by disloyal masters "forever free of their servitude" and ordered that they be "not again held as slaves." It thus went far beyond the First Confiscation Act, whose provisions had touched only those slaves employed in Confederate service. Although the new confiscation act assigned to the federal courts ultimate responsibility for determining the loyalty of individual slaveholders, it designated the slaves "captives of war," placing them under the jurisdiction of the Union army. The act also enhanced the antislavery provisions of the additional article of war adopted the previous March. The article had not prevented army officers so disposed from opening their camps to slaveholders in pursuit of runaway slaves, so long as no soldier actually assisted in the capture. The Second Confiscation Act forbade persons in federal service to decide upon the validity of a claim to a slave "under any pretence whatever" or to "surrender up" any slave to a claimant. In effect, the new law deemed free all fugitive slaves who came into army lines professing that their

---

[66] *Statutes at Large*, vol. 12, p. 432; Richard O. Curry, *A House Divided: A Study of Statehood Politics and the Copperhead Movement in West Virginia* (Pittsburgh, Pa., 1964), pp. 100–130.

[67] Lincoln, *Collected Works*, vol. 5, pp. 317–19. Two days after their meeting with Lincoln, twenty of the border-state congressmen formally rejected compensated emancipation. A minority of eight approved the President's appeal.

owners were disloyal, as well as those slaves who fell under army control as Union troops occupied enemy territory. Furthermore, it held out a promise of protection from recapture and reenslavement. Bowing to the President's continued interest in removing black people from the United States – a popular idea among many white Northerners – the new confiscation act also encouraged the transfer of freed slaves to some tropical country willing to grant them "the rights and privileges of freemen."[68]

Despite lip service to colonization, Congress contemplated another role for the freed slaves. The Second Confiscation Act authorized the President to employ "persons of African descent" in any capacity to suppress the rebellion. The Militia Act, which became law on the same day, provided for their employment in "any military or naval service for which they may be found competent" and granted freedom to slave men so employed, as well as to their families, if they, too, were owned by disloyal masters.[69] Together, the Second Confiscation Act and the Militia Act made manifest the North's determination both to punish rebel slaveholders and to employ black men and women in the Union war effort.

Five days after signing the two acts, Lincoln issued an executive order translating the new legislation into instructions for the Union army and navy. He authorized military commanders operating in the seceded states to "seize and use any property, real or personal, which may be necessary or convenient for . . . military purposes," and he instructed them to "employ as laborers . . . so many persons of African descent as can be advantageously used for military and naval purposes, giving them reasonable wages for their labor." Although he also reiterated customary injunctions against wanton or malicious destruction of private property and required that records be kept to permit compensation to slaveholders "in proper cases," there was no mistaking the import of Lincoln's order.[70] Federal army officers understood it as an indication

---

[68] *Statutes at Large*, vol. 12, pp. 589–92.

[69] *Statutes at Large*, vol. 12, pp. 597–600.

[70] Lincoln's executive order, dated July 22, 1862, was promulgated to the armies in the field by a War Department order of August 16. (*Official Records*, ser. 3, vol. 2, p. 397.)

that thereafter no rebel property – slaves included – would escape military appropriation, and that fugitive slaves – at least the able-bodied men – should be welcomed into Union lines and put to work.[71]

The momentous events of July 1862 did not stop with the confiscation and military employment of slaves. On July 22, Lincoln informed the cabinet of his intention to issue a proclamation of general emancipation in the seceded states. Although he solicited comments from his advisers, he made clear his determination to act before the new year, regardless of opposition. At the cabinet's recommendation, however, Lincoln agreed to withhold his pronouncement until the occasion of a Union victory at arms, so that emancipation could be presented as an act of strength rather than weakness.[72] The summer dragged on without offering such an opportunity, and in September matters took an even more ominous turn. The Confederates invaded both Maryland and Kentucky, panicking the Northern population, forcing federal troops into defensive retreat, and marking a low point for the Union.

The battle of Antietam, though hardly the hoped-for triumph, halted the Confederate offensive in Maryland and at last provided the occasion for Lincoln's announcement. On September 22, 1862, he issued the preliminary Emancipation Proclamation, serving notice that on January 1 he would declare "then, thenceforward, and forever free" all the slaves in those states still in rebellion. Lincoln pledged that the United States government would protect their freedom and, moreover, would do nothing to repress any actions taken by the slaves themselves to secure their own liberty. While thus – as slaveholders saw it – virtually inviting slave insurrection, Lincoln also renewed his call for voluntary, gradual, and compensated emancipation in the border states, voiced support for colonizing freed slaves "upon this continent or elsewhere," and promised to recommend that all loyal owners be compensated for the loss of their slaves.[73]

---

[71] For examples of changes in military policy following the Second Confiscation Act, the Militia Act, and Lincoln's executive order, see *Destruction of Slavery*, docs. 93–94, 96–97.

[72] Franklin, *Emancipation Proclamation*, chap. 2.

[73] *Statutes at Large*, vol. 12, pp. 1267–68.

The new departures had immediate repercussions in the field. Abolitionist officers, who believed that slaveholders were enemies of the
Union, whatever their purported loyalty, welcomed the new legislation
and presidential pronouncements, and applied them with enthusiasm.
Other commanders, less principled than pragmatic, were unconcerned
about the fate of slavery but desperate for laborers; they, too, welcomed
the change. General William T. Sherman, whose reluctance to meddle
with slavery had become notorious, simply accepted fugitive slaves into
his ranks, employed those who could work, and left the others to shift
for themselves. His policy of keeping strict account of the labor performed by fugitive slaves, but withholding wages until the courts
should rule on their owners' loyalty, found wide acceptance among like-
minded officers.[74]

The change wrought by legislation and proclamation could be seen
even in the actions of military officers who had long deferred to the
rights of slaveholders. They too marched to a different beat. General
McClellan, stalled on the Virginia peninsula, republished Lincoln's
executive order almost upon receipt, adding, with full-throated indig-
nation, "we are engaged in supporting the Constitution and laws of the
United States and in suppressing rebellion . . . we are not engaged in a
war of rapine, revenge, or subjugation." Despite this petulant restatement of his long-established position, McClellan made haste to imple-
ment the President's edict, asserting that black laborers "have always
understood that after being received into the military service of the
United States in any capacity they could never be reclaimed by their
former holders."[75]

By the late summer of 1862, black men in large numbers – as well
as some black women – were already laboring for the Union army and
navy. Some had been accepted under the First Confiscation Act, others
in direct violation of the policy of exclusion. Now their numbers increased rapidly as federal commanders discovered what Confederate
officers had known all along: Slaves and free-black people were the most

[74] For Sherman's policy, see *Destruction of Slavery*, docs. 92, 94, 96.
[75] *Official Records*, ser. 1, vol. 11, pt. 3, pp. 362–64.

43

readily available – sometimes the only – source of military labor. Nearly every army post, supply depot, and wood yard acquired a contingent of black men to clear camps, build roads, construct fortifications, chop wood, and transport supplies. Few naval vessels lacked a handful of black men who handled the dirty and difficult business of coaling. Union commanders also found that black men, free and slave, possessed a variety of skills and were knowledgeable wagoners, scouts, and pilots. White workers – Northern and Southern – disdained certain kinds of labor as "nigger work," but black men and women stood able and often willing to take up the task – particularly if it would assure their liberty. The generally accepted notion that white people could not labor in tropical climates further increased reliance on black workers as the Union army marched south.

Military labor offered thousands of black men an opportunity to escape slavery and gain the protection of the Union army. Still, they found much to criticize in their new position. Their work frequently took them away from family and friends, and the military and civilian overseers who supervised them could be as abusive as any master – sometimes more so. Despite the specification of pay and rations in the Militia Act, the government often had difficulty meeting its payroll. Black laborers routinely received their wages late, and sometimes not at all – a circumstance that left them at the mercy of sharp traders in the army and out. The burden of work for the Yankee army led some black men to flee military labor as they had fled slavery. When they did, Union officers frequently resorted to impressment, much as had Confederate labor agents. Still, whatever its liabilities, military labor provided fugitive slaves with obvious advantages. Even those who deserted federal labor gangs seldom returned to their erstwhile owners.[76]

The Union army's willingness, indeed its need, to employ able-bodied black men did little to assist the black women, children, and old or infirm men who also made their way into Union lines in increasing numbers. Some women found employment as laundresses, cooks,

---

[76] On the experience of black military laborers, see *Wartime Genesis: Upper South*; *Wartime Genesis: Lower South*.

seamstresses, and hospital attendants, but the demand for such workers paled in comparison with the calls for men to construct fortifications, move supplies, and chop wood. Old people and children had even fewer opportunities to gain a livelihood. Like the women, they generally had to rely upon fathers, husbands, and sons who labored in federal service. But the massive exodus from bondage had disrupted black life, and the reconstitution of families was hindered by the chaos of war. Many of those who escaped slavery had no way to support themselves.

The mass of destitute black refugees posed monumental problems for Union authorities. Anxious to secure their liberty, unattached women, children, and elderly people, along with the families of black laborers, crowded around military depots and posts. As much as they tried to ingratiate themselves with their liberators, army commanders generally objected to their presence. Officers complained that the former slaves clogged roads and impeded the movement of soldiers and supplies, and that the refugees' squalid quarters and impoverished condition bred disease and vice.[77]

Union commanders found a variety of ways to deal with the fugitive slaves, all of them makeshift. Some left them to fend for themselves. A few sent them North. Some placed them under the care of civilian superintendents assigned to the occupied South by Northern churches and benevolent societies. But as the number of black military laborers swelled, the army itself was forced to accept at least some responsibility for the refugees within its lines. Indeed, the black men who labored for the army often made it clear that they would not work unless their families were provided with food and shelter. During the fall of 1862, federal commanders began to organize contraband camps, placing sympathetic officers – generally regimental chaplains or other men of humanitarian bent – in charge.[78]

[77] On the problems posed by the black refugees, see *Destruction of Slavery*, docs. 61, 63, 69n.; *Black Military Experience*, docs. 41, 194; *Wartime Genesis: Upper South*, doc. 11; *Wartime Genesis: Lower South*, docs. 65, 149, 157, 160.

[78] On the evolution of federal policy regarding the black refugees, see *Wartime Genesis: Upper South*; *Wartime Genesis: Lower South*; Louis S. Gerteis, *From Contraband to Freedman: Federal Policy toward Southern Blacks, 1861–1865* (Westport, Conn., 1973).

Former slaves who labored for the Union army or took refuge in the contraband camps did not remain satisfied with their own escape from slavery. Almost as soon as they reached the safety of federal lines, they began plotting to return home and liberate families and friends. Some traveled hundreds of miles into the Confederate interior, threading their way through enemy lines, eluding Confederate pickets, avoiding former masters, and outrunning the slave catchers hired to track them down. Not all succeeded, but when they did, their courage helped hundreds escape bondage and informed still others of the possibility of freedom. Occasionally, these brave men and women received assistance from sympathetic Union soldiers and commanders, who accompanied former slaves back to the old estates or provided material assistance to those intent upon returning to free others. The bargain seemed mutually beneficial – the Union army gained additional laborers, and the former slaves secured the liberty of their loved ones.[79]

The growing importance of black labor increased support for emancipation in the North. Abolitionists publicized the role of black laborers, arguing that their service to the Union made them worthy of freedom and citizenship. Other Northerners, indifferent or even hostile to the extension of civil rights to black people, also saw value in the exchange of labor for freedom. Expropriation of the slaveholders' property seemed condign punishment for treason. And they noted that by doing the army's dirty work, black laborers freed white soldiers for the real business of war. Samuel J. Kirkwood, governor of Iowa, was appalled to learn that one of his state's regiments had *"sixty men on extra duty* as teamsters &c. whose places could just as well be filled with *niggers."* He urged the military authorities to employ additional black laborers to do such *"negro work."* Indicating the drift of Northern opinion, Governor Kirkwood added a few words on the subject of enlisting black men as soldiers: "When this war is over & we have summed up the entire loss of life it has imposed on the country I shall not have any regrets if it is found that a part of the dead are *niggers* and that *all* are not white men."[80]

[79] *Destruction of Slavery*, docs. 12, 17, 101, 176.
[80] *Black Military Experience*, docs. 24–25.

Cynical though they were, such sentiments strengthened the hand of abolitionists, white and black, who urged the arming of black men with muskets as well as shovels. They had long maintained that enlisting black soldiers would enhance the military might of the Union, while also securing emancipation and pushing the nation toward racial equality. Their earlier efforts to introduce black men into military service had been peremptorily dismissed, sometimes with sharp rebuke. But as public opinion turned against slavery, the proponents of black enlistment met with increasing success. In the summer and fall of 1862, the first black soldiers entered Union ranks in the Sea Islands of South Carolina, in southern Louisiana, and in Kansas.[81]

As its advocates had hoped, the enlistment of black soldiers provided a powerful instrument in the war against slavery. Even before they had seen active service, news of the black men in blue uniforms had an electrifying effect on those still in bondage, encouraging many to strike out for the Yankee lines. When the first black regiments took the field, their subversive force increased manyfold. Black soldiers, the vast majority of them former slaves, coveted the liberator's role. Moving from plantation to plantation – up the tidal rivers of the South Atlantic coast and through the bayous and swamps of southern Louisiana – they urged slaves to abandon their owners and aided them in doing so. Indeed, black soldiers had such a destructive impact on slavery that they sometimes frightened their own commanders. In late 1862, General Godfrey Weitzel, who ended his wartime career at the head of the only all-black army corps, sought to be relieved of his first command of black troops from fear that they would incite a general slave revolt. When officers of steadfast antislavery conviction took command of black regiments, the work of dismantling slavery proceeded apace, transforming the liberated into liberators at dizzying speed. Black soldiers freed slaves and escorted them to the safety of Northern encampments, where recruiting officers inducted the able-

---

[81] For a full discussion of the earliest instances of black recruitment, see *Black Military Experience*, chap. 1. See also *Destruction of Slavery*, doc. 168.

bodied men into federal ranks and began drilling them for missions of their own.[82]

The possibility of military service opened the door to freedom for some slaves only to close it for others. As the enlistment of black men and the general increase of federal military activity provoked slaveholders to tighten plantation discipline, escape became more difficult and punishment more severe. Some masters called upon Confederate authorities to execute recaptured fugitive slaves as traitors in time of war, and at least one Confederate commander instituted court-martial proceedings against runaways.[83] Other slaveholders, choosing the risks of removal over the hazards of remaining within reach of federal raids, refugeed their slaves deep into the Confederate interior.

Thus, even with the aid of federal arms, freedom advanced slowly and not always directly. Individual slaveholders could aggravate the difficulties of escape to the Yankees, and Southern armies could recapture black people who had already reached Union lines. Confederate military offensives provided harsh reminders that the Northern commitment to emancipation amounted to little without military success. Indeed, any Union retreat or rebel attack could reverse the process of liberation and throw men and women who had tasted freedom back into bondage.[84]

The Confederate invasion of Kentucky in August and September 1862 dramatized the fragility of wartime emancipation. As the Union army withdrew from northern Alabama and middle Tennessee to counter the rebel threat, thousands of black people fell once again under Confederate control, their title to liberty under the federal confiscation acts rendered valueless. Many found themselves cast back into the

---

[82] On black soldiers as liberators, see *Destruction of Slavery*, docs. 14A-B, 31–32, 34, 189; *Black Military Experience*, docs. 78, 80A-B, 205E, 207, 299–301; *Wartime Genesis: Upper South*, doc. 180. For Weitzel's apprehensions, see *Destruction of Slavery*, doc. 69.

[83] On the tightening of slave discipline in response to emancipation and black enlistment, see *Destruction of Slavery*, docs. 15, 32, 319, 326–27. On Confederate military punishment of recaptured runaways, see *Destruction of Slavery*, docs. 318A-B, 320.

[84] In addition to the episode discussed in the next paragraph, see, for example, *Wartime Genesis: Upper South*, doc. 39; *Wartime Genesis: Lower South*, docs. 96, 168.

hands of their old masters – who had not forgotten how their slaves had turned on them and cooperated with the hated Yankees. Other former slaves, scrambling to retain the protection of the Union army, joined the forced march to Kentucky as pioneers, teamsters, and officers' servants. Still others trailed the retreating federal force – footsore, hungry, and fearful of what lay ahead, but certain of what remained behind. Many fell by the wayside and were captured by guerrillas or jailed by local authorities as runaway slaves. Even those who succeeded in reaching Kentucky learned firsthand of the insecurity of wartime freedom. State and local officials arrested hundreds of them under Kentucky's fugitive-slave law, advertised for their masters, and sold them to new owners when no one registered a claim. In the spring of 1863, federal authorities began to intervene in such instances of reenslavement, but many men, women, and children who had escaped bondage in the Confederate states endured the remainder of the war as slaves in Kentucky.[85] Their travail testified to the link between the military success of the Northern armies and the liberty of Southern slaves.

On New Year's Day, 1863, President Lincoln gave that connection the full weight of federal authority. The Emancipation Proclamation fulfilled his pledge to free all slaves in the states still in rebellion. Differences between the preliminary proclamation of September and the final pronouncement of January suggest the distance Lincoln and other Northerners had traveled in those few months. Gone were references to compensation for loyal slaveholders and colonization of former slaves. In their place stood the determination to incorporate black men into the federal army and navy. As expected, the proclamation applied only to the seceded states, leaving slavery in the loyal border states untouched, and it exempted Tennessee and the Union-occupied parts of Louisiana and Virginia. Nonetheless, its simple, straightforward declaration – "that all persons held as slaves" within the rebellious states "are, and henceforward shall be, free" – had enormous force.[86]

As Lincoln understood, the message of freedom required no embel-

[85] *Destruction of Slavery*, docs. 209–10, 213A-B, 215, 216n., 217B, 218, 223A-B; *Wartime Genesis: Upper South*, doc. 203.

[86] *Statutes at Large*, vol. 12, pp. 1268–69.

lishment. However deficient in majesty or grandeur, the President's words echoed across the land. Abolitionists, black and white, marked the occasion with solemn thanksgiving that the nation had recognized its moral responsibility, that the war against slavery had at last been joined, and that human bondage was on the road to extinction. But none could match the slaves' elation. With unrestrained – indeed, unrestrainable – joy, slaves celebrated the Day of Jubilee. Throughout the South – even in areas exempt from the proclamation – black people welcomed the dawn of a new era.[87]

In announcing plans to accept black men into the army and navy, the Emancipation Proclamation specified their assignment "to garrison forts, positions, stations, and other places, and to man vessels" – evidently proposing no active combat role and, in fact, advancing little beyond the already established employment of black men in a variety of quasi-military positions. Nonetheless, black people and their abolitionist allies – who viewed military service as a lever for racial equality, as well as a weapon against slavery – seized upon the President's words and urged large-scale enlistment. Despite continued opposition from the advocates of a white man's war, the grim reality of mounting casualties convinced many Northerners of the wisdom of flexing the sable arm. Moreover, once the Emancipation Proclamation had made the destruction of slavery a Union war aim, increasing numbers of white Northerners thought it only fitting that black men share the burden of defeating the Confederacy.[88]

Proponents of black enlistment adapted their cause to the new circumstances. They had few scruples about clothing their principled convictions in the rhetoric of military necessity, and such arguments found sympathetic listeners in Washington, where administration officials and legislators had awakened to the implications of protracted warfare and increasing manpower needs. As the number of white volunteers dwindled, Congress prepared legislation (adopted in March 1863)

[87] Franklin, *Emancipation Proclamation*, chaps. 4–5. For examples of celebrations of emancipation, see McPherson, *Negro's Civil War*, pp. 49–52, 61–65; *Destruction of Slavery*, doc. 73; *Wartime Genesis: Lower South*, doc. 36.

[88] *Black Military Experience*, pp. 74–76; *Wartime Genesis: Lower South*, docs. 159–60.

providing for national military conscription. At the same time, the War Department took the first steps toward systematic recruitment of black soldiers. In January, Secretary of War Stanton yielded to the importunities of John A. Andrew, antislavery governor of Massachusetts and long-time advocate of the sable arm, authorizing him to raise a black regiment. Other governors received similar permission, and recruiters – many of them black – fanned out across the free states, politicizing and inspiring black communities as never before. Eventually, nearly three-quarters of the military-age black men in those states enlisted in federal military service.[89]

The War Department also expanded recruitment of black men in Union-occupied areas of the Confederacy, sending recruiting officers of high rank to tidewater North Carolina and southern Louisiana. In March 1863, the department crowned its new policy by dispatching General Lorenzo Thomas, adjutant general of the army, to the Mississippi Valley, where he propounded its virtues to Union commanders and troops and launched full-scale recruitment of black men. Thomas's appointment signaled a shift from haphazard recruitment by interested parties and independent commanders to a centrally coordinated effort under War Department auspices. The Bureau of Colored Troops, established in May 1863, provided bureaucratic embodiment of that shift. From the spring of 1863 to the end of the war, the federal government labored assiduously to maximize the number of black soldiers. The Northern public and officials in Washington came to understand what field commanders had discovered at first hand: Every slave placed in federal military service represented a double gain – one lost to the Confederacy and one added to the Union.[90]

As black soldiers joined white soldiers in expanding freedom's domain, the Union army became an army of liberation. Although the Emancipation Proclamation implied an auxiliary role, black soldiers would not permit themselves to be reduced to military menials. They longed to confront their former masters on the field of battle, and they

---

[89] *Black Military Experience*, chap. 2; Table 1 and note 38 in Chapter 3, this volume.
[90] *Black Military Experience*, chap. 3, and pp. 9–10.

soon had their chance. The earliest black regiments acquitted themselves with honor at the battles of Port Hudson, Milliken's Bend, and Fort Wagner in the spring and summer of 1863, and black soldiers thereafter marched against the Confederacy on many fronts. Meanwhile, scores of black regiments served behind the lines – protecting railroads, bridges, and telegraph lines; manning forts; and fending off guerrillas and rearguard rebel attacks. Their services became essential to the Union war effort as Northern armies advanced deep into Confederate territory, lengthening the lines of communication and supply. The subversive effect of black soldiers on slavery, first demonstrated on the South Atlantic coast and in southern Louisiana, increased with the number of black men in federal ranks. By war's end, nearly 179,000 – the overwhelming majority slaves – had entered the Union army, and another 10,000 had served in the navy.[91]

Military service provided black men with legal freedom and more. In undeniable ways, it countered the degrading effects of Southern slavery and Northern discrimination. Soldiering gave black men, free as well as slave, a broader knowledge of the world, an acquaintance with the workings of the law, access to some rudimentary formal education, and a chance to demonstrate their commitment to freedom for themselves and their people. Battlefield confrontations with the slaveholding enemy exhilarated black soldiers by proving in the most elemental manner the essential equality of men. In their own eyes, in the eyes of the black community, and, however reluctantly, in the eyes of the nation, black men gained new standing by donning the Union blue.[92]

Large-scale enlistment of black soldiers deepened the federal government's commitment to all former slaves. Although black men contributed to the Northern cause both as laborers and as soldiers, it seemed more difficult to deny support to the families of those who shouldered muskets than to the families of those who wielded shovels. When the army mustered black soldiers from the Confederate states, it implicitly –

---

[91] On the combat and noncombat duties of black soldiers, see *Black Military Experience*, chaps. 10–11. For the number of black men in the army and navy, see Table 1 and note 38 in Chapter 3, this volume.

[92] *Black Military Experience*, especially chaps. 9, 11, 14.

and sometimes explicitly – agreed to protect and provide for their families and friends. Adjutant General Thomas understood the relationship between recruiting soldiers and caring for their families as fully as any federal officer. When he began recruiting black regiments in the Mississippi Valley, he organized contraband camps as he established recruitment stations; often the two were the same. Commanders in other parts of the Union-occupied Confederacy followed a similar course, though their efforts never kept pace with the number of black refugees.[93]

As the population of the contraband camps swelled, the superintendents began settling former slaves on plantations abandoned by their owners, usually as laborers in the employ of Northerners who leased the estates, occasionally as independent farmers.[94] But, at best, the camps and abandoned plantations provided only short-term solutions to the problems created by the growing number of fugitive slaves within Union lines. Indeed, these temporary arrangements merely raised larger questions about the future of black people once slavery was abolished. To address these questions, Secretary of War Stanton appointed the American Freedmen's Inquiry Commission in March 1863, instructing the three commissioners to investigate the condition of the refugee slaves and report how they might best defend and support themselves. Creation of the commission signaled the federal government's recognition of its necessary role in shaping the future of the slaves freed by the President's proclamation.[95]

Important Union victories in the summer of 1863 marked a turning point in the war and increased the urgency of regularizing federal policy

[93] For Thomas's first thoughts on the problem of black refugees, see *Black Military Experience*, doc. 194. On federal policy regarding black soldiers' families in the Union-occupied Confederacy, see *Black Military Experience*, chap. 16, and docs. 158B, 194; *Destruction of Slavery*, doc. 110; *Wartime Genesis: Upper South*, docs. 22, 26, 33–34, 40, 42–43, 47A, 101–2, 108–11, 129; *Wartime Genesis: Lower South*, docs. 37, 59, 107, 172, 187, 204, 212.

[94] On plantation leasing in 1863, confined chiefly to the Mississippi Valley and southern Louisiana, see *Wartime Genesis: Lower South*, chaps. 2–3.

[95] For Stanton's instructions to the commissioners, see *Official Records*, ser. 3, vol. 3, pp. 73–74. The commission issued a preliminary report in June 1863 and a final report in May 1864. (*Official Records*, ser. 3, vol. 3, pp. 430–54; ser. 3, vol. 4, pp. 289–382.) See also John G. Sproat, "Blueprint for Radical Reconstruction," *Journal of Southern History* 23 (Feb. 1957): 25–44.

respecting former slaves. Northern military successes liberated slaves in unprecedented numbers, especially in the Mississippi River Valley, where the fall of Vicksburg opened the way to federal control of the great river and severed the Confederacy. Tens of thousands of slaves thereby fell into Union hands, and thousands more fled to Union lines from Confederate territory on both sides of the river. Federal officials, drawing on established policy, promptly enlisted the men into the army and sent the women, children, and old people to safety behind the lines. To accommodate the influx, they established new contraband camps and expanded the plantation-leasing system, with the understanding that Northern lessees would employ the soldiers' families. To defend the plantations and contraband camps against Confederate raids, federal commanders assigned some of the newly enlisted black soldiers to guard duty, making them protectors of their parents, wives, and children.[96]

As the Union army transformed plantations into recruiting stations and contraband camps, the struggle over black manpower escalated. Responding to the federal challenge and the pleas of their own military commanders, Confederate leaders laid greater claim to the South's black labor force. In October 1863, Secretary of War James A. Seddon ordered the implementation of legislation, approved the previous March, that had increased the Confederacy's power to impress black military laborers. But that legislation, the first of a series of enactments expanding authority over slave and free-black men, stopped far short of granting unrestricted power to overrule slaveholders and claim the labor of their slaves.[97] Even as the Southern army retreated before the

[96] On the expansion of plantation leasing in the Mississippi Valley, see *Wartime Genesis: Lower South*, pp. 638–47, and docs. 180–81, 185, 189, 196–97. On the assignment of black soldiers to guard plantations and contraband camps, see *Wartime Genesis: Upper South*, doc. 205n.; *Wartime Genesis: Lower South*, docs. 168, 207, 213; *Black Military Experience*, docs. 53, 194.

[97] For the various laws and some of the orders implementing them, see *Official Records*, ser. 4, vol. 2, pp. 469–72, 897–98; ser. 4, vol. 3, pp. 112, 207–9, 897–99, 1082–83. See also Bernard H. Nelson, "Confederate Slave Impressment Legislation, 1861–1865," *Journal of Negro History* 31 (Oct. 1946): 392–410. On Confederate use of slave labor, see James H. Brewer, *The Confederate Negro: Virginia's Craftsmen and Military Laborers, 1861–1865* (Durham, N.C., 1969); Mohr, *On the Threshold of Freedom*, chap. 5; Robinson, "Day of Jubilo," chap. 3; Wiley, *Southern Negroes*, chap. 7.

Northern enemy, many slaveholders ignored requests for laborers and refused to hire their slaves to Confederate quartermasters, engineers, and medical officers. State officials – claiming that the states and not the general government had jurisdiction over slavery – sometimes went so far as to countermand Confederate orders and recall slaves who had been impressed.[98]

Slaveholders resisted impressment in part because it revealed to the slaves the limits of their owners' authority and thereby undermined slavery. Confederate officers, often of junior grade, sometimes rode roughshod over the masters. Observing the derogation of their owners' power – especially the ability to protect their slaves against outsiders – slaves became less willing to accord them the old deference. They worked slower and answered faster – in a tone that chilled their owners.

Confederate military commanders fumed at the slaveholders' cupidity and despaired at the narrow preoccupations of state officials. Some impugned the slaveholders' patriotism, a charge that resonated loudly within the lower ranks of the Southern army. When slave owners ridiculed the accusation and continued to ignore requests for laborers, hard-pressed field officers simply took them, sometimes with the permission of officials in Richmond and sometimes on their own authority. The resulting struggles set off ripples of recrimination. Slaveholders denounced military officers, state officials challenged the general government, small slaveholders condemned large ones, and nonslaveholders rebuked slaveholders in general for their unwillingness to sacrifice their slaves while the yeomanry sacrificed its sons. The widespread conviction that manpower burdens were being borne unequally was reinforced by complaints about inequity in taxation, conscription, and the distribution of food and other scarce commodities.[99]

[98] On the reluctance or refusal of slaveholders to surrender their slaves to Confederate authorities, see *Destruction of Slavery*, docs. 266–67, 272, 290, 328; *Black Military Experience*, doc. 121; Harrison A. Trexler, "The Opposition of Planters to the Employment of Slaves as Laborers by the Confederacy," *Mississippi Valley Historical Review* 27 (Sept. 1940): 211–24.

[99] For examples of the internecine conflicts occasioned or exacerbated by the impressment of slaves, see *Destruction of Slavery*, docs. 265, 274B, 277–78, 290, 292, 295, 298A, 316.

Slaves studied the divisions in Southern society with great care, dreading the prospect of being dragged into Confederate service. Impressment almost always removed slave men from home and family. Labor superintendents often treated them roughly. Having no interest in impressed slaves as property, they worked them hard with scant concern for their well-being. Often they drove slaves far beyond the usual demands of plantation labor, despite protests by their owners. Meanwhile, as impressment agents and slaveholders debated terms of service and responsibility for rations, clothing, shelter, and medical care, the impressed laborers went hungry and cold, fell ill, and died in numbers that appalled even the most hard-hearted.[100] The terrifying possibility of impressment set slaves in motion. Many fled to the woods; others turned toward Union lines, where recruiters waited to fit the men for a blue uniform.[101]

Fearing that they would soon face their slaves on the field of battle if they did not lose them to Confederate labor agents, slaveholders searched for a safe harbor, distant from the dangers of both escape and impressment. During the summer of 1863, refugeeing assumed unprecedented proportions, especially in the Mississippi Valley and in lowcountry Georgia and South Carolina. Slaveholders moved thousands – indeed, tens of thousands – of slaves to the interior and to Texas.[102]

Properly executed, refugeeing effectively slowed the exodus from the plantations. But attempted relocation, rather than securing slave property, often became the occasion for its loss. Understanding the diminished opportunities to escape from the interior, and unwilling in any

[100] On the physical treatment and working conditions of slaves impressed for Confederate military labor, see *Destruction of Slavery*, docs. 260F, 260H, 268–69, 274–75, 281–83, 290n., 316.

[101] On the flight of slaves to avoid impressment or to escape Confederate military labor, see *Destruction of Slavery*, docs. 266, 276, 278–79, 280n., 281–82, 283n., 290–91, 295, 299n., 324, 328.

[102] On refugeeing slaves to the Confederate interior and to Texas, see *Destruction of Slavery*, pp. 675–77, and docs. 14B, 103, 123, 307–14; *Wartime Genesis: Lower South*, docs. 101, 185, 190; *Black Military Experience*, doc. 116; Wayne K. Durrill, *War of Another Kind: A Southern Community in the Great Rebellion* (New York, 1990), chaps. 3, 6; Mohr, *On the Threshold of Freedom*, chap. 4; Robinson, "Day of Jubilo," chap. 5.

case to leave their homes, slaves resisted removal. Everywhere efforts to refugee slaves spurred flight.[103] Sometimes they escaped to the woods, awaited their owner's departure, and then returned to the old plantation to farm on their own. Despite their vulnerability to rebel raids, these independent settlements served as examples to slaves on neighboring plantations and, before long, as rendezvous for runaways. Even successfully executed refugeeing did not entirely serve the slaveholders' purpose. The swollen slave population of the interior placed enormous burdens on scanty food supplies and disrupted local economies. In effect, refugeeing transferred the disorder of the war zone to areas not yet directly touched by the conflict. With the arrival of refugeed slaves in the interior, the number of runaways surged, as did the fear of insurrection.[104]

Insurrection was only one concern of those who governed plantation life. With the impressment and refugeeing of large numbers of able-bodied young men, the burden of plantation labor increasingly devolved upon slave women and those men who remained. Embittered by the enforced absence of their loved ones and resentful of the heavy work load, they could not – and would not – continue to labor at the same pace. The motley collection of white women, disabled soldiers, and old men who presided over the great estates seemed incapable of maintaining the old discipline.[105]

The Confederate tax-in-kind and the impressment of draft animals and farm implements further reduced agricultural production.[106] And, with animals and tools in short supply, slaves saw little reason to work beyond their own personal needs. In the early years of the war, planters had been encouraged to switch from staple crops to food production; as the war dragged on, many of them drifted from commercial

---

[103] On the flight of slaves in anticipation of or during refugeeing, see, for example, *Destruction of Slavery*, docs. 311, 313, 318A.

[104] *Destruction of Slavery*, doc. 313; *Black Military Experience*, doc. 116.

[105] On the problem of maintaining slave discipline in the Confederacy, see *Destruction of Slavery*, docs. 281, 294, 302, 307, 313, 315–31.

[106] Richard C. Todd, *Confederate Finance* (Athens, Ga., 1954), pp. 141–48; James L. Nichols, "The Tax-in-Kind in the Department of the Trans-Mississippi," *Civil War History* 5 (Dec. 1959): 382–89.

agriculture to subsistence farming. As the Confederacy shrank, even self-sufficiency became difficult, and inflation increasingly put market purchases out of reach. A subsistence crisis of considerable magnitude gripped the South. For many slaves, the failure of their owners to feed and clothe them severed the last threads of allegiance. When they did not abandon the plantation, they simply raised food crops for their own tables.[107]

The disorder on the home front worried those on the war front. Confederate soldiers petitioned for leave of absence to attend to their families' needs, and, when short-handed commanders rejected their pleas, they deserted in droves. Those who did not desert complained bitterly that their own families went hungry while slaves fed the slaveholders' kin. Disaffection among white Southerners sometimes gave slaves new allies. For a few dollars, deserters and other disaffected whites shepherded runaways to freedom, or they joined slaves in the swamps to form interracial outlaw gangs.[108] As the war dragged on, slaves occasionally found assistance within the ranks of the Confederate army. Soldiers, military overseers, and labor agents sold passes to impressed slaves, allowing them to escape labor and sometimes bondage.[109]

Caught between Confederate impressment officers and Yankee recruiters, reluctant to refugee their slaves for fear of losing them, growing numbers of slaveholders were driven to make new concessions to keep them at home and at work. Negotiations began tentatively and proceeded awkwardly, since slaveholders would not concede their loss of mastery and slaves would not accept the legitimacy of bondage. Often the bargaining assumed an air of unreality, as slaveholders-turned-employers offered a "gift" at harvest time, while slaves-turned-employees demanded more concrete remuneration. Some slaves and

[107] On the problem of agricultural production in the Confederacy, see *Destruction of Slavery*, docs. 292–98, 304, 314, 328; Wiley, *Southern Negroes*, chap. 3; Robinson, "Day of Jubilo," chap. 2; Paul W. Gates, *Agriculture and the Civil War* (New York, 1965), pt. 1.
[108] See, for example, *Destruction of Slavery*, doc. 27.
[109] See, for example, *Destruction of Slavery*, doc. 324.

their owners bartered labor for a promise of manumission at some future date, others haggled over a portion of the crops, and still others dickered about wages in cash or in kind. Whatever the terms agreed upon, neither party rested satisfied. Slaveholders were sure they conceded too much, slaves convinced they received too little. At the first promising opportunity, each party abandoned concessions and pressed for the ideal – the slaveholders, for reinstatement of the old regime; the slaves, for full independence from it.[110]

The breakdown of these fragile accords sent slaves or slaveholders – and sometimes both – flying to safety. Slaves moved toward Union lines, slaveholders deeper into the shrinking Confederacy. Black people who remained on the old estates entered an ill-defined world between slavery and freedom. Where their owners abdicated, slaves cultivated food crops on the abandoned land they now considered their own. The presence of these independent black farmers had a ruinous effect on slavery in areas under Confederate control.[111]

Slavery suffered more serious damage in the portions of the Confederacy occupied by the Union army. Slaveholders – even in Tennessee and southern Louisiana, which were exempt from the Emancipation Proclamation – found themselves unable to halt the steady disintegration of their authority. Time and again, unionist masters learned the futility of trying to control their slaves when those owned by rebel masters worked independently upon abandoned land, labored for the Union army, or enlisted as Union soldiers. With the slaves' options increasing, the old modes of discipline no longer carried the same force. The wisest slaveholders accepted the demands of the emerging order and did what was necessary to keep their slaves at work. Some welcomed, indeed urged, the establishment of federally sponsored labor systems – like those enacted by General Butler and his succes-

---

[110] For examples of privately negotiated free-labor arrangements during the war, see *Destruction of Slavery*, docs. 111, 122–23; *Wartime Genesis: Upper South*, docs. 89, 107, 112, 116, 125, 127–28, 130; *Wartime Genesis: Lower South*, docs. 104–5, 156, 203, 211, 214, 231–32.

[111] For examples of independent occupation of land by former slaves, see *Wartime Genesis: Lower South*, docs. 79, 91, 97, 190, 196, 209.

sor, General Nathaniel P. Banks, in Louisiana – that required planters to pay wages but pledged Yankee assistance in maintaining plantation discipline.[112] In the absence of federal interference, slaveholders in the Union-occupied South – like their counterparts in the Confederacy – were forced to relinquish old prerogatives if they hoped to retain their labor force.

The federal government's introduction of wage labor formed part of a larger effort to create loyal governments in the occupied states of the Confederacy. Familiar with the sources of Republicanism in the free states, Lincoln hoped to foster similar coalitions in the South by drawing together disaffected yeoman farmers, urban workingmen and shopkeepers, and planters and businessmen of Whig antecedents. Black men – first, free blacks and soon, former slaves – tried to join these nascent unionist parties, but they were hampered by their exclusion from citizenship. The expansion of the territory under federal control, especially after the fall of Vicksburg in July 1863, gave struggling unionists in Louisiana, Tennessee, and Arkansas an aura of legitimacy they had previously lacked. Meanwhile, the destruction of slavery by federal arms undercut the influence of proslavery unionists in the state coalitions and in Washington, rendering them progressively more isolated and impotent. Feeding upon the debility of proslavery unionism and enjoying the sponsorship of federal military commanders, antislavery unionists pressed their cause and found new adherents as its prospects improved. Their demand for emancipation pushed slavery to the edge in those parts of the Confederacy exempted from Lincoln's proclamation.[113]

[112] On the labor systems of Butler and Banks, see *Wartime Genesis: Lower South*, chap. 2; Gerteis, *From Contraband to Freedman*, chaps. 4–6; C. Peter Ripley, *Slaves and Freedmen in Civil War Louisiana* (Baton Rouge, La., 1976), especially chaps. 2–5; William F. Messner, *Freedmen and the Ideology of Free Labor: Louisiana, 1862–1865* (Lafayette, La., 1978), especially chaps. 3–6. On the system established by Adjutant General Lorenzo Thomas along the Mississippi River, and later extended to middle Tennessee and northern Alabama, see *Wartime Genesis: Lower South*, chap. 3; *Wartime Genesis: Upper South*, doc. 109; Gerteis, *From Contraband to Freedman*, chaps. 7–10.

[113] On unionist politics in the occupied Confederate states, see Peyton McCrary, *Abraham Lincoln and Reconstruction: The Louisiana Experiment* (Princeton, N.J., 1978); Joe Gray Taylor, *Louisiana Reconstructed, 1863–1877* (Baton Rouge, La., 1974), chap.

The deterioration of slavery in the Union-occupied Confederacy had no immediate effect on the institution in the Union's own slave states. Having stood by the old flag when the other slave states seceded, Delaware, Maryland, Kentucky, and Missouri were not included in the Emancipation Proclamation. Insistent upon slavery's full legal standing under the federal constitution, slaveholders in the border states rejected Lincoln's repeated urgings that they adopt some plan of gradual, compensated emancipation. Indeed, their minority position as slaveholders in the Union seemed only to stiffen their resolve. Rather than bend to the winds of change, they deployed old defenses of their right to human property and fashioned new ones. Border-state legislatures bolstered antebellum slave codes, which were rigorously enforced by local officials. State courts not only upheld these laws and sustained the rights of slaveholders, but also entertained suits against anyone who interfered with slavery, including officers of the United States army.[114]

The legality of slavery narrowed the avenues to freedom in the border states, but slaves hazarded them nonetheless. From the earliest months of the war, many of them had found refuge with Northern regiments,

2; C. Peter Ripley, *Slaves and Freedmen in Civil War Louisiana* (Baton Rouge, La., 1976); James W. Patton, *Unionism and Reconstruction in Tennessee, 1860–1869* (Chapel Hill, N.C., 1934); Thomas S. Staples, *Reconstruction in Arkansas, 1862–1874* (New York, 1923), chaps. 1–2. Efforts by black people to influence wartime unionist politics were most salient in Louisiana. See Donald E. Everett, "Demands of the New Orleans Free Colored Population for Political Equality, 1862–1865," *Louisiana Historical Quarterly* 38 (Apr. 1955): 43–64; David C. Rankin, "The Impact of the Civil War on the Free Colored Community of New Orleans," *Perspectives in American History* 11 (1977–78): 379–416, and "The Origins of Negro Leadership in New Orleans during Reconstruction," in *Southern Black Leaders of the Reconstruction Era*, ed. Howard N. Rabinowitz (Urbana, Ill., 1982), pp. 155–89; Ted Tunnell, *Crucible of Reconstruction: War, Radicalism, and Race in Louisiana, 1862–1877* (Baton Rouge, La., 1984), chap. 4; "State Convention of the Colored People of Louisiana," in *Proceedings of the Black State Conventions, 1840–1865*, ed. Philip S. Foner and George E. Walker, 2 vols. (Philadelphia, 1979–80), vol. 2, pp. 243–53; *Wartime Genesis: Lower South*, doc. 139. On the participation of black Tennesseans in the formal politics of emancipation, see John Cimprich, "The Beginning of the Black Suffrage Movement in Tennessee, 1864–65," *Journal of Negro History* 45 (Summer 1980): 185–95; *Black Military Experience*, doc. 362.

[114] *Destruction of Slavery*, docs. 143–46, 173, 183, 202D-G, 203–5; *Wartime Genesis: Upper South*, docs. 184, 189, 213B, 215; *Black Military Experience*, docs. 72, 74, 85.

and some gained employment as military laborers. In Missouri, especially along the Kansas border, a virtual civil war within the Civil War provided slaves with opportunities to leave their owners, and in Maryland, proximity to the District of Columbia afforded fugitive slaves a safe haven.[115] The slaves' persistence and the receptivity of federal troops and army quartermasters forced border-state slaveholders into rearguard actions that undermined their unionist credentials. By the end of 1863, exasperated army officers and federal officials had tired of feuding with masters who appeared to care more for their property than for the Union. As Lincoln had predicted, the "friction and abrasion" of war were eroding slavery in the border states.[116]

Wartime wear and tear also encouraged indigenous white opponents of slavery in the border states. These men and women felt most at home in the great regional centers of trade and production — Baltimore, Louisville, and St. Louis. White wage-workers — many of them immigrants — had in large measure displaced slaves in these cities. They brought with them notions of the moral and material superiority of free labor, beliefs inimical to slavery. Opposition to slavery could also be found in the countryside, especially among yeoman farmers who had long distanced themselves from both slaveholders and slaves. Many antislavery farmers, like urban employers, depended upon free workers, including free blacks. The active role played by white workers and their employers — urban and rural — in preventing secession had given them an important place in the unionist coalition of each border state, and they battled the slaveholding unionists for leadership. Antislavery unionists enjoyed greatest success in Maryland and Missouri, but even there they failed to gain parity with proslavery unionists until the fall of 1863.

---

[115] On the flight of Maryland slaves to the District of Columbia, see *Destruction of Slavery*, docs. 41, 44, 46, 51, 135–37, 144–45A; *Wartime Genesis: Upper South*, docs. 157, 158B; *Black Military Experience*, doc. 72. On the exodus of Missouri slaves to Kansas, see Richard B. Sheridan, "From Slavery in Missouri to Freedom in Kansas: The Influx of Black Fugitives and Contrabands into Kansas, 1854–1865," *Kansas History* 12 (Spring 1989): 28–47; *Destruction of Slavery*, docs. 168, 190, 195; *Black Military Experience*, doc. 85; *Wartime Genesis: Upper South*, doc. 161.

[116] For full discussions of the erosion of slavery in the border states, see *Destruction of Slavery*, chaps. 6–8.

As the federal government enunciated its commitment to emancipation, antislavery partisans in the border states grew bolder. They campaigned openly for an end to slavery, gaining support from nonslaveholding farmers and artisans. Long denied access to black labor by the slaveholders' monopoly, many farmers and tradesmen welcomed the disruption of the old regime. Some of them hired fugitive slaves with few questions asked. When slaveholders threatened prosecution under state codes that prohibited hiring a slave without the owner's permission, employers either had to dismiss their workers or defy the slaveholders. The emergence of a viable antislavery movement made their choice easier. As nonslaveholders cast their weight on the side of freedom, the ground shifted beneath the slaveholders.[117]

Still, slavery did not give way in the border states until black men began entering the Union army in large numbers.[118] In the summer of 1863, with the enlistment of black men already proceeding in the North and in the Union-occupied Confederacy, federal authorities inaugurated black recruitment in Maryland and Missouri. Reluctant to offend slaveholding unionists, President Lincoln and the War Department at first authorized the enlistment only of free blacks and of slaves whose owners were disloyal. But black men – including the slaves of loyal owners – volunteered so enthusiastically that it proved nearly impossible to restrict enlistment. This was particularly true once nonslaveholding white men recognized that black recruits reduced conscription quotas that they would otherwise have to fill. Nonslaveholders demanded that slaves be enlisted as well as – and sometimes instead of – free blacks. In Maryland, where nonslaveholding farmers feared that the enlistment of free-black men would diminish their work force

---

[117] For examples of antislavery unionism in the border states and assessments of its growing strength, see *Destruction of Slavery*, docs. 140, 175, 179, 185–86, 188; *Wartime Genesis: Upper South*, doc. 186; *Black Military Experience*, docs. 71, 76, 87, 99, 108. On the obstacles posed by the continued legal standing of slavery, see *Destruction of Slavery*, docs. 242, 244, 246, 248–49, 251–52, 254–55; *Wartime Genesis: Upper South*, docs. 184, 189, 193, 215, 238–39; *Black Military Experience*, doc. 112.

[118] On the recruitment of black soldiers in the border states, see *Black Military Experience*, chap. 4.

while leaving that of the slaveholders intact, this demand reached its highest pitch. In all the border states, antislavery partisans united in urging the elimination of distinctions between slaves of the loyal and those of the disloyal. With the ready compliance of black volunteers, recruiters stepped up enlistment, circumventing regulations regarding the status of the recruits or the politics of their owners.

Recruiters of an abolitionist stamp warmed to the task of dismantling slavery in the border states. In Maryland and Missouri, they raided plantations and farms, offering freedom in exchange for military service. Slaveholders denounced the federal government's betrayal of its promise not to interfere with slavery, but masters who a year earlier could command the full attention of cabinet officers now received short shrift from bureaucrats of the lowest rank. Complaints from slaveholders and their representatives about the recruiters' high-handed tactics brought temporary relief at best. In the fall of 1863, over the opposition of border-state slaveholders, the War Department authorized the systematic enlistment of slave men in Maryland, Missouri, and Delaware, including slaves owned by loyal masters. General Order 329 promised freedom to the recruits and compensation to loyal owners.[119] Thousands of black men answered the call.

By the end of 1863, only black men in Kentucky remained off-limits to army recruiters. Many of them took matters into their own hands and fled to neighboring states to enlist, especially after recruitment began in Tennessee. Kentucky slaveholders managed to forestall black enlistment by marshaling the assistance of sympathetic Union commanders – many of them slaveholding natives – and by flexing their still considerable political muscle. But in the spring of 1864, with the demand for soldiers increasing and the success of black recruitment evident, federal authorities ended Kentucky's special standing. Following the earlier pattern in Maryland and Missouri, recruiters began by accepting free-black volunteers, as well as slaves owned by disloyal masters or by loyal masters who consented to their

---

[119] General Order 329, which provided for black recruitment in Maryland, Missouri, and Tennessee, was issued on October 3, 1863. Its provisions were extended to Delaware on October 26. (*Official Records*, ser. 3, vol. 3, pp. 860–61, 925.)

enlistment. Again, slaves thronged the recruiting stations in defiance of their owners' wishes. In the face of such massive volunteering, the restrictions could not hold, and by early summer, federal officials had sanctioned the enlistment of any able-bodied black man who reached a recruitment office, regardless of his owner's loyalty or consent.[120]

The recruitment of black men dealt a death blow to slavery in Delaware, Maryland, and Missouri, and terminally weakened it in Kentucky. Black men in the border states joined the army in staggering proportions: In Delaware, enlistees equaled 25 percent of eligible black men; in Maryland, 28 percent; in Missouri, 39 percent; in Kentucky, 57 percent. Altogether, nearly 42,000 black men from the border states served in the Union army, and 2,400 more – mostly from Delaware and Maryland – enlisted in the navy.[121] What wartime disruption, slave flight, and antislavery agitation had begun, the massive drain of able-bodied black men accomplished in short order.

Border-state black men paid a price for freedom over and above their military service. Slaveholders, understanding the subversive effects of armed service, spared nothing to prevent the transformation of their slaves into soldiers. Unprotected until they reached the safety of a recruitment office, slaves braved arrest, physical assault, even death. Many of them traveled great distances by night to avoid violent encounters with slave masters and their hired thugs. Volunteers rejected by recruiters as physically unfit faced similar dangers.[122]

To dissuade slave men from enlisting and to punish those who did, border-state slaveholders turned upon their families. Inveighing against ungrateful servants, some slaveholders drove off the parents, wives, and

[120] On black recruitment in Kentucky, see *Destruction of Slavery*, docs. 227–28, 230, 233–34; *Black Military Experience*, chap. 4.
[121] See Table 1 and note 38 in Chapter 3, this volume. These figures exclude the numerous border-state black men who fled to free territory before enlisting in the army, notably Maryland slaves who enlisted in the District of Columbia and Missouri slaves who enlisted in Kansas. The District of Columbia, whose black population in 1860 included 1,823 men of military age, was credited with 3,269 black soldiers. Kansas, with a black military-age population of only 126, enlisted 2,080 black soldiers.
[122] *Destruction of Slavery*, docs. 146, 188, 190, 227n.; *Wartime Genesis: Upper South*, doc. 136; *Black Military Experience*, docs. 74, 87–88, 90A-B, 100–101, 103, 105.

children of black soldiers, leaving them to fend for themselves. Others avenged the desertion of slave men by whipping and otherwise abusing their families. The soldiers' kin also bore the burden of enlistment in the form of additional chores, including backbreaking work previously reserved for young men. Fearful that this harsh regimen would encourage flight, slaveholders resorted to preventive measures such as locking up the slaves' shoes and clothing at night. But, in the end, even the most ruthless violence could not sustain slavery.[123]

To escape vindictive owners, slave women and children frequently accompanied their husbands, sons, and fathers to the recruitment centers. Others fled on their own and settled near army camps and military posts or squatted on patches of unoccupied land. In the face of relentless harassment by slaveholders whose legal authority was undiminished, black soldiers demanded protection for their families. Their pleas, joined by those of sympathetic white officers, ascended the military chain of command. But Union officials, severely handicapped because the soldiers' families had no legal claim to freedom, could do little to prevent them from being abused or even reenslaved. At times the army itself contributed to their difficulties by evicting them from military posts and nearby shantytowns, thereby exposing them to recapture by their owners or the civil authorities.[124]

Unable to prevent black men from exchanging slavery for military service and freedom, border-state slaveholders executed a series of obstructionist maneuvers to salvage what remained of their eroding power. Some Missouri slaveholders forwarded their slaves to Kentucky, slavery's last sanctuary within the Union. The most optimistic relocated their entire operations, much like the rebel planters who had migrated to the interior of the Confederacy. But many simply sold out, dispatching their slaves to Kentucky slave marts for whatever price they

---

[123] *Destruction of Slavery*, docs. 191–93, 231, 233, 235, 237; *Wartime Genesis: Upper South*, docs. 181, 193, 225B, 226; *Black Military Experience*, docs. 74, 79, 83, 90B, 91–94, 106–7, 294, 296–98, 302–4, 312B.

[124] *Destruction of Slavery*, docs. 146, 192, 228A, 233; *Wartime Genesis: Upper South*, docs. 173, 177, 179, 193, 196, 219; *Black Military Experience*, docs. 83, 90B, 91, 93, 97, 102A-C, 105, 107, 110–11, 312A-B, 333, 336, 341.

would fetch. This revival of the interstate slave trade evoked a mighty protest and eventual military interdiction, but not before many Missouri slaves had been sold from their homes and families.[125]

While slaveholders lashed out at those slaves still under their control, the new order began to take shape. Increasing numbers of border-state slaveholders – like their counterparts in the Union-occupied Confederacy – were forced to bargain with their slaves, offering inducements in cash or kind to keep them from enlisting in the army or simply running away. Nonslaveholders also began to bid for the services of fugitive slaves. Black men and women took advantage of this competition, seeking the most attractive terms of employment.[126] When nonslaveholders became employers of black laborers, they linked arms politically with antislavery unionists, and the momentum of emancipation became irresistible. By January 1865, both Maryland and Missouri had abolished slavery.[127]

As slavery withered in the border states, the war entered its final phase. In a succession of hard-fought Union advances that culminated in the fall of Atlanta in September 1864, General William T. Sherman – now chief commander in the western theater – positioned his army to dismember the Confederacy. After Atlanta, the end came quickly. Sherman's troops swept through Georgia to the sea, taking Savannah in December. He set his sights next on South Carolina, the seedbed of secession, and in early 1865 struck out across the state, his inexorable march cutting a swath of destruction and terror.[128] Areas not scarred by the advancing federal army felt the effects of masters and slaves fleeing desperately for safety. Upcountry Georgia and South Carolina slaveholders experienced belatedly what had already become common throughout

---

[125] *Destruction of Slavery*, docs. 184A-B, 223A; *Wartime Genesis: Upper South*, docs. 165, 171n.; *Black Military Experience*, pp. 189–90, and docs. 91–94.

[126] *Wartime Genesis: Upper South*, docs. 139, 186, 188–89, 191, 196–97, 222, 228; *Black Military Experience*, doc. 96.

[127] Francis N. Thorpe, comp., *The Federal and State Constitutions*, 7 vols. (Washington, 1909), vol. 3, pp. 1741–79, vol. 4, pp. 2191–2219. The Maryland emancipation constitution took effect in November 1864, and a Missouri constitutional convention abolished slavery in January 1865.

[128] See Joseph T. Glatthaar, *The March to the Sea and Beyond: Sherman's Troops in the Savannah and Carolinas Campaigns* (New York, 1985).

the war zone. Slaves grew impertinent and insubordinate. They refused to be refugeed, and movement at gunpoint bred still greater discontent. Refugeed slaves sought to return to their old homes, especially when their families had been left behind. If they could not do so, they ran toward the Yankees instead of away from them. The reverberations from Sherman's march echoed wherever slavery remained intact. The entire Confederacy shuddered with apprehension.

Slaves not evacuated before Sherman's army followed in its rear. Ragged and frightened, exhausted but determined, they hazarded an uncertain future. Stragglers fell by the wayside, often becoming victims of slave catchers who continued to ply their gruesome trade. But Sherman had no intention of delaying his march to accommodate black refugees. Even those who matched Sherman's columns step for step could not count on the sympathy, much less the support, of his army. Sherman had never disguised his contempt for black people, and both officers and men took their cue from him. Moreover, as the commander of an army on the march in enemy territory, living off the land, Sherman felt no obligation to care for those whose lives it crossed and transformed. The thousands of black stalwarts who followed in his train praised Sherman's troops for breaking their shackles, but had precious little else for which to thank them. Union soldiers stripped slave cabins of their meager contents with the same spirit in which they rifled the masters' mansions, often leaving slaves without food or clothing.[129] Nevertheless, the mass of black refugees who crowded upon his ranks provoked Sherman to bestow upon them a gift worthy of their faith in the Union, with far-reaching consequences for postwar reconstruction. In January 1865, after consulting with black leaders in Savannah, Sherman issued Special Field Order 15, which set aside the coastal lands of South Carolina and Georgia, from Charleston southward, for the exclusive occupation of black people and established procedures by which black settlers might acquire "possessory title" to forty-acre plots.[130]

---

[129] For examples, see *Destruction of Slavery*, docs. 36–38.

[130] For Sherman's order, see *Wartime Genesis: Lower South*, doc. 59. For an account of the meeting that preceded its issue, see *Wartime Genesis: Lower South*, doc. 58.

The Destruction of Slavery

In other theaters of the war, the work of destroying slavery proceeded less dramatically but no less surely. Union troops in the Mississippi Valley steadily extended the territory under their control and maintained the vital supply lines that supported Sherman's Atlanta campaign. In Virginia, enormous federal armies under General-in-Chief Ulysses S. Grant hounded the Confederates into the trenches of Petersburg and Richmond, and then laid siege to the last remnants of Robert E. Lee's once mighty legion. In all these military operations, black soldiers played conspicuous parts. They manned forts, guarded railroad bridges, protected contraband camps and government plantations, skirmished with guerrillas, and dug and fought in the trenches. The deployment of black soldiers sped the decline of slavery and assured fugitive slaves a friend in the field.[131]

With slavery in shambles and Northern victory increasingly sure, unionists in much of the occupied South concluded the business of emancipation. Federal officials and army commanders turned on their slaveholding allies and made it clear that the liquidation of slavery was prerequisite for readmission to the Union. Antislavery unionists, previously stymied by slaveholding loyalists, took control of the unionist coalitions and pressed for immediate abolition. Early in 1864, Arkansas loyalists enacted constitutional changes ending slavery. Unionists in states partly or wholly exempt from the Emancipation Proclamation followed suit, in Louisiana late in 1864 and in Tennessee early in 1865.[132] As Lincoln had hoped, these new state constitutions placed emancipation upon firmer ground, beyond the reach of judicial challenge to the confiscation acts or the Emancipation Proclamation.

Union military success also strengthened the North's own commitment to freedom. Sherman's triumph at Atlanta helped Lincoln beat back a challenge for the presidency by George B. McClellan, the former general-in-chief. The previous spring, with reelection in doubt, congressional support for emancipation had faltered. The Senate had approved a constitutional amendment abolishing slavery, but when it

---

[131] See *Black Military Experience*, chaps. 10–11.
[132] Thorpe, *Federal and State Constitutions*, vol. 1, pp. 288–306, vol. 3, pp. 1429–48, vol. 6, p. 3445.

came before the House, the Democratic opposition had denied it the two-thirds majority required for passage. In January 1865, with Lincoln reelected and the Republicans securely in power, the House approved the amendment and forwarded it to the states for ratification.[133] As the state legislatures opened their debates, the President and the Congress turned in earnest to the task of postwar reconstruction. In early March, Lincoln signed legislation creating the Bureau of Refugees, Freedmen, and Abandoned Lands (or Freedmen's Bureau, as it became known) to supervise the transition from slavery to freedom. A joint resolution adopted the same day liberated the wives and children of black soldiers, regardless of their owners' loyalty, and thereby provided a claim to freedom for tens of thousands of border-state slaves whose bondage had been impervious to law or presidential edict.[134]

The value of emancipation to the Union did not escape Confederate leaders. They realized that by employing black men, first as laborers and then as soldiers, and by demonstrating a commitment to universal freedom, the North had transmuted the Confederacy's cornerstone into its tombstone. In their last desperate hour, a few Southern leaders tried to reverse that alchemy. They began deliberations on the enlistment of black soldiers into Confederate ranks, with the understanding that freedom would be offered in exchange for military service. In November 1864, President Jefferson Davis asked the Confederate Congress to consider the government's relationship to the slave as person, rather than as property. With the support of General Lee, legislation authorizing black enlistment was finally adopted in March 1865, too late for any slave soldiers to strike a blow for Southern independence. In early April, as Confederate recruiters took to the streets, Lee surrendered.[135]

In the aftermath of Appomattox, word of freedom spread to areas of the Confederacy that had escaped wartime Union occupation. Dis-

[133] Wilson, *History of Antislavery Measures*, chap. 13. See also LaWanda Cox and John H. Cox, *Politics, Principle, and Prejudice, 1865–1866: Dilemma of Reconstruction America* (New York, 1963), chap. 1.

[134] *Statutes at Large*, vol. 13, pp. 507–9, 571.

[135] *Official Records*, ser. 4, vol. 3, pp. 797–99; *Black Military Experience*, pp. 281–82, and docs. 123–26; Durden, *The Gray and the Black*, chap. 7.

charged black soldiers sometimes carried the news. Men who had fled their homes as slaves now returned as liberators, uniformed in Union blue and carrying rifles (which they, like other federal soldiers, could purchase upon muster-out). Along with word of freedom, they also bore the special experience of having participated in the Union's greatest triumph. Black soldiers still in service also traversed the South, forming part of the postwar army of occupation. As representatives of federal power in the former Confederacy, they enjoyed great authority in bringing freedom to fruition and interpreting its meaning.[136] Still, the message did not reach some slaves until well into the summer, or even later. In Texas, where the Confederate surrender came a full two months after Appomattox, black people celebrated "Juneteenth" as emancipation day. In a few places, slaveholders who were determined to maintain the old order used force to keep their slaves locked in bondage. The liquidation of these vestiges of slavery continued long after the cessation of hostilities, eventually aided by the Thirteenth Amendment. In the concise, clipped language of the law, the new amendment – ratified in December 1865 – summarized the monumental changes wrought by the war: "Neither slavery nor involuntary servitude, except as a punishment for crime whereof the party shall have been duly convicted, shall exist within the United States, or any place subject to their jurisdiction."[137]

The promulgation of freedom followed no set pattern. Sometimes, army officers and Freedmen's Bureau agents made the rounds of plantations and farms, armed with the Emancipation Proclamation or an order by the local Union army commander. To hastily called assemblages, they announced the demise of slavery, often appending long disquisitions on the meaning of freedom – the need for freedpeople to work hard, respect rightful authority, and support themselves and their dependents.

Usually, however, word of slavery's death preceded the arrival of federal officers. With rumors of freedom rife and some slaves silently

[136] See *Black Military Experience*, chaps. 17–18.
[137] *Statutes at Large*, vol. 13, pp. 774–75.

departing their owners' domain, slaveholders understood that if they did not act promptly they would soon face rows of empty slave cabins, if not angry and unruly laborers. In quick order, they called "their people" together to enact a drama for which neither they nor their audience was fully prepared. Masters and slaves shifted uneasily, their eyes glued to some formal document or distant object, as they tried desperately to avoid direct confrontation. Struggling to maintain their composure, slaveholders gave deadpan renditions of the proclamation or a military order taken from the local press. Slaves strained to decipher the strange words and peculiar cadence of these official edicts, but the meaning was clear enough from their owners' demeanor. The slaveholders often concluded with words of their own. Some blurted out an oath, cursed their former slaves, and damned their posterity. Others wished the freedpeople well and asked them to remain through the harvest – perhaps agreeing only to feed and clothe them "as usual," perhaps promising a part of the crop, a token payment, or "to do well by them at Christmas." The men and women whose freedom was thus conceded rarely responded directly. Indeed, despite the momentous implications of the occasion, they displayed little emotion. Instead, they returned to the quarters to sort out the meaning of what had transpired, to plan for the future, and to celebrate among themselves. They were slaves no more.

As often as not, however, there was no final confrontation, no moment of truth when master and slave stood eye to eye for the last time. Some slaves, learning of abolition, waited for their owners to make amends or offer some better arrangement. Erstwhile slaveholders, unable to conceive of a world without slaves, remained strangely silent – hoping against hope that life would go on as in former times. For a while it might, but then, one morning, the household would be strangely silent, and former masters and mistresses would have to try their hands at unfamiliar tasks. Not all slaveholders let it come to this. As news of freedom spread, they began to bargain with their one-time slaves – much as slaveholders in the Union-occupied Confederacy had been forced to do during the war. Some black men and women accepted these new arrangements; many did not. Although they marched into an uncertain future in either case, they too were slaves no more.[138]

The last chapter of the story of emancipation was not written exclusively in the disloyal South. Through the end of 1865, while Northerners celebrated the triumph of freedom over slavery and army officers and Freedmen's Bureau agents liberated black people illegally enslaved in the former Confederacy, other black people remained legally bound in loyal Delaware and Kentucky. Delaware contained only a handful, but Kentucky slaveholders still held tens of thousands who had no claim to liberty. The end of the war no more deterred these die-hard slaveholders than did congressional passage of the constitutional amendment abolishing slavery or its ratification by a steady progression of states. Indeed, the more hopeless their situation, the more adamant they became. They indignantly rejected the amendment and anything else that smacked of abolition, and loudly asserted their right to their slaves. Progressively isolated as emancipation became increasingly inevitable, they held out until the bitter end, making the end as bitter as possible for their slaves.[139]

Until the constitutional amendment was ratified, military enlistment remained the only avenue to freedom for Kentucky slaves. By liberating the wives and children of black soldiers, the congressional joint resolution of March 1865 stimulated a new surge of enlistments. But state courts obligingly declared the resolution unconstitutional, and state and local officials continued to enforce the slave code. Moreover, many Kentucky black soldiers were stationed far from home, in Virginia before Appomattox and in Texas after the Confederate surrender. With the soldiers unable to intervene, would-be slaveholders continued to regard the families of these men as slaves; indeed, they heaped upon them unprecedented abuse. And as discharged black soldiers began returning to Kentucky, they met extraordinary violence. Both slaveholders and nonslaveholders who capitulated to the inevitable end of slavery

---

[138] Litwack, *Been in the Storm So Long*, chap. 4.

[139] On the postwar struggle for emancipation in Kentucky, see *Destruction of Slavery*, pp. 514–18, and docs. 239–56; *Wartime Genesis: Upper South*, docs. 231–42; *Black Military Experience*, docs. 112, 172, 261, 304, 307A-B, 312B, 327.

faced the scorn and judicial persecution of neighbors who still contested emancipation and who remained in control of local government.

Fortunately for Kentucky slaves, the federal commander assigned to their state was an avowed enemy of slavery. General John M. Palmer, himself Kentucky-born, had moved to Illinois as a youth, where he developed a keenly honed hatred of the South's "domestic institution" and participated in the formation of the Republican party. Wartime military service had sharpened his antislavery convictions. Utilizing existing legislation, notably the joint resolution, Palmer undertook the liquidation of slavery in Kentucky. He wielded his military authority to override state laws and to protect black people, and circumvented the slaveholders' power by issuing passes to their slaves. Still, even a commander as determined as Palmer could not overcome all the obstacles created by the continued legality of slavery, especially after martial law was lifted in October. Not until December 1865, when the Thirteenth Amendment was ratified, could slavery be dismantled. In elevating war-won emancipation to constitutional status, the amendment gave many Kentucky slaves their first claim to freedom.

After the war, freedpeople and their allies – some newly minted, some of long standing – gathered periodically to celebrate the abolition of slavery. They spoke of great deeds, great words, and great men, praising the Emancipation Proclamation and the Thirteenth Amendment and venerating their authors. A moment so great needed its icons. But in quieter times, black people told of their own liberation. Then there were as many tales as tellers. Depending upon the circumstances of their enslavement, the events of the war, and the evolution of Union and Confederate policy, some recounted solitary escape; others, mass defections initiated by themselves or the Yankees. Many depicted their former owners in headlong flight, and themselves left behind to shape a future under Union occupation. Others told of forced removals from home and family to strange neighborhoods and an enslavement made more miserable by food shortages, heightened discipline, and bands of straggling soldiers. Still others limned a struggle against slaveholders whose unionist credentials sustained their power. More than a few black people shared the bitter memory of escaping slavery only to be re-enslaved when the Northern army retreated or they ventured into one of the Union's own slave states. Some recalled hearing the news of freedom from an exasperated master who reluctantly acknowledged the end of the old order; others, from returning black veterans, bedecked in blue uniforms with brass buttons. Those who had escaped slavery during the war often had additional stories to relate. They told of serving the Union cause as cooks, nurses, and laundresses; as teamsters and labor-ers; as spies, scouts, and pilots; and as sailors and soldiers. Even those who had remained under the dominion of their owners until the defeat of the Confederacy and had been forced to labor in its behalf knew that their very presence, and often their actions, had played a part in destroy-ing slavery.

These diverse experiences disclosed the uneven, halting, and often tenuous process by which slaves gained their liberty, and the centrality of their own role in the evolution of emancipation. The Emancipation Proclamation and the Thirteenth Amendment marked, respectively, a turning point and the successful conclusion of a hard-fought struggle. But the milestones of that struggle were not the struggle itself. Neither its origins nor its mainspring could be found in the seats of executive and legislative authority from which the great documents issued. In-stead, they resided in the humble quarters of slaves, who were con-vinced in April 1861 of what would not be fully affirmed until Decem-ber 1865, and whose actions consistently undermined every settlement short of universal abolition.

Over the course of the war, the slaves' insistence that their own enslavement was the root of the conflict – and that a war for the Union must necessarily be a war for freedom – strengthened their friends and weakened their enemies. Their willingness to offer their loyalty, their labor, and even their lives pushed Northerners, from common soldiers to leaders of the first rank, to do what had previously seemed unthink-able: to make property into persons, to make slaves into soldiers, and, in time, to make all black people into citizens, the equal of any in the Republic. White Southerners could never respond in kind. But they too came to understand the link between national union and universal liberty. And when the deed was done, a new truth prevailed where slavery had reigned: that men and women could never again be owned and that citizenship was the right of all. The destruction of slavery transformed American life forever.

2

The Wartime Genesis of Free Labor 1861–1865

A S SLAVERY DETERIORATED during the American Civil
War, fundamental questions arose about the social order that
would take its place.[1] Amid the tumult and danger of war, former
slaves – usually designated "contrabands" or "freedmen" – struggled
to secure their liberty, reconstitute their families, and create institutions befitting a free people. But no problem loomed larger than finding a means of support. Having relinquished the guarantee of subsistence that accompanied slavery, freedpeople faced numerous obstacles
to gaining a livelihood. Many had fled their homes with little more
than the clothes on their backs. Others had been abandoned by their
owners. Nearly all began life in freedom without tools or land, with no
certain source of food, clothing, or shelter, and with no means to
provide for the old, the young, the sick, or the disabled. For generations the slaves' labor had enriched their owners. Now, in freedom,
would they or others benefit from their toil?

Military operations in the slave states compelled Northern officials to
confront the same questions. Fugitive slaves poured into federal lines,
searching for protection and freedom. Other slaves came under Union
control as Northern forces occupied parts of the Confederacy. From the
first, military considerations encouraged officers in the field and officials in Washington to mobilize former slaves on behalf of the Union
war effort. Provision also had to be made for those who could not be

---

[1] This essay, like the others in this volume, is based primarily upon documents
published in *Freedom: A Documentary History of Emancipation* and other documents
from the National Archives of the United States. For published primary sources and
general secondary works pertaining to slavery and emancipation during the Civil
War, most of which touch on labor arrangements, see note 1 in Chapter 1, this
volume. Other especially useful studies of wartime labor include Eric Foner, *Reconstruction: America's Unfinished Revolution, 1863–1877* (New York, 1988), chaps. 1–
2; Louis S. Gerteis, *From Contraband to Freedman: Federal Policy toward Southern
Blacks, 1861–1865* (Westport, Conn., 1973); Edward Magdol, *A Right to the Land:
Essays on the Freedmen's Community* (Westport, Conn., 1977), chap. 4; Lawrence N.
Powell, *New Masters: Northern Planters during the Civil War and Reconstruction* (New
Haven, Conn., 1980); C. Peter Ripley, *Slaves and Freedmen in Civil War Louisiana*
(Baton Rouge, La., 1976); Armstead L. Robinson, " 'Worser dan Jeff Davis': The
Coming of Free Labor during the Civil War, 1861–1865," in *Essays on the Postbellum
Southern Economy*, ed. Thavolia Glymph and John J. Kushma (College Station, Tex.,
1985), pp. 11–47; Willie Lee Rose, *Rehearsal for Reconstruction: The Port Royal
Experiment* (Indianapolis, Ind., 1964).

usefully employed by the army or navy. Once emancipation became official federal policy, attention turned as well to the task of constructing free labor upon the ruins of slavery. Throughout the Union-occupied South, intertwined questions of labor and welfare forced themselves upon officials concerned chiefly with waging the war.

Federal military authorities were not alone in claiming the labor of the former slaves. Antislavery Northerners hoped to demonstrate the superior productivity of free labor, and Yankee entrepreneurs saw profits to be made in the bargain. Slave owners insisted that the former slaves were still theirs by right, and owners-turned-employers demanded preferential access to the labor of people they had lost as property. White Southerners who had never owned slaves saw an opportunity to break the slaveholders' monopoly of black workers. As the confiscation acts, the Emancipation Proclamation, and the success of federal arms extended freedom, the questions of how former slaves would work and for whose benefit assumed ever-greater importance.

In the course of a complex struggle among many contestants, free labor slowly took root throughout the Union-occupied South. Owing more to wartime necessities than to carefully considered plans, the new arrangements were ad hoc responses, not systematic designs for the future. They were restricted, moreover, to the narrow bounds of Union-held territory, themselves subject to the overriding requirements of the war. Provisional by their very nature, wartime labor programs were certain to be revamped or even jettisoned upon the return of peace. Nevertheless, measures adopted as temporary expedients had far-reaching implications. As the victorious North evaluated wartime developments, precedents solidified that opened certain possibilities and foreclosed others. Meanwhile, thousands of former slaves and former slaveholders entered the postwar world already experienced in the ways of free labor. Reconstruction of the defeated South would begin where wartime measures left off.

Four related circumstances influenced the wartime evolution of free labor: the notions of freedom espoused by Northerners, the beliefs and material resources of former slaves and free blacks, the extent and character of federal occupation, and the policies of federal authorities. If no one circumstance operated independently of the others, each was of special significance at particular moments and in particular places.

Free labor emerged in the Union-occupied South as freedom was being redefined in the North. During the first half of the nineteenth century, Northern merchants and manufacturers had reorganized work arrangements and, in the process, gained unprecedented control over production. They thereby elevated themselves to new positions of social and economic preeminence and set in motion changes that ousted artisans from their crafts and farmers from their land. On the eve of the Civil War, most small towns and farming communities had not yet been touched by these revolutionary changes. But in all the major cities of the Northeast and Midwest, as well as in many small towns, workshops employing dozens of workers and factories employing hundreds had become common. In these places, wage-workers may have outnumbered landed farmers, propertied artisans, and self-employed shopkeepers.

Changing patterns of ownership and production created overlapping and, often, contradictory conceptions of freedom. From one perspective, freedom derived from a man's ownership of productive property, real and personal, which guaranteed a competency and the ability to establish an independent household. Ownership of productive property ensured respectability within a community and membership in its polity. The ideal citizen was a male proprietor whose control over his own labor and its products underlay both economic and political independence. Since men of independent means could not be bought or bribed, they alone – at least until the 1820s, in most states – could vote, hold office, serve on juries, and enjoy the other manifestations of full citizenship. As heads of households, such men could extend some of the benefits of freedom to others under their jurisdiction – wives, children, servants, apprentices, and journeymen – whom they represented in the polity. Depending on their age, sex, and color, these dependents might travel without restriction, assemble at will, bear arms, testify in court, and enjoy other rights, but they were not and could not be citizens in the fullest sense.

The social and economic changes that eroded property-based independence created a different understanding of freedom. From the new perspective, freedom derived not from the ownership of productive property, but from the unfettered sale of one's labor power – itself a commodity – in a competitive market. "Political freedom rightly defined," proclaimed a Union general, "is liberty to work, and to be protected in the full enjoyment of the fruits of labor."[2] Voluntary rather than obligatory labor, represented by contracts based on mutual consent, became the hallmark of the new order. Ideal citizens thus included not only independent farmers, artisans, and shopkeepers, but also upwardly mobile wage-workers who by dint of ambition, industry, and luck improved themselves. Indeed, to the apostles of the emerging order, the process of self-improvement itself made for better workers, better citizens, and better men, thereby affirming the natural – if not providential – origins of the new ideal.

Individual men, able to rise and fall according to their own ability and energy, began breaking away from traditional household structures. By the early nineteenth century, indentured servitude had all but disappeared, apprenticeship was falling into disuse, and the master-journeyman system – increasingly unable to regulate prices, training, or the quality of workmanship – was crumbling. Changes that undermined personal subordination in the workplace also altered domestic relationships. Although fathers retained much of their traditional power and full political rights were not extended to women, the departure of production from the household allowed some women a new authority over domestic life.[3]

---

[2] *Wartime Genesis: Upper South*, doc. 26. The general was Benjamin F. Butler.
[3] On the transformation of economy and society in the free states, see David Montgomery, *Beyond Equality: Labor and the Radical Republicans, 1862–1872* (New York, 1967), especially chap. 1 and appendix A; Alfred D. Chandler, *The Visible Hand: The Managerial Revolution in American Business* (Cambridge, Mass., 1977), chaps. 1–3; Alan Dawley, *Class and Community: The Industrial Revolution in Lynn* (Cambridge, Mass., 1976); David M. Gordon, Richard Edwards, and Michael Reich, *Segmented Work, Divided Workers: The Historical Transformation of Labor in the United States* (Cambridge, U.K., 1982), chap. 3; Steven Hahn and Jonathan Prude, eds., *The Countryside in the Age of Capitalist Transformation: Essays in the Social History of Rural America* (Chapel Hill, N.C., 1985), chaps. 1–4, 8–11; Peter Dobkin Hall, *The*

As Northerners came to advocate internally generated initiative, rather than personal obligation and external force, as the proper stimulus to industry, they assaulted those social relations that smacked of direct coercion. Southern slaveholders represented everything that advocates of the new freedom despised. By denying the two great incentives to self-improvement – the stick of hunger and the carrot of property accumulation – slaveholders debased both their slaves and themselves and created a social order that was tyrannical, exploitative, and corrupt. Only free labor could make for a society of free and independent men.[4]

The new conception of freedom existed side by side with the old, and rather than see them as mutually exclusive, most Northerners embraced elements of both. Indeed, for many of them, the opportunities of the market offered a way to achieve the old ideal of freehold independence.

Organization of American Culture, 1700–1900: Private Institutions, Elites, and the Origins of American Nationality (New York, 1982); Mary P. Ryan, *Cradle of the Middle Class: The Family in Oneida County, New York, 1790–1865* (Cambridge, U.K., 1981); Anthony F. C. Wallace, *Rockdale: The Growth of an American Village in the Early Industrial Revolution* (New York, 1978); Sean Wilentz, *Chants Democratic: New York City and the Rise of the American Working Class, 1788–1850* (New York, 1984). The decline of the master-apprentice system is traced in W. J. Rorabaugh, *The Craft Apprentice: From Franklin to the Machine Age in America* (New York, 1986). For the ideological changes that accompanied and articulated the social transformation, see Eric Foner, *Free Soil, Free Labor, Free Men: The Ideology of the Republican Party before the Civil War* (New York, 1970), chaps. 1–2, and *Politics and Ideology in the Age of the Civil War* (New York, 1980), chaps. 3–4, 6–7; Jonathan A. Glickstein, *Concepts of Free Labor in Antebellum America* (New Haven, Conn., 1991); Robert J. Steinfeld, *The Invention of Free Labor: The Employment Relation in English and American Law and Culture, 1350–1870* (Chapel Hill, N.C., 1991); Barbara J. Fields and Leslie S. Rowland, "Free Labor Ideology and Its Exponents in the South during the Civil War and Reconstruction," *Labor History* (in press). The changing role of women is analyzed in Nancy F. Cott, *The Bonds of Womanhood: "Woman's Sphere" in New England, 1780–1835* (New Haven, Conn., 1977); Ryan, *Cradle of the Middle Class*; Kathryn Kish Sklar, *Catharine Beecher: A Study in American Domesticity* (New Haven, Conn., 1973); Christine Stansell, *City of Women: Sex and Class in New York, 1789–1860* (New York, 1986).

4 David Brion Davis, *The Problem of Slavery in the Age of Revolution, 1770–1823* (Ithaca, N.Y., 1975), especially chaps. 8–10; Jonathan A. Glickstein, " 'Poverty Is Not Slavery': American Abolitionists and the Competitive Labor Market," in *Antislavery Reconsidered: New Perspectives on the Abolitionists*, ed. Lewis Perry and Michael Fellman (Baton Rouge, La., 1979), pp. 195–218; Foner, *Free Soil, Free Labor, Free Men*; Louis S. Gerteis, *Morality and Utility in American Antislavery Reform* (Chapel Hill, N.C., 1987).

The promise of social mobility bridged the gap between propertyless proletarian and independent proprietor, suggesting that any industrious individual could attain independent standing. "There is [no] such thing," declared Abraham Lincoln, "as the free hired laborer being fixed to that condition for life. . . . The prudent, penniless beginner in the world labors for wages awhile, saves a surplus with which to buy tools or land for himself, then labors on his own account another while, and at length hires another new beginner to help him."[5] With similar optimism, Northerners also argued that there was no inherent conflict between the propertied and the propertyless. To the contrary, a "harmony of interests" united capital and labor. Governed by the universal "laws" of political economy, that harmony was embodied in the voluntary contractual relations that joined employer and employee.

A growing number of wage-workers discerned conflict, not harmony, between labor and capital. While struggling to improve themselves, they began to articulate new ideas that denied the preeminence of the market and the right of employers to determine their employees' place in society. Those who subsisted by selling their labor power demanded and received title to privileges previously reserved for property-owning freemen. The suffrage and other political rights became prerogatives of dependent proletarians as well as independent proprietors.[6]

The older ideas about independence corresponded to particular notions of dependence. In a community of independent freeholders, households were responsible for the support of their own dependents, be they children, elderly parents, servants, journeymen, or apprentices. Through networks of family and community, households also

---

[5] Lincoln's statement appears in his annual message to Congress of December 1861. (Abraham Lincoln, *Collected Works*, ed. Roy P. Basler, Marion D. Pratt, and Lloyd A. Dunlap, 9 vols. [New Brunswick, N.J., 1953–55], vol. 5, pp. 35–53.)

[6] On the development of the American working class during the antebellum years, see Herbert G. Gutman, *Work, Culture, and Society in Industrializing America: Essays in American Working-Class and Social History* (New York, 1976), especially chap. 1; Dawley, *Class and Community*, chaps. 1–3, 5; Gordon et al., *Segmented Work, Divided Workers*, chap. 3; Wallace, *Rockdale*, chap. 4; Wilentz, *Chants Democratic*. Changes in the requirements for suffrage and officeholding are outlined in Richard P. McCormick, *The Second American Party System: Party Formation in the Jacksonian Era* (Chapel Hill, N.C., 1966).

succored orphans, the physically and mentally ill, and other unfortunates. When such men, women, and children held no claim upon a particular household, local authorities assigned them to one and provided a subsidy from public funds. Respectable men and women who had fallen on hard times were often supported in their own homes – so-called outdoor relief – both to meet their immediate needs and to maintain the integrity of the community. The care of dependents thus lent support to the social order in communities in which face-to-face relations were the standard. Strangers and those deemed not respectable were either "warned out" of town or given short shrift, no matter how desperate.

The new notions of independence altered ideas about dependence. Relief assumed a new form as mobile, unattached individuals began to outnumber settled householders. In the seaboard metropolises of the Northeast, the arrival of thousands of newcomers from the countryside and from foreign lands transformed neighbors into strangers. In response, associations of benevolent individuals, in alliance with public officials, assumed responsibilities once borne by households. Sponsoring an array of new institutions – schools, poorhouses, penitentiaries, and asylums – these reformers offered a new discipline that would guard against permanent impoverishment in the absence of the traditional rewards and restraints. Reformers wanted to ensure that the freedom of propertyless men and women did not lead to license. They sought to demonstrate that even without a foundation in property ownership, civic responsibility and social discipline could rest upon industry, frugality, and sobriety, the personal virtues taught in common schools and Protestant churches and enforced by the market.[7]

---

[7] Intertwined ideas of public charity, private philanthropy, reform, and welfare are discussed in Paul Boyer, *Urban Masses and Moral Order in America, 1820–1920* (Cambridge, Mass., 1978), chaps. 1–7; Michael B. Katz, *In the Shadow of the Poorhouse: A Social History of Welfare in America* (New York, 1986), chaps. 1–4; Benjamin Joseph Klebaner, *Public Poor Relief in America, 1790–1860* (New York, 1976); David J. Rothman, *The Discovery of the Asylum: Social Order and Disorder in the New Republic* (Boston, 1971). Robert H. Bremner, *The Public Good: Philanthropy and Welfare in the Civil War Era* (New York, 1980), chaps. 1–5, is especially helpful on the war years.

On the eve of the Civil War, the conflicting notions about freedom and independence, work and welfare, were far from reconciled. Fighting a war for national reunification heightened the contradictions. Mobilization under the banner of "Union and Liberty" brought together diverse Northern constituencies with different understandings of both terms: New Englanders and midwesterners, factory workers and yeoman farmers, Protestant reformers and Catholic immigrants, antislavery Republicans and proslavery Union Democrats. Contention over the meaning of freedom divided Northerners even as opposition to secession united them.

Southern slaves had their own conceptions of freedom, derived from their experience as slaves within the American republic. Themselves property, they were denied control over their labor and its product. Without independent standing in the eyes of the law, they were subject to the personal will of their owners. Slaves could be sold, disciplined, and moved without recourse, and they had no right to marry, educate their children, or provide for their parents. They could bear arms, assemble, hold property, and travel only with their owners' consent.

Slaves expected the destruction of their owners' sovereignty to open a world of new possibilities. If slavery denied them the right to control their persons and progeny, freedom would confer that right. If slavery required that they suffer arbitrary and often violent treatment, freedom would enable them to protect themselves against such abuse. If slavery allowed their owners to expropriate the fruits of their labor, freedom would at least guarantee compensation if not the entire product of their labor. As free people, former slaves expected to be able to organize their lives in accordance with their own sense of propriety, establish their families as independent units, and control productive property as the foundation of their new status.

But freedom was not merely slavery's negative. Even before the war, slaves established families, created churches, selected community leaders, and carved out a small realm of independent economic activity. An elaborate network of kinship – with its own patterns of courtship, rites of marriage, parental responsibilities, and kin obligations – linked slaves together. Throughout the South, slaves organized churches –

formal congregations in cities and on some large plantations, informal gatherings on small farmsteads. Black ministers articulated a different interpretation of Christianity from that heard in the churches of slave owners. In addition to preachers, slaves chose other leaders from their own ranks. Often these were drivers or artisans, but sometimes men and women of no special status in the owners' view.

While subject to their owners' overwhelming power, slaves struggled to increase the possibilities of independent action in all areas of their lives. They pressed for nothing more relentlessly than control over their own labor, denial of which constituted the very essence of chattel slavery. Conceding what they could not alter, slaves worked without direct compensation but claimed the right to a predictable portion of what they produced. They expected their owners to feed, clothe, and house them in accordance with customary usage and irrespective of age, infirmity, or productivity.

Through a continuous process of contest and negotiation with individual owners, many slaves also established a right to some time of their own in which to cultivate gardens, hunt, fish, raise poultry and hogs, make baskets and practice other handicrafts, hire themselves to neighboring farmers and artisans, or receive payment for overwork. Some slaves were permitted to sell the products of such independent activities, often to their own masters and sometimes to others. Although their property usually had no standing at law, it gained recognition in practice, enabling them to accumulate small and generally perishable resources by which they improved their own lives and gave the next generation "a start." The slaves' self-directed economic activities, like their families and religious congregations, fostered a vision of an independent life and shaped their expectations of the postemancipation world.[8]

[8] The best general studies of Southern slavery in the nineteenth century are Eugene D. Genovese, *Roll, Jordan, Roll: The World the Slaves Made* (New York, 1974), and Kenneth M. Stampp, *The Peculiar Institution: Slavery in the Ante-Bellum South* (New York, 1956). On the family life of slaves, see Herbert G. Gutman, *The Black Family in Slavery and Freedom, 1750–1925* (New York, 1976); on religion, Albert J. Raboteau, *Slave Religion: The "Invisible Institution" in the Antebellum South* (New York, 1978); on the slaves' independent economic activity, Ira Berlin and Philip D.

While the slaves' ideas about freedom everywhere derived from slavery, slavery was not everywhere the same. Regional and local differences affected the character of emancipation. Many of the four million slaves in the South in 1860 lived and worked alongside their owners, sharing intimately, if never equally, in the daily routine. Others hardly knew their owners and instead stood at the end of a chain of command that extended from a black driver or foreman through a white overseer before it reached an absentee master. Some slaves had roots in the land they worked that reached back for generations; others were newcomers, recently torn from old homes and transplanted to a strange and distant place. Some slaves spent their entire lives on one great estate, rarely venturing beyond its boundaries. Others lived on small farms or in cities, interacted regularly with nonslaveholding whites and free blacks, traveled widely, and were sometimes rented out by their owners to different hirers. A few privileged slaves hired themselves out, paying their owners a monthly "wage" and retaining for themselves whatever remained.

Slaves also worked in different ways. Most were agricultural workers, chiefly field hands. Although they shared the experience of tilling the soil, the regimen of different crops and particular forms of labor organization fostered divergent patterns of work. Some slave men and women were assigned daily tasks, after the completion of which they could engage in self-directed activities that supplemented their diets and sometimes generated a small surplus. The majority of plantation slaves, however, worked from sunup to sundown in closely supervised gangs and had relatively little time to cultivate garden plots or accumulate property of any sort. Still other agricultural slaves, especially those in mixed-farming regions, labored at a variety of seasonally defined tasks that required flexible schedules and considerable freedom of movement. Work outside the field – in artisan shops, in urban warehouses and factories, and in the big house – created other distinctive patterns. The

Morgan, eds., "The Slaves' Economy: Independent Production by Slaves in the Americas," special issue of *Slavery and Abolition* 12 (May 1991), especially the introduction and the essays by John Campbell, Roderick A. McDonald, and John T. Schlotterbeck.

slaves' various work routines influenced both their lives in slavery and their ideas about freedom.[9]

Black people with prior experience in freedom, approximately a quarter-million on the eve of the Civil War, also contributed to the emergence of free-labor relations. Most free blacks resided in the Upper South, where they were so mixed and intermarried with slaves as to have become socially inseparable. Others, particularly those in the port cities of the Lower South, styled themselves "free people of color" and held themselves apart from the mass of rural, black slaves. But no matter how they tried to distinguish themselves, free blacks lived within the close confines of a society that presumed people of African descent to be slaves. Southern lawmakers denied them many liberties enjoyed by white people, forbidding them to travel freely, to testify in court or sit on juries, to bear arms, or (in some states) to hold property in their own names. Yet free blacks were not slaves. They enjoyed the right to marry, establish independent households, control their own labor, and accumulate property. Drawing on their skills and their personal connections with white patrons, a few ambitious free blacks managed to amass considerable wealth and attain a degree of respectability even in the eyes of slaveholders. Their experience engendered a special social outlook and an understanding of freedom that could be as different from that of the liberated as it was from that of the liberators.[10]

No matter what expectations black people brought to freedom, their intentions — like those of everyone else — collided with the realities of war. In some regions of the South, notably the South Carolina Sea Islands and certain areas of the Mississippi Valley, the arrival of federal troops caused slaveholders to abandon both their estates and their slaves. Transformed into de facto freedpeople by their owners' exodus,

[9] The spatial diversity and temporal development of slavery in the United States are captured in Willie Lee Rose, ed., *A Documentary History of Slavery in North America* (New York, 1976); and Ira Berlin, "Time, Space, and the Evolution of Afro-American Society on British Mainland North America," *American Historical Review* 85 (Feb. 1980): 44–78.

[10] Ira Berlin, *Slaves without Masters: The Free Negro in the Antebellum South* (New York, 1974).

such former slaves pursued an independent livelihood on their home plantations, surrounded by a familiar landscape, kinfolk, and friends. In much of the seceded South, however, and in the border states that remained in the Union, slaves gained freedom only by flight. Since solitary fugitives stood a better chance of success – especially early in the war – runaways often had to leave family and friends behind. Many fugitive slaves followed familiar paths to hideaways in forests and swamps, while others occupied abandoned farms and plantations. But the vast majority of fugitives sought safety in or near federal encampments, trusting their future to perfect strangers.

Still other slaves secured freedom with their owners in residence. Most notably in southern Louisiana, Tennessee, and the border states, slaves confronted owners who were determined to maintain their old dominance in fact if not at law. Many such slaveholders, professing loyalty to the Union, called upon federal authorities to sustain their claims to black laborers; the officials, hesitant to alienate much-needed allies, frequently complied. Occasionally, even disloyal masters brazenly demanded military backing.[11]

Above all, the march of contending armies determined the possibilities available to former slaves. Where federal lines were secure, freedpeople could sink roots, reconstitute their families, organize churches and schools, and earn a livelihood. Such places were few in number. Enormous though it became, the federal army was never large enough simultaneously to protect the loyal states, defend the occupied regions of the Confederacy, and mount offensives against the rebels. Confederate troops held Union armies at bay during the first two years of the war and enjoyed the ability to counterattack in force well into 1864. Federal lines shifted in the ebb and flow of military campaigns, sometimes incorporating slaves from Confederate territory, sometimes uprooting freedpeople and sending them in search of another safe haven. Certain districts nominally under Union control became the site of guerrilla activity that widened into a war of all against all. If many

---

[11] The uneven evolution of legal freedom in different parts of the South is described in *Destruction of Slavery*.

slaves gained freedom on the run, subsequent events often kept them in motion. Few black men and women passed from slavery to freedom untouched by the uncertainty of military events.[12]

Vagaries of federal policy likewise affected the wartime experience of former slaves. The Union war effort entailed thousands of official decisions, great and small, made by an array of politicians, bureaucrats, and military officers. Although their policies aimed first to secure victory, other considerations also weighed heavily. In the field, soldiers and officers acted to safeguard their lives. In Washington, elected officials and civil servants protected their careers, scrutinizing possible courses of action against their prospects of reelection and advancement. Officials, elected and appointed, kept an eye on the interests of their friends, constituents, and political parties. Only incidentally, if at all, did they consider the effect of their decisions upon the freedpeople. Nevertheless, programs implemented to recruit soldiers, to execute a particular military strategy, to bolster the national treasury, or to determine the ownership of captured property had important implications for the lives of former slaves.[13]

Nothing had prepared federal officials for the mobilization that followed the outbreak of war. The army and navy needed tons of food and uniforms, herds of horses and mules, miles of wagons and railroad cars, and thousands of rifles, cannons, and caissons – a veritable mountain of materiel – all of which would have to be purchased by a government that had no national tax save a tariff. It would have been difficult enough to amass and pay for the necessities of war under normal conditions, and these were not normal times. Secession had shaken established patterns of commerce and industry and disrupted financial

---

[12] Patterns of federal occupation and their implications for the destruction of slavery are discussed in *Destruction of Slavery*.

[13] Studies of federal policy include Robert P. Sharkey, *Money, Class, and Party: An Economic Study of Civil War and Reconstruction* (Baltimore, 1959); Leonard P. Curry, *Blueprint for Modern America: Nonmilitary Legislation of the First Civil War Congress* (Nashville, 1968); Fred A. Shannon, *The Organization and Administration of the Union Army, 1861–1865*, 2 vols. (Cleveland, 1928).

markets throughout the Union, requiring wholesale reordering of agricultural and industrial production.

The demands of making war exceeded the resources of the peacetime nation and strained the Northern labor force. While the leaders of the Confederacy assumed that slave labor would undergird their war effort,[14] Union officials at first evinced little interest in black laborers, either free or slave. Few in number, generally assumed to be unskilled and untutored, free blacks cut a poor figure in the eyes of most white Northerners, who viewed them as the refuse of slave society. Slave laborers seemed no more desirable or – if desired – attainable. Although slaves constituted a large portion of the laboring population in the loyal border states of Kentucky, Maryland, and Missouri, their services could be secured only with the consent of politically powerful slaveholders. Fearful that such a request might push the border states over the brink of secession, Union officials dared not ask.[15]

Border-state slaves, by contrast, were not deterred by the loyal standing of their owners. As soon as Union soldiers appeared in the border states, so did runaway slaves. But federal commanders went out of their way to safeguard the property rights of slaveholders. Fugitive slaves who offered their services to the Union army met a stern and sometimes violent rebuke. The heavy work associated with armies on the move therefore fell chiefly upon Northern soldiers themselves, with an occasional assist from private citizens laboring for wages.[16]

The federal government's respect for slavery extended to the seceded states as well. By reiterating a commitment to honor and protect slavery wherever it existed, President Abraham Lincoln and the Republican-controlled Congress hoped to win over not only border-

---

[14] Confederate mobilization of slave and free-black laborers is discussed in *Destruction of Slavery*, chap. 9.

[15] On Northern free blacks, see Leon F. Litwack, *North of Slavery: The Negro in the Free States, 1790–1860* (Chicago, 1961). On federal policy regarding slavery in the border slave states, see *Wartime Genesis: Upper South*, chaps. 4–6; *Destruction of Slavery*, chaps. 6–8; *Black Military Experience*, chap. 4. On early military employment of black laborers in the border states, see *Wartime Genesis: Upper South*, doc. 131; *Destruction of Slavery*, doc. 197.

[16] *Destruction of Slavery*, pp. 332, 397–99, 495–98, and docs. 127–29, 153–54, 157, 160A-C, 197, 199–201.

state slaveholders and Northern Democrats but also lukewarm Confederates. Accordingly, when Union armies entered areas in rebellion, commanders disavowed any intention to unsettle relations between master and slave. Judicious policy, a War Department official explained, would "avoid all interference with the Social systems or local institutions" of the seceded states.[17]

While Lincoln and his subordinates courted slaveholders, slaves demonstrated their readiness to risk all for freedom and to do whatever they could to aid their owners' enemy. At every turn, federal soldiers met fugitive slaves bearing information, providing food and drink, and volunteering their labor. Determined to make the most of the presence of the Union army, slaves did whatever they could to ingratiate themselves to the invaders. It did not take long for Northern soldiers to see the wisdom of receiving and protecting them, if only to ease the burdens of military life and prevent the rebels from doing the same. Although officially denied entry to Union army lines, frequently manhandled, and sometimes returned to their owners, slaves continued to offer their services. In time, some found shelter in federal encampments, and many more gained residence in their shadow. Before long, the wisdom of common soldiers began to ascend the chain of command. A glimmer of this dynamic appeared in the border states, where most military operations transpired during 1861 and early 1862; it emerged in full brilliance when Union forces advanced into the seceded South.[18]

Events unleashed by the invasion and occupation of Confederate territory transformed federal policy regarding fugitive slaves and their labor. In May 1861, Union troops reinforced Fortress Monroe, a federal installation in tidewater Virginia. The following November, a joint army and navy expedition invaded Port Royal Sound, in the South Carolina Sea Islands, to establish a coaling station for the blockading squadron. The presence of federal troops disrupted slavery in both

---

[17] *Destruction of Slavery*, doc. 18.

[18] See, for example, *Destruction of Slavery*, docs. 1A, 6, 19, 41, 61, 81, 131A, 160B, 163, 197. The commander of a Union army division in northern Alabama echoed the sentiment of many of his men when he observed that, among local residents, the slaves "are our only friends." (*Destruction of Slavery*, doc. 86n.)

tidewater Virginia and the Sea Islands. At Fortress Monroe, fugitive slaves from the nearby countryside arrived in search of freedom and military protection. At Port Royal, most of the white residents and virtually all the slaveholders fled when Union gunboats drew near, leaving the slaves in possession of the islands' great estates, including their crops of long-staple cotton. In both regions, federal commanders were confronted by large numbers of slaves whose owners were avowed enemies, not wavering friends. [19]

Far from their base of supply, army and navy officers found themselves badly in need of laborers. White Southerners, even those who professed loyalty to the federal government, displayed little inclination to work on its behalf. Northern laborers, whose wages had increased rapidly with the onset of war, proved difficult to lure south. With few alternatives, Union officials followed the traditional army practice of assigning soldiers to various fatigue duties, offering them "extra-duty pay" for work performed on their own time. [20] But the employment of soldiers had its limits, especially with Confederate troops menacing isolated Union outposts.

Military commanders therefore put able-bodied slaves to work. At Fortress Monroe and at Port Royal, runaway slaves soon composed the bulk of the labor force in the army's quartermaster, engineer, and subsistence departments. Navy officers employed fugitive slaves aboard ship and on shore. For those slaves who were able to work, military employment offered food, protection, and freedom in return for their labor. Women, children, and old or disabled people – who, in the eyes

---

[19] On the Union occupation of tidewater Virginia and the South Carolina Sea Islands, see *Destruction of Slavery*, chaps. 1–2.

[20] On the military use of Northern laborers in the occupied South, see, for example, *Wartime Genesis: Upper South*, docs. 16, 27; testimony of Gen. Dix before the American Freedmen's Inquiry Commission, 9 May 1863, filed with O-328 1863, Letters Received, ser. 12, Records of the Adjutant General's Office, RG 94, NA [K-68]; Capt. R. Saxton to Capt. L. H. Pelouse, 12 Mar. 1862, Letters Received, ser. 2254, SC Expeditionary Corps, Records of U.S. Army Continental Commands, RG 393 Pt. 2 No. 130, NA [C-1642]. (A bracketed number at the end of a citation is the document's control number in the files of the Freedmen and Southern Society Project.) On the employment of "extra duty soldiers," see *Wartime Genesis: Upper South*, doc. 6.

of the generals, could contribute nothing substantial to the war effort – posed a problem for Union officers, as no provision had been made for their support. At Fortress Monroe, General Benjamin F. Butler and his successor, Genéral John E. Wool, applied the earnings of those contrabands employed as military laborers toward the support of those not so employed. At Port Royal, General Thomas W. Sherman paid military laborers a small wage and issued rations to those unable to work.[21]

Ad hoc employment of fugitive-slave men and meager relief for their dependents failed to satisfy those Northerners who were determined to use every available means to punish treason and reunite the nation. Seeing slavery as the root of the rebellion, practical-minded Republicans had no qualms about accepting fugitive slaves into federal lines, if only to punish the rebels. It was foolhardy not to do so, they argued, for the Confederates had already mobilized slaves in behalf of their own war effort. Abolitionists, black and white, turned that utilitarian argument to their own purposes. Seizing the opportunity to realize the egalitarian promise of the American Revolution, they denounced the narrow ground upon which Lincoln and the Congress were fighting the war. They called for outright abolition of slavery and the employment of former slaves as both soldiers and laborers.

Rather than rely upon the half-hearted efforts of federal commanders, abolitionists mobilized on behalf of the former slaves accumulating within Union lines. During the fall and winter of 1861–1862, antislavery men and women – often in league with other "educated and philanthropic" Northerners – organized contraband relief societies (subsequently known as freedmen's aid societies). These groups gathered clothing, bibles, schoolbooks, and medical supplies for the destitute ex-slaves at Fortress Monroe, Port Royal, and the District of Columbia. Convinced of their ability "to provide for all [the freedpeople's] proper wants," they assured the Lincoln administration that "there is no necessity for any Governmental charity."[22] But the abolitionists and their allies had no intention of confining themselves to rolling bandages and

---

[21] *Wartime Genesis: Upper South*, doc. 2; *Destruction of Slavery*, doc. 1A; *Wartime Genesis: Lower South*, docs. 1, 4.

[22] *Wartime Genesis: Upper South*, doc. 4.

collecting old clothes. They would guide the passage of the former slaves to freedom.

Before long, philanthropic gentlemen and ladies were taking up stations in the Union-occupied South. Most of them were young men and women of high social standing, who had been raised in the abolitionist tradition and saw their service as a culmination of the long struggle against slavery. As teachers, ministers, and physicians, they brought useful skills and a heightened respect for the former slaves' humanity into federal camps. While these Yankees shared many of the racial preconceptions common among white Northerners, they were sure of both the iniquity of slavery and the superiority of free labor. They assumed that, once freed of the vices of slavery and tutored in the virtues of free labor, evangelical Christianity, and republican citizenship, former slaves would take their place as productive and responsible members of the body politic.[23]

Although united in their determination to free the slaves and transform the South, antislavery Northerners did not share a vision of the social order that would replace the slaveholders' regime. They agreed that abolishing property rights in man and substituting the discipline of voluntary contracts for that of the lash were necessary conditions for a free South. But they disagreed about whether those steps were sufficient. A sizable contingent believed that self-ownership without possession of productive property did not constitute true freedom, but thereafter they too divided among themselves. Some of them recommended that freedpeople be required to purchase such property with wages earned after their liberation; the others maintained that years of uncom-

---

[23] On Northern reformers in the wartime South, see Bremner, *The Public Good*, chap. 5; Robert F. Engs, *Freedom's First Generation: Black Hampton, Virginia, 1861–1890* (Philadelphia, 1979), chap. 3; McPherson, *Struggle for Equality*, especially chaps. 7, 11; Frederick Law Olmsted, *The Papers of Frederick Law Olmsted*, ed. Charles Capen McLaughlin and Charles E. Beveridge, 5 vols. to date (Baltimore, 1977–), vol. 4, *Defending the Union: The Civil War and the U.S. Sanitary Commission, 1861–1863*, ed. Jane Turner Censer, pp. 3–4, 20–26, and chap. 4; Joe M. Richardson, *Christian Reconstruction: The American Missionary Association and Southern Blacks, 1861–1890* (Athens, Ga., 1986), chaps. 1–2; Rose, *Rehearsal for Reconstruction*, especially chaps. 2–3; Henry L. Swint, *The Northern Teacher in the South, 1862–1870* (Nashville, 1941).

pensated toil entitled the ex-slaves outright to the land they had "watered . . . with their tears and blood." Charles B. Wilder, a Massachusetts abolitionist assigned to Fortress Monroe by the American Missionary Association, regarded wage labor not as an end in itself, but an opportunity for former slaves to "buy a spot of land" where they could "have a little hut to live in with their families like any body else." Mansfield French, a Methodist clergyman sent to the Sea Islands by the same association, urged the government to endow freedpeople with land as indemnification for past injustice. "[T]he negroes had made [the land] what it was and . . . it belonged to them, and them only," he declared.[24]

The freedpeople's Northern friends drew upon their own notions of dependence as well as their ideas of independence. Antislavery men and women were alert to the development of new modes of poor relief. Many of them had ministered to the downtrodden and preached the gospel of industry, frugality, and sobriety in the North's growing cities. To them, destitute former slaves resembled other impoverished people. The imperative to work or starve would bear upon freedpeople no more lightly than it did upon newly arrived foreigners or rural migrants. The need to support themselves and their families and the opportunity to improve themselves and accumulate property would spur former slaves to diligent and faithful labor just as they did other people. "The negro is actuated by the same motives as other men," asserted one opponent of slavery, "& we must appeal to the *human nature* & make it appear for his interest to work & then he *will* work." To be sure, the freedpeople would require temporary assistance. But only temporary. Opponents of slavery feared replacing one form of dependency with another and believed that charity would create permanent dependency. "Irish souphouses" and other "socialistic institutions" would not make former slaves industrious workers and exemplary citizens.[25]

[24] *Wartime Genesis: Upper South*, docs. 16, 28, 43; statement of William B. Lucas, 30 Jan. [1864], enclosed in Wm. Henry Brisbane to Hon. Joseph J. Lewis, 15 Feb. 1864, General Correspondence, ser. 99, SC, Records of or Relating to Direct Tax Commissions in the Southern States, Records of the Internal Revenue Service, RG 58, NA [Z-3]. See also *Wartime Genesis: Lower South*, docs. 44–45.

[25] *Wartime Genesis: Upper South*, doc. 4; *Wartime Genesis: Lower South*, doc. 40.

Agents of Northern aid societies generally received a welcome from federal commanders, who shared many of their ideas about the relationship between private philanthropy and public charity and also saw "the contraband problem" as one of destitution and its relief. This shared perspective propelled some agents of Northern benevolence into positions of authority, with responsibility for distributing government rations and funneling donations from the North to needy freedpeople. At Fortress Monroe, General Wool appointed Wilder to supervise the "Vagrants or Contrabands." In the District of Columbia, where federal officers had initially lodged fugitive slaves in a jail, it seemed fitting to select Danforth B. Nichols, who had once directed a Chicago reformatory, as superintendent of contrabands.[26] Nowhere, however, did Northern reformers play a more prominent role than in the South Carolina Sea Islands.

During the first weeks after the arrival of Union troops, Sea Island slaves supported themselves from the corn and potatoes they had recently harvested and from the larders abandoned by their fugitive owners.[27] But soon, looking to the future, they also began to prepare the fields for a new year's cultivation. Placing their highest premium upon subsistence, they showed no interest in picking the cotton still in the fields or ginning what had already been harvested. Neither had they any intention of planting anew the crop that had "enriched [their] masters but had not fed them."[28]

Although the freedpeople ignored cotton, cotton would not be ignored. War-induced shortage of the staple had driven its price to record levels, and the long-staple cotton of the Sea Islands fetched the highest price of all. The partly harvested crop of 1861 immediately drew the notice of Treasury Department agents, who espied a source of revenue

[26] *Wartime Genesis: Upper South*, docs. 4n., 60. In coastal North Carolina, Vincent Colyer, who in 1862 had charge of both fugitive slaves and white refugees, was given the title "Superintendent of the Poor." (*Wartime Genesis: Upper South*, doc. 7.)

[27] On the Sea Islands under Union occupation, see Rose, *Rehearsal for Reconstruction*; Julie Saville, "A Measure of Freedom: From Slave to Wage Laborer in South Carolina, 1860–1868" (Ph.D. diss., Yale University, 1986), chap. 2; *Wartime Genesis: Lower South*, chap. 1.

[28] *Wartime Genesis: Lower South*, docs. 4, 8, 19, 21.

for the Union war effort. While the agents urged the freedpeople to gather the cotton still in the fields, offering to pay them for the work, Northern entrepreneurs clamored for an opportunity to operate the plantations the following year.[29]

To abolitionists, far more was at stake than public revenue and private profit. Inspired by the opportunity to institute free labor on the plantations of some of the South's most notorious rebels, they mobilized under the direction of Edward L. Pierce, a Boston attorney who had briefly supervised former slaves near Fortress Monroe. In February 1862, Secretary of the Treasury Salmon P. Chase — who construed his authority over trade in the occupied South to include operation of the Sea Island estates — appointed Pierce a special agent to oversee cultivation of the 1862 crop and guide the transformation of slaves into free workers. Assisted by freedmen's aid societies in Boston, New York, and Philadelphia, Pierce selected some fifty men to supervise the plantations. A contingent of ministers, teachers, and physicians also joined the enterprise. By March 1862, the flower of Northern abolitionism — young men and women whose mission earned them the sobriquet "Gideonites" — had taken up stations in the Sea Islands.[30]

Prepared to introduce former slaves to the rigors of free labor, the plantation superintendents discovered that their charges had already initiated a new order of their own. To be sure, Sea Island freedpeople generally welcomed the interlopers. They eagerly attended the Gideonites' schools and churches and accepted their gifts of clothing, medicine, and other supplies. But the former slaves contested the newcomers' belief that freedom could be validated only through the cultivation of cotton for wages. Although some plantation superintendents discerned a laudable "republican spirit" in the old slave quarters, they feared that the former slaves would retreat into mere self-sufficiency.

[29] *Wartime Genesis: Lower South*, docs. 3, 5–7.
[30] *Wartime Genesis: Lower South*, docs. 8, 10, 36; Edward L. Pierce, "Persons recommended by the 'Educational Commission' of Boston . . ." and "Persons approved by the 'National Freedman's Relief Association' of New York . . . ," [Mar. 1862], vol. 19, #80, Port Royal Correspondence, 5th Agency, Records of the Civil War Special Agencies of the Treasury Department, RG 366, NA [Q-9]; Rose, *Rehearsal for Reconstruction*, chap. 2.

Eager to demonstrate the efficiency of free labor in growing cotton and dependent upon revenue from the staple to fund their "experiment," the Northerners insisted that the former slaves take their accustomed place in the cotton fields. When the freedpeople were slow to comply, the superintendents did not hesitate to deny them rations.[31]

The exigencies of war rapidly eroded the sources of subsistence that had enabled the freedpeople to decline work in the cotton fields. Confederate troops raided outlying islands with alarming frequency. Even when they failed to capture and reenslave the inhabitants, the rebels succeeded in ravaging the plantations, burning houses, and carrying off food and livestock. In the wake of such raids, federal commanders relocated former slaves from endangered localities to the more secure islands around Port Royal Sound. There they were forced to rely upon the government for food and shelter. Northern soldiers and sailors also laid claim to the property and people on Sea Island plantations. On numerous islands, uniformed Yankees both with and without authorization stripped the estates of useful items. Military employers and Treasury Department cotton agents detailed hands to suit their own needs and convenience, leaving many plantations to be worked largely by women, children, and old people. When fugitive slaves arrived from the mainland, officials quickly siphoned off able-bodied men for military labor and remanded all others to the plantations. The destitute new arrivals added to the burdens of the resident plantation population. Having begun the year with high hopes of subsisting themselves through their own self-directed labor, freedpeople found their goal increasingly difficult to achieve.[32]

Former slaves elsewhere in the South faced many of the same difficulties, and their numbers grew rapidly when the federal army launched its spring campaign. Invasion of coastal North Carolina in March 1862 resulted in the establishment of Union posts at Roanoke Island, New Berne, and other points on the perimeter of Pamlico and Albemarle sounds. By April, army and navy operations had brought additional

[31] *Wartime Genesis: Lower South*, docs. 10–11, 13, 21.
[32] *Wartime Genesis: Lower South*, docs. 2, 8, 11–13, 21.

South Carolina Sea Islands into the Union fold, along with a few Georgia islands and small coastal enclaves at Fernandina and St. Augustine, in northern Florida. Events moved more quickly, and with more momentous implications, in the western theater. By early spring, forces of the Department of the Gulf commanded by General Butler had captured New Orleans and the southern Louisiana parishes between the city and the Gulf of Mexico. At about the same time, federal armies farther north embarked from winter quarters in Kentucky and Missouri for a three-pronged offensive into Arkansas and Tennessee. By midsummer 1862, the Union army had established major posts at Nashville and Memphis, Tennessee; Helena, Arkansas; Huntsville, Alabama; and Corinth, Mississippi; as well as lesser points along strategic waterways and railroads. These operations in the western theater left Union forces well situated for further strikes into the Confederate interior.

As federal troops advanced, slaves gained their freedom under circumstances as different from each other as they were from those in the Sea Islands. In southern Louisiana, many slaveholders fled their estates, but a substantial proportion remained, proclaiming loyalty to the United States government and demanding that it sustain the slave regime. Eager to reassure slaveholding unionists, General Butler acceded to their entreaties during the first months of occupation. But before long, slaves had successfully challenged their owners and undermined Butler's policy. By the fall of 1862, slave insubordination and flight had disrupted the old order in the sugar parishes and forced Butler to reorganize plantation labor, requiring planters to pay wages and employing federal troops to enforce labor discipline. Taking the pragmatic stand that such intervention was necessary to save the region's crop, control unruly black workers, and restore peace in the countryside, Butler pushed legal slavery to the edge but stopped short of outright emancipation.[33]

As was true in southern Louisiana, the agricultural year was well under way when federal forces secured footholds in middle and west

---

[33] On Union occupation and the undermining of slavery in southern Louisiana, see *Destruction of Slavery*, chap. 4. On wartime labor arrangements, see *Wartime Genesis: Lower South*, chap. 2.

Tennessee, eastern Arkansas, northern Mississippi, and northern Alabama. Many slaveholders remained in residence, although few possessed the unionist credentials of their counterparts in the sugar parishes. In the vicinity of Union posts, slavery retreated and free labor slowly began to emerge. Federal installations became magnets for fugitive slaves. Most of them were young men who had left their families behind. Although they arrived tired and hungry, they were ready to do whatever was necessary to gain freedom and protection.[34]

Federal commanders had plenty for them to do. With the expansion of Union-held territory during the spring and summer of 1862, the army and navy experienced persistent shortages of laborers. Setting aside reservations about the employment of former slaves, quartermaster, commissary, and engineer officers hired freedmen as artisans, teamsters, and common laborers. Medical officers put freedwomen to work as nurses and laundresses and freedmen as hospital attendants. Individual officers and common soldiers found countless jobs for both men and women, from policing camps to washing clothes and preparing food.

The employment of black laborers received growing support from Washington. As hopes of quick victory and easy reunification dwindled, Lincoln and his advisers became convinced that defeating the rebellion demanded more than the mobilization of Southern white unionists and the conversion of deluded secessionists. It required the destruction of Southern armies, occupation of substantial territory in the Confederate states, and demoralization of those who supported the rebellion. To achieve these goals, the Union needed all the help it could get. "It is a military necessity to have men and money," the President observed in July 1862, "and we can get neither in sufficient numbers or amounts if we keep from or drive from our lines slaves coming to them."[35]

---

[34] On military developments and the destruction of slavery in the Mississippi Valley (including middle and east Tennessee and northern Alabama), see *Destruction of Slavery*, chap. 5. Wartime labor arrangements in Union-occupied territory along the Mississippi River are considered in *Wartime Genesis: Lower South*, chap. 3; those in middle and east Tennessee and northern Alabama are treated separately in *Wartime Genesis: Upper South*, chap. 3.

[35] *Official Records*, ser. 1, vol. 53, pp. 529–30.

That same month, the Congress and the President ratified the practice of accepting fugitive slaves into Union lines and putting them to work. The Second Confiscation Act and the Militia Act, both enacted on July 17, 1862, declared free the slaves of disloyal owners, authorized the President to mobilize "persons of African descent" against the rebellion, and granted freedom to any slave so employed. Within days, Lincoln ordered his commanders in the seceded states to "employ as laborers" as many black people "as can be advantageously used for military and naval purposes, giving them reasonable wages for their labor."[36] By the fall of 1862, the Union war effort rested in large measure upon the labor of former slaves. That dependence enabled federal commanders at last to comprehend abolitionist arithmetic: Every slave employed by the army or navy represented a double gain, one subtracted from the Confederacy and one added to the Union. Some officers learned the lesson too well, adopting dragnet methods of labor recruitment. Slave men who had once begged to enter federal camps found themselves dragooned into service by *"forcible persuasion."*[37]

Most former slaves needed no coaxing. Understanding the connection between Union victory and their own liberty, large numbers volunteered for military labor. Freedpeople in coastal North Carolina, reported one military superintendent, "consider it a duty to work for the U.S. government" and "tabooed" any of their fellows who refused to do so. Accustomed to long workdays under hard taskmasters and eager to secure their freedom, former slaves tolerated conditions that other workers would not. Irish laborers brought to Fortress Monroe, noted Charles Wilder, "are crabbed and will work only so many hours a day." Freedmen, by contrast, "if they are decently paid . . . will work nights or any time and do any thing you want done."[38]

That commitment convinced numerous military employers of the superiority of black workers over Northern and immigrant laborers,

---

[36] *Statutes at Large*, vol. 12, pp. 589–92, 597–600; *Official Records*, ser. 3, vol. 2, p. 397.

[37] On the impressment of black laborers, see, for example, *Wartime Genesis: Upper South*, docs. 19–20, 25.

[38] *Wartime Genesis: Upper South*, docs. 7, 16.

and especially over soldiers. Among such employers in the Mississippi Valley, reported a superintendent of contrabands, "the lowest estimate is . . . that one negro is worth three soldiers." Union officers commonly rationalized their preference for black laborers with stereotypes of African docility or the putative ability of black people to withstand the subtropical sun and lowland diseases. While these notions obscured both the commitment of the former slaves to the Union cause and their desperate circumstances, they also reflected the centrality of black workers to the federal war effort.[39]

Military labor assumed different forms, each with its own implications for the ex-slave employees. Thousands of fugitive slaves found work as personal servants to Union officers or soldiers, or hired on as company cooks or regimental laundresses. So prevalent was the employment of black servants at Helena, Arkansas, in the summer of 1862 that it seemed as if "[e]very other soldier" had one. Living in close quarters and sharing the rigors and camaraderie of camp life, servants often developed strong personal relationships with their employers. Yankee soldiers who hired black men and women simply because "we can get no others" frequently found that they had come to "like them as servants . . . and to feel an interest in their welfare." Such connections offered fugitive slaves a measure of protection from pursuing owners, as well as from hostile Northern soldiers. That same personal dependency also rendered black servants liable to exploitation by their employers, some of whom demanded the performance of degrading duties, refused to pay agreed-upon compensation, or inflicted physical abuse. Women were especially vulnerable to sexual assault. Yet the promise of protection counterbalanced such risks, especially during the first year of the war when the status of fugitive slaves remained largely undefined.[40]

While thousands of former slaves worked as servants, tens of thousands toiled as common laborers. They performed the army's most taxing, tedious, and dangerous tasks: building fortifications, felling

---

[39] *Wartime Genesis: Upper South*, docs. 27, 62, 206; *Wartime Genesis: Lower South*, doc. 159.

[40] *Wartime Genesis: Upper South*, doc. 119B; *Destruction of Slavery*, docs. 158, 160B; *Wartime Genesis: Lower South*, docs. 150, 157, 160.

trees, constructing roads, laying railroad track, repairing levees, and digging canals. Laborious even under the best of circumstances, such work was often done double-time, in unhealthy surroundings, and under hostile fire. Supervisors drove the workers hard and frequently afforded them insufficient rest and food. Such usage took its toll, as debilitated workers fell prey to disease. At one post in southern Louisiana, where federal officers had assumed authority over the maintenance of levees, military laborers toiled for three long months without a single day's rest. Shoeless, clad in rags, living in filthy quarters, and given meager rations of rice and sugar, the laborers endured conditions that moved one Northern officer to declare, *"My cattle at home are better cared for than these unfortunate persons."*[41]

Unlike personal servants, who usually worked for individual employers, laborers stood at the bottom of a vast hierarchy. Most worked in large groups, sometimes encompassing several hundred men (and, occasionally, a smattering of women). In their sheer size, such units exceeded all but the largest field forces in the slave South and rivaled the huge labor gangs on the great antebellum canal and railroad projects. Working under the immediate supervision of white overseers or foremen – usually civilians or junior officers – black gang workers seldom knew the higher-ranking officers who employed them. They were subject to an impersonal regimentation and discipline resembling that of unskilled factory operatives. Engineer employees at Fort Clinch, Florida, wore numbers on their hats to simplify monitoring the work completed by each hand.[42] Such impersonality distanced workers from their bosses. It also encouraged a solidarity with their fellow workers that, among other things, facilitated collective protest against unacceptable conditions.

Many black military workers endured neither the suffocating closeness experienced by personal servants nor the regimentation of gang laborers. Instead, they worked singly or in small groups, driving

---

[41] *Wartime Genesis: Upper South*, docs. 4, 52, 90, 102; *Wartime Genesis: Lower South*, doc. 80.

[42] On the scale and organization of military labor gangs, see *Wartime Genesis: Upper South*, docs. 52, 90, 102–3; *Wartime Genesis: Lower South*, doc. 24.

teams, caring for sick and wounded soldiers, and performing a host of other duties. Like other military laborers, these freedpeople found themselves assigned to tasks shunned by others. Army medical authorities in Washington, for example, put black men to work "cleansing cesspools, scrubbing privies and policing the grounds" – work white civilians spurned and soldiers performed only "under the fear of punishment."[43] The hours were as long as the labor was arduous, especially when "military necessity" demanded prompt completion of a job.

Whether they toiled indoors or out, individually or in gangs, black men and women often found that their work for military employers failed to fulfill the most elemental promise of free labor – compensation. Unlike most Northern wage-labor arrangements, in which workers were responsible for purchasing their own and their families' necessities, military labor was generally accompanied by a guarantee of subsistence in the form of rations and sometimes clothing and shelter. Many military employers made similar provision for the immediate families of their employees, usually deducting the cost from the laborers' wages. Former-slave and free-black military laborers, who had few other resources with which to provide for their families, relied heavily on such allowances. Some federal officers therefore reckoned that the boon of freedom, plus nonmonetary remuneration, was compensation enough. Rejecting the appeal of one group of black military laborers for wages, Quartermaster General Montgomery C. Meigs contended that "[s]ustenance & freedom given at great cost by the United States has fully compensated" the claimants.[44]

For many ex-slaves fresh from bondage, sustenance and freedom were compensation enough, at least at first. But even on Meigs's terms, freedpeople found reason to complain. The quality of rations and clothing issued by military employers often fell below what their owners had provided. Even if rations and clothing were furnished to black workers' families, they still required money to meet other expenses, and when-

---

43 *Wartime Genesis: Upper South*, docs. 65A-B; *Wartime Genesis: Lower South*, doc. 20.
44 For examples of the monetary and nonmonetary compensation of black military laborers, see *Wartime Genesis: Upper South*, docs. 2–3, 54–55, 87n.; *Wartime Genesis: Lower South*, docs. 8, 15, 24, 64–65, 148, 160.

ever military laborers had to purchase their families' subsistence, they depended on regular wages.

Few federal officials recognized the depth of this dependence. Confusion within various government bureaus, as well as simple negligence, kept many laborers from receiving compensation. Because of faulty record keeping, hundreds of black men who worked at Fortress Monroe during the first months of the war were still awaiting their wages at war's end. Negligence was compounded by corruption, as the freedpeople's illiteracy and incomplete documentation of their employment made them easy targets for dishonest employers and paymasters. Often, however, the problem stemmed from the enormous wartime strain on the national treasury. At times, the army simply could not meet its payroll.[45]

The complexity of federal policy also contributed to difficulties in paying military laborers. The Militia Act stipulated that black military laborers were entitled to rations and wages of $10 per month (minus $3 for clothing), and Lincoln's executive order called for payment of "reasonable wages." But the law also stipulated that "in proper cases," compensation might be made to loyal slaveholders.[46] Pending official determination of which cases were "proper," many military employers hesitated to pay laborers whose owners might yet enter a claim. In some places, especially in the border states, paymasters issued vouchers or wages to putative owners rather than to the workers themselves. Such procedures made one military employer "ashamed to look a negro in the face." Indefinite and sometimes contradictory instructions from Washington and from field commanders put military employers in an awkward position, because army and navy regulations made them personally liable for improper expenditures. Even officers who wished to pay their workers fully and fairly could not do so without the authorization of superiors and, when proper records were lacking, could not do so at all.[47]

---

[45] *Wartime Genesis: Upper South*, docs. 1, 12, 14, 17, 20, 59A, 87; *Wartime Genesis: Lower South*, docs. 157–58, 160, 226.

[46] *Statutes at Large*, vol. 12, pp. 597–600; *Official Records*, ser. 3, vol. 2, p. 397; *Black Military Experience*, doc. 64.

[47] On complications involving payment of wages to the owners of military laborers who were legally still slaves, see *Destruction of Slavery*, doc. 26B; *Wartime Genesis: Upper South*, docs. 92, 99, 103, 132, 217; *Wartime Genesis: Lower South*, doc. 148.

Newly arrived fugitives might endure such shabby treatment for a time, out of gratitude for freedom and the protection of federal arms. But before long, the hard work, the abuse, and the inability to support themselves and their families drove many of them away. Much to the disgust of military employers, black workers "deserted" in large numbers to find employers who would treat them decently and pay them regularly.[48]

While affording large numbers of former slaves employment with the Northern army or navy, Union occupation also created opportunities for free labor on different terms. A federal presence over the ridge or around the bend enabled slaves to negotiate new conditions of labor with their masters and mistresses. The slaves pressed for working arrangements that accorded them a measure of self-direction, increased their access to the resources of farms and plantations, or provided compensation. A good many slaveholders met such demands, knowing that if they refused, their slaves would leave them to work for the Yankees. Other farmers and planters, who despaired of making a crop under wartime conditions, abandoned their estates. Often they left their property in the custody of their slaves, who were promised that they could keep a portion – sometimes the entirety – of what they produced. Desperate to salvage some financial return, a few slaveholders renounced slavery altogether and rented land to their former slaves. Other intrepid ex-slaves did not depend upon negotiation to attain independent occupation of land. They simply squatted on abandoned tracts.[49]

Wherever and by whatever means freedpeople secured a chance to farm independently, they demonstrated a preference for food production similar to that exhibited by former slaves in the Sea Islands. They cultivated fields of corn or other grains, planted gardens, raised poultry, and hunted, fished, and foraged in the wild. At times they availed themselves of the smokehouses, corncribs, and poultry yards of the estates, or appropriated hogs ranging in the forests and swamps. As

---

[48] On turnover among military laborers, see, for example, *Wartime Genesis: Upper South*, docs. 3, 16, 56, 92; *Wartime Genesis: Lower South*, docs. 157, 182.

[49] *Wartime Genesis: Upper South*, docs. 112–13, 116–17, 127; *Destruction of Slavery*, doc. 123; *Wartime Genesis: Lower South*, docs. 104–5, 156.

their crops matured, many of them sold or bartered their surplus with Yankee soldiers, neighboring farmers, or the residents of nearby towns. Independent occupation of land could entail a rugged and dangerous existence, especially in disputed territory, but those ex-slaves who managed to gain a foothold clung to their hard-won independence.

In some places, military officials supported the freedpeople's attempts to farm on their own. Charles B. Wilder legitimated the self-organized settlements just inside federal lines in tidewater Virginia, and he permitted other fugitives to "cultivate the Ground and use the property of Rebels in Arms against the Government." At Helena, Arkansas, General Samuel R. Curtis, commander of the Army of the Southwest, went a step further. Deeming the former slaves who had remained on nearby plantations to be the rightful owners of the cotton they had grown as slaves, he and other officers paid them for whatever they brought in. Curtis's policy permitted former slaves to support themselves on the old estates and gave them a small endowment of capital with which to begin their lives in freedom. But Wilder and Curtis had few imitators among federal officials in the occupied South. A military court of inquiry chastised Curtis for his actions.[50]

The war made it difficult and dangerous for freedpeople to farm on their own. Independent black farmers drew the ire of neighboring slaveholders, who attacked them personally or enlisted Confederate raiders to do so. Union troops foraged in the freedpeople's fields, gardens, and stockpens, and sometimes dismantled buildings in which they had taken refuge. Even under agreements with former owners and with guarantees of federal protection, independent black farmers stood on precarious ground, as new terms of employment could revert to the old when lines of military occupation shifted. Nonetheless, a handful of black men and women braved the danger to gain the independence they had long desired. Believing themselves entitled to the land, they sometimes took up arms against those who contested their right to it.[51]

---

[50] On Wilder, see *Wartime Genesis: Upper South*, doc. 5. On Curtis, see *Wartime Genesis: Lower South*, doc. 151.

[51] *Destruction of Slavery*, docs. 20, 25A-B; *Wartime Genesis: Upper South*, docs. 12, 112, 116, 127; *Wartime Genesis: Lower South*, docs. 23, 91, 97, 104, 114, 156.

Former slaves in the Union-occupied zones who could not or dared not farm independently sought other ways to earn a living. For all its attendant hardships, the war allowed many freedpeople new latitude to pursue self-directed activities. Army camps and garrisons housed customers aplenty for anyone with cordwood, meat, fish, produce, milk, eggs, or baked goods to sell. Similarly, Union occupation created an unprecedented demand for wood to fuel the engines of steamers and locomotives. Black men and women who as slaves had occasionally sold food or wood now did so routinely, and some managed to support themselves entirely by huckstering or wood chopping. At military posts, where men generally outnumbered women several times over, freedwomen took in laundry or cooked for soldiers; some turned to prostitution to support themselves and their families.[52]

Pursuit of such opportunities often drew former slaves from the countryside. Cities in the Union-occupied South expanded rapidly, particularly those like Washington and Nashville that served as bases for Northern military operations. Their warehouses, arsenals, repair shops, stables, and naval yards employed tens of thousands. Freedpeople in these and other cities and towns also found work catering to enlarged civilian and military populations as barbers, stable keepers, draymen, laundresses, cooks, and domestic servants. The wartime boom allowed some of them to establish businesses of their own. Carpenters became contractors, draymen established their own stables, and cooks opened small restaurants or saloons. Former slaves who lacked marketable skills frequently tried to earn an independent livelihood as peddlers. Some of this entrepreneurship stood outside the law. Cookshops and groceries could serve as fronts for illicit trade, in which contraband or proscribed articles were exchanged for other goods or for cash.[53]

[52] See, for example, *Wartime Genesis: Upper South*, docs. 7–8, 17, 58; *Wartime Genesis: Lower South*, doc. 212.

[53] On black petty proprietors, see *Wartime Genesis: Upper South*, docs. 10, 20, 97–98, 118. Useful studies of Southern cities under Union occupation include Peter Maslowski, *Treason Must Be Made Odious: Military Occupation and Wartime Reconstruction in Nashville, Tennessee, 1862–65* (Millwood, N.Y., 1978), chap. 6; James T. Currie, *Enclave: Vicksburg and Her Plantations 1863–1870* (Jackson, Miss., 1980),

Union-occupied cities and towns emerged as centers of black institutional life. Long-established black churches gained new standing, and Northern missionaries – black and white – founded new congregations. Churches both old and new sponsored schools where former slaves could gain the rudiments of literacy. Mutual-aid societies and other associations took shape to address the particular concerns of members and the general concerns of former slaves at large. In these organized settings, and less formally wherever freedpeople congregated, they discussed old times and new possibilities. By such exchanges, they apprised each other of the going wages, the reputations of various employers, and the opportunities for self-employment.[54]

Yet life in the cities and towns was no easier than in the countryside. Although wages were high, wartime inflation drove prices higher. Even in Washington, where most black military laborers were paid $25 per month, more than twice the rate specified by the Militia Act, former slaves and free blacks had a difficult time making ends meet. Heavy migration swelled urban populations so that the number of workers outpaced expanding employment, creating pitiless competition. Women found their opportunities especially limited and their pay inadequate to support themselves, much less children and other dependents. Former slaves – like other rural migrants – discovered urban housing to be scarce and expensive. The shortage of housing forced black people to reside in alleys, outbuildings, or shanties on the edge of town. Crowded and lacking clean water or sanitary facilities, such quarters bred disease, fueling frightful mortality and driving many black city-dwellers back to the countryside.[55]

In city and countryside alike, the changing composition of the

especially chaps. 1–2; Gerald M. Capers, *Occupied City: New Orleans under the Federals, 1862–1865* (Lexington, Ky., 1965), especially chap. 10; Constance McLaughlin Green, *Washington: Village and Capital, 1800–1878* (Princeton, N.J., 1962), chaps. 10–11, and *The Secret City: A History of Race Relations in the Nation's Capital* (Princeton, N.J., 1967), chaps. 4–5.

54 On urban schools and churches, see *Wartime Genesis: Upper South*, docs. 30–31, 102, 170–72. On benevolent societies, see *Wartime Genesis: Upper South*, docs. 30, 84.

55 On urban living conditions, see *Destruction of Slavery*, doc. 107; *Wartime Genesis: Upper South*, docs. 17, 30, 53, 55–57, 59A-B, 64, 66, 76, 179n.

fugitive-slave population added to the freedpeople's woes. Beginning in the fall of 1862, the government's guarantee of freedom for all who reached Union lines encouraged slaves to flee not individually or in small groups, but en masse. The arrival of families, and sometimes entire plantation units, increased the number of women, children, and old people under federal jurisdiction. The approach of winter added to the rush, as tens of thousands of fugitive slaves made for Union lines in hopes of obtaining food, shelter, and protection during the cold months.[56]

Many Northern officers welcomed the families of black men and women who labored for the government. They offered them shelter and rations not only as a matter of justice, but also because the able-bodied freedpeople would not work if their families were neglected or abused. But other officers saw their employees' dependents as impediments to efficient military operations. Such officials made no provision for their support and did much to discourage them – damning the women as whores and the parents and children as so many "useless mouths."[57] Despite the abuse, the women, children, and old people remained, erecting makeshift villages and scratching out a living as best they could. Their stolid persistence forced federal officials in the field and in Washington to reconsider the "contraband question."

As they had before the war, numerous white Northerners proposed removing former slaves from the United States. From the founding of the Republic, some white Americans had advocated the "repatriation" of black people – particularly free blacks – to Africa or their removal to another nation in the Americas. During the antebellum years, proponents of "colonization" had promoted Liberia as a home for free blacks and manumitted slaves. Despite the vehement opposition of the vast majority of black people, colonizationist sentiment continued to find considerable support among antislavery politicians and their constituents.[58]

[56] On the changing character of the fugitive-slave population in late 1862, see *Destruction of Slavery*, pp. 32–34. See also *Wartime Genesis: Lower South*, docs. 71, 152–54.
[57] *Official Records*, ser. 1, vol. 6, pp. 201–3.
[58] On the colonization movement during the late antebellum and wartime years, see P. J. Staudenraus, *The African Colonization Movement, 1816–1865* (New York,

Among the proponents of removal was Abraham Lincoln. During the first year of the war, the President entertained various proposals from foreign nations and private individuals concerning colonization, and in December 1861 he recommended that the government acquire territory outside the United States in which to resettle slaves freed by the First Confiscation Act. Prodded by Lincoln, Congress enacted several measures in support of colonization during the spring and summer of 1862. In April, the law emancipating slaves in the District of Columbia set aside $100,000 to defray the cost of relocating any black people in the District who might "desire to emigrate to the Republics of Hayti or Liberia, or such other country . . . as the President may determine." Subsequent legislation appropriated additional funds for colonization, and the President frequently pledged federal assistance in removing emancipated slaves and free blacks.[59]

Although most black people spurned colonization, a few held so dim a view of their prospects in the United States that it seemed an attractive possibility. During the 1850s, support for emigration had grown among free blacks, who faced harsh discriminatory legislation throughout the nation, mob violence in the North, and threats of deportation and enslavement in the South. While suspicious of the colonizationists' motives, a number of black men and women tried to turn the wartime legislation and the President's proposals to their own purposes. In April 1862, just days after slavery was abolished in the District of Columbia, at least sixty free blacks petitioned Congress to provide a homeland in Central America where they could "secure, by their own industry, that mental and physical development which will allow them an honorable position in the families of God's great world." But the growing Northern commitment to emancipation, embodied in the Second Confisca-

---

1961); Floyd J. Miller, *The Search for a Black Nationality: Black Emigration and Colonization, 1787–1863* (Urbana, Ill., 1975); Willis D. Boyd, "Negro Colonization in the National Crisis, 1860–1870" (Ph.D. diss., University of California, Los Angeles, 1953).

59 Jason H. Silverman, " 'In the Isles beyond the Main': Abraham Lincoln's Philosophy on Black Colonization," *Lincoln Herald* 80 (Fall 1978): 115–21; Lincoln, *Collected Works*, vol. 5, pp. 35–53; *Statutes at Large*, vol. 12, pp. 376–78, 422–26, 589–92.

tion Act and in Lincoln's preliminary Emancipation Proclamation, rapidly deflated such sentiment.[60] By the end of 1862, virtually all black Americans had rejected emigration.

While colonization foundered, the transfer of "surplus" contrabands to the North seemed more practical. In the absence of instructions from Washington, some military commanders saw the relocation of former slaves as a convenient way to rid themselves of people who clogged their lines, devoured their supplies, and demoralized their soldiers. Besides, "help" was increasingly hard to find in the free states, as the military enlistment of white men shrank the civilian labor force. Accordingly, in September 1862, General Ulysses S. Grant, commander of the Department of the Tennessee, proposed to transport former slaves from Union encampments in the Mississippi Valley to Cairo, Illinois, where arrangements had been made to hire them to civilian employers. About the same time, General John A. Dix, commander of the Department of Virginia, asked the governors of several northeastern states to receive some of the contrabands who had accumulated at Fortress Monroe.[61]

Initially Grant's proposal received approval from the War Department. But the merest whisper that former slaves were to be shipped North evoked impassioned protest in the free states, some of which had erected legal barriers against the immigration of black people. Hostility to such migration crested during the latter half of 1862, as Democrats exploited the "Negro Influx Question" in state and congressional elections. Fearful that federal sponsorship of migration would undermine support for the war, Republican politicians made their objections known to the Lincoln administration. Even abolitionists like John A. Andrew, governor of Massachusetts, opposed the relocation of black people from the slave states. Andrew objected on the grounds that

---

[60] For the petition from free blacks in the District of Columbia, see *Wartime Genesis: Upper South*, doc. 51. On opposition by black people to wartime colonization, see William Seraile, "Afro-American Emigration to Haiti during the American Civil War," *The Americas* 35 (Oct. 1978): 185–200; Ira Berlin, Wayne K. Durrill, Steven F. Miller, Leslie S. Rowland, and Leslie Schwalm, " 'To Canvass the Nation': The War for Union Becomes a War for Freedom," *Prologue* 20 (Winter 1988): 241–42.

[61] *Official Records*, ser. 3, vol. 2, p. 569; *Wartime Genesis: Upper South*, doc. 11; *Wartime Genesis: Lower South*, doc. 154; *Black Military Experience*, doc. 41n.

black men should remain in the South and be armed as soldiers, but other Republican leaders cared only that freedpeople stay out of the North.[62]

Determined not to be outflanked by racist Democrats, the Lincoln administration squelched proposals to settle former slaves in the free states. Secretary of War Edwin M. Stanton, who had approved Grant's plan, abruptly reversed himself. After Governor Andrew exposed Dix's scheme to public view, Dix let the matter drop. In his annual report of December 1862, Stanton assured the Northern public that "no colored man will leave his home in the South if protected in that home"; putting freedpeople to work in the South would ensure that they had "neither occasion nor temptation . . . to emigrate to a northern and less congenial climate."[63] By the end of 1862, the Lincoln administration had decided that whatever the fate of the former slaves, it would be in the South.

Unable or unwilling to ship former slaves to Africa, to Central America, or to the North, Union military commanders sought means to support them within the occupied South. From the outset, the war had created unprecedented relief problems, and the number of displaced and destitute people – black and white – increased exponentially as continued fighting suspended agricultural production, disrupted local economies, and sent refugees in search of a safe haven. As Union forces occupied Confederate territory, army rations constituted the principal form of aid to impoverished civilians. Whatever the justice of providing relief from federal coffers, other demands upon the treasury encouraged both niggardly assistance and a determination to

---

[62] *Wartime Genesis: Upper South*, doc. 13; *Black Military Experience*, doc. 41. On Northern opposition to immigration by former slaves, see V. Jacque Voegeli, *Free But Not Equal: The Midwest and the Negro during the Civil War* (Chicago, 1967), chap. 4; *Black Military Experience*, docs. 30, 194. One Northerner proposed to keep former slaves out of the free states by hiring them to " 'poor white' Southrons," who would be allowed to purchase forty-acre plots from confiscated plantations. Such a solution, he argued, would retain the former slaves' "trained labor on cotton & tobacco." (Robert A. Maxwell, "To Save Fall elections on Negro Influx Question," 25 July 1862, Miscellaneous Letters Received: K Series, ser. 103, General Records of the Department of the Treasury, RG 56, NA [X-243].)

[63] *Official Records*, ser. 3, vol. 2, pp. 663, 897–912.

find alternative sources of support. Northern churches and aid societies assumed part of the burden, but private charity could not begin to meet the need. In some places, Union commanders levied special assessments upon prominent secessionists, on the theory that those who had caused the rebellion should help alleviate the consequent suffering. Such assessments, however, were both locally unpopular and difficult to enforce. More important, they, too, were inadequate to the task. With respect to relief for former slaves, federal officials turned increasingly to the idea that able-bodied freedpeople who succeeded in finding employment should be required to support those who remained dependent and unemployed.[64]

Generalizing from longstanding Northern welfare policies, some Union officers insisted first that individual families must care for their own. But in the midst of war, it was difficult for former slaves to fulfill these expectations, however much they struggled to do so. Even when families had fled bondage together or were reunited behind Union lines, they were often separated when military authorities redeployed black laborers or relocated their dependents. In such circumstances, federal officials sought to extend the principle of familial obligation. The idea, in the words of one army chaplain, was to "[keep] families together in responsibility if not in fact."[65]

On the assumption that all Southern black people were members of a single community, federal authorities in some jurisdictions charged relief expenses against the earnings of black military laborers. In September 1862, when a quartermaster in west Tennessee requested instructions regarding provision for black women and children, Quartermaster General Meigs urged that a portion of the wages owed to

---

[64] Bremner, *The Public Good*, pp. 91–92. For examples of assessments upon secessionists, see *Official Records*, ser. 1, vol. 15, pp. 538–39, and ser. 3, vol. 2, pp. 720–25, 731–32; Andrew Johnson, *The Papers of Andrew Johnson*, ed. Leroy P. Graf, Ralph W. Haskins, and Paul H. Bergeron, 8 vols. to date (Knoxville, Tenn., 1967-), vol. 5, pp. 623–25. For an order issued late in the war that proposed to assess "avowed rebel sympathizers" for the care of "sick, helpless, and needy" former slaves, see *Wartime Genesis: Upper South*, doc. 142.

[65] *Wartime Genesis: Lower South*, doc. 158n.

black military laborers be set aside to assist the needy. "The labor of the men & those women able to work," Meigs reasoned, "should support the whole community of negros at any station." Secretary of War Stanton approved. By the same logic, the War Department authorized a $5 monthly deduction from the wages of black military laborers in the District of Columbia and nearby Alexandria, Virginia. Similar assessments were later made upon black wage-earners in other jurisdictions.[66]

Former slaves expected to support their families and frequently went out of their way to assist the needy, even those to whom they bore no kinship obligations. However, black military laborers objected to taxes that took a large portion of their wages. In the District of Columbia, black freemen – many of whom had never been slaves – thought it unfair that the federal government tax them for the benefit of destitute ex-slaves, especially since white workers were not similarly assessed. Authorities brushed aside such protests and continued to take deductions for the "contraband fund."[67]

Revenue realized through these levies defrayed some of the expense of supporting former slaves. However, it went but a small way toward ameliorating the problems of health, sanitation, and housing created by the presence of large numbers of ex-slaves within federal lines. With winter fast upon them, necessity – as well as humanity – impelled field commanders to establish makeshift bivouacs or "contraband camps" for the reception, relief, and employment of black refugees. In doing so, they placed all freedpeople under direct military oversight and simplified the distribution of rations, clothing, and medical supplies. By the end of 1862, large camps had been established at LaGrange, Bolivar, and Memphis in west Tennessee and at Corinth in northern Mississippi. "Contraband colonies" on the outskirts of New Orleans housed several thousand residents. In the eastern theater, Craney Island, near Norfolk, Virginia, was set aside for unemployed

---

[66] *Wartime Genesis: Upper South*, docs. 54–55; *Wartime Genesis: Lower South*, docs. 153, 166n.

[67] *Wartime Genesis: Upper South*, docs. 56, 66, 69–70, 82.

contrabands, as was Camp Barker in the District of Columbia, only blocks from the President's mansion.[68]

As they established separate settlements for former slaves, federal commanders assigned subordinate officers to supervise their labor and welfare. Many of the new superintendents of contrabands came from the ranks of army chaplains, including John Eaton, Jr., and most of his subordinates in the Department of the Tennessee. Some, such as Lieutenant George H. Hanks in the Department of the Gulf, were quartermasters whose duties had involved mobilizing black laborers. Nearly all had connections to Northern aid societies, and a few were themselves agents of those societies. The appointment of the superintendents thus conferred official recognition upon some abolitionists and the organizations they represented. Although their formal incorporation into the Union chain of command gave them new authority, it also signified that private philanthropy would play a subaltern role. The superintendents operated within the framework of military bureaucracy and were subject to the dictates of superior officers.[69]

The new superintendents organized residents of the contraband camps into working parties according to age and physical condition. Healthy men and some women were assigned to the quartermaster, commissary, medical, and engineer departments of the army. The remaining women, children, and old and disabled men did what work they could. Virtually every camp required such freedpeople to police grounds, construct and repair buildings, and generally maintain the premises. Beyond that, the character of their labor depended upon the location of the camp and the timing and circumstances of its establishment. Residents of contraband camps in northern Mississippi and west Tennessee harvested cotton under the direction of government

[68] *Wartime Genesis: Upper South*, docs. 13n., 17–18, 42, 60; *Wartime Genesis: Lower South*, docs. 64–65, 71, 154–55, 160; Registers of Freedmen at Camp Barker, June 1862–Dec. 1863, ser. 570, Camp Barker DC, Records of the Bureau of Refugees, Freedmen, and Abandoned Lands, RG 105, NA [A-10092]. See also Cam Walker, "Corinth: The Story of a Contraband Camp," *Civil War History* 20 (Mar. 1974): 5–22.

[69] *Wartime Genesis: Upper South*, docs. 4n., 22, 64, 72; *Wartime Genesis: Lower South*, docs. 110, 155, 157n.

overseers, sometimes from abandoned fields, other times from the fields of resident owners who paid the government for the labor. At Camp Barker, in Washington, the superintendents hired hundreds of former slaves to civilian employers, including slaveholders. Some camps were poorly situated to provide employment. On desolate Craney Island, there was little but make-work; despite the freedpeople's desire to be "of some account," their superintendent had nothing to offer but unpaid labor refurbishing grain sacks and sewing Union uniforms.[70]

Even in the most favorable circumstances, residents of the contraband camps had to rely upon the government for at least a portion of their livelihood. Not only did the army regularly remove those men and women best able to support themselves and their dependents, but it also made no provision to distribute the earnings of laborers to their relatives and friends. Attempts at self-support were overwhelmed by the continued influx of fugitive slaves. And because most camps were not established until the fall of 1862, their inhabitants could not plant food for immediate consumption. At best, they could forage from nearby woods and abandoned fields.

For all its privations, life in the contraband camps permitted former slaves some latitude in shaping their own lives. Although most residents received only subsistence, some earned modest wages outside the camp, with which they purchased additional food, clothing, and amenities like bibles and schoolbooks or tobacco and liquor. In the camps, many freedpeople reconstituted families separated during slavery or in the travail of war. They eagerly attended schools taught by the agents of Northern aid societies, sympathetic officers and soldiers, or the literate within their own ranks. They organized both informal prayer meetings and formal congregations of the faithful, celebrated weddings, and – all too often – mourned the dead. Freedpeople shouldered much of the responsibility for their own medical care – a considerable burden because disease flourished among the crowded, ill-housed, and mal-

[70] *Wartime Genesis: Upper South*, docs. 17–18, 60–61; *Wartime Genesis: Lower South*, doc. 160.

nourished inhabitants of the camps. With army physicians and nurses in short supply, black "aunties" and "grannies" ministered to the sick, applying the healing skills they had learned as slaves. Although rude, the contraband camps were the first home in freedom for many former slaves.[71]

The contraband camps and large-scale employment of black military laborers epitomized the transformation of Union policy toward former slaves. By the end of 1862, the necessity of mobilizing former slaves had become apparent to all but the most intransigent federal officials. In defending the Union, declared Quartermaster General Meigs, "it is impossible to cast aside the millions of recruits who will offer themselves for the work, accustomed to the climate, inured to labor, acquainted with the country, and animated by the strong desire not merely for political but for personal liberty." Secretary of War Stanton urged that the Union "turn against the rebels the productive power that upholds the insurrection." "By striking down this system of compulsory labor, which enables the leaders of the rebellion to control the resources of the people," Stanton intoned, "the rebellion would die of itself."[72]

The Emancipation Proclamation, issued by President Lincoln on New Year's Day, 1863, at once ratified developments of the previous year and set new terms for the subsequent evolution of free labor. The proclamation declared free all slaves in the Confederacy, except those in Tennessee and in the Union-occupied parts of southern Louisiana and tidewater Virginia. Congress had already abolished slavery in the District of Columbia and the western territories. The Militia Act had liberated slaves who worked for the Union army or navy. The Second Confiscation Act had extended freedom to those slaves coming under Union control whose owners were disloyal. Now Lincoln's proclamation made emancipation an official aim of the war. Thenceforward, as federal

---

[71] On everyday life in the contraband camps see, for example, *Wartime Genesis: Upper South*, docs. 17–18, 60–61, 72–74; *Wartime Genesis: Lower South*, docs. 160, 164, 170.

[72] *Official Records*, ser. 3, vol. 2, pp. 786–809, 897–912.

troops advanced into the Confederate heartland, they marched as agents of freedom.[73]

The Emancipation Proclamation closed some doors as it opened others. Whereas the preliminary proclamation of September 1862 had included the customary pledge to support the removal of freed slaves from the United States, the final edict was silent on the subject. The folly of exiling the very men and women whom Union commanders were trying to mobilize – and who showed no interest in emigrating – seemed increasingly manifest. No less important, the heads of several Central American states had bluntly refused to accept black immigrants. Although Lincoln later gave occasional lip service to colonization, it had become a lost cause. In early 1864 the widely publicized debacle of a government-sanctioned venture in Ile à Vache, Haiti, where unscrupulous Northern promoters abandoned several hundred black emigrants to sicken and die, ended the administration's involvement in such schemes.[74]

While it silently rejected colonization, the Emancipation Proclamation explicitly authorized a larger role for former slaves in the Union war effort. The President enjoined persons freed by the proclamation, "in all cases when allowed, [to] labor faithfully for reasonable wages." More important, he invited black men to support the Union cause as soldiers. Northern free blacks and their abolitionist allies had long viewed military service as a lever for racial equality, as well as a weapon against slavery, and they rushed to accept the President's invitation. In mid-January 1863, Massachusetts Governor Andrew secured permission from Secretary of War Stanton to organize a black regiment, and within weeks volunteers from all over the North were enlisting in the 54th Massachusetts Infantry.[75]

---

[73] For the Emancipation Proclamation, see *Statutes at Large*, vol. 12, pp. 1268–69. For the earlier emancipation measures, see *Statutes at Large*, vol. 12, pp. 376–78, 432, 597–600. For an example of federal officers arming former slaves and sending them back to their home plantations as *"missionaries"* of freedom, see *Destruction of Slavery*, doc. 101.

[74] Boyd, "Negro Colonization in the National Crisis," chaps. 5, 7, 13.

[75] *Statutes at Large*, vol. 12, pp. 1268–69. On the recruitment of black soldiers in the North, see *Black Military Experience*, chap. 2.

As winter turned to spring, events in the North reemphasized the connection between emancipation and the success of federal arms. In March, Congress authorized the enrollment and conscription of Northern white men. The draft created a firestorm of opposition to the Lincoln administration and to the war itself. In part to shift the burden from Northern whites, the War Department moved quickly to enlist black men, expanding recruitment first to free blacks throughout the North and then to Southern slaves liberated by Lincoln's proclamation and congressional emancipation measures. By the end of April, Secretary of War Stanton had dispatched specially commissioned officers to virtually every part of the Union-occupied Confederacy to organize black regiments. Only the border states and middle Tennessee remained off-limits, and they not for long.[76]

With the nation committed to emancipation and black men marching under the American flag, Northerners contemplated a future in which all black people would be free. To plan for that day, Stanton impaneled the American Freedmen's Inquiry Commission in March 1863, instructing its members to recommend "practical measures for placing [the former slaves] in a state of self-support and self-defense, with the least possible disturbance to the great industrial interest of the country," and asking them to suggest how the government might "[render] their services efficient in the present war." In the year that followed, the three commissioners traveled throughout the Union-occupied Confederacy and the border slave states, interviewing military officers, white civilians, free blacks, and former slaves about slavery and freedom, work and property, God and family. In May 1864, the commission submitted its blueprint for reconstructing the South and the nation.[77]

In the meantime, with the beginning of both the spring military campaign and the agricultural season of 1863, the freedpeople's desper-

---

[76] On the expansion of recruitment in the North and its extension to the Union-occupied South, see *Black Military Experience*, chaps. 2–3.

[77] *Official Records*, ser. 3, vol. 3, pp. 73–74. For the commission's preliminary and final reports, dated June 30, 1863, and May 15, 1864, see *Official Records*, ser. 3, vol. 3, pp. 430–54, and ser. 3, vol. 4, pp. 289–382. An excerpt from a supplement to the final report is printed in *Wartime Genesis: Lower South*, doc. 115.

ate condition required more immediate measures. President Lincoln concluded that it was time for former slaves to start "digging their subsistence out of the ground."[78] His terse formulation struck a sympathetic chord with many Northerners who agreed that the interests of the Union and of the freedpeople themselves would be best served by putting them to work on land abandoned by their erstwhile owners. In the view of Secretary of War Stanton, the loyalty of former slaves and the treason of their former owners made it both right and necessary to give black people "protection and employment upon the soil which they have thus far cultivated, and the right to which has been vacated by the original proprietors."[79]

Putting the freedpeople to work on abandoned plantations promised to solve many of the problems created by fighting a war for both national unity and universal liberty. By providing former slaves with a way to earn their own food, clothing, and shelter, it would reduce federal expenditures for relief. The resumption of cotton production would stoke the Northern economy and return revenue to the national treasury via wartime taxes on the staple and on commerce in the occupied zones. Furthermore, it would speed the transformation of slaves into free workers. Liberated by the President's proclamation, former slaves would learn to labor for wages in the Union-occupied South.

Its many advantages notwithstanding, the decision to establish freedpeople on abandoned plantations and farms raised numerous practical questions. One of the most important involved ownership of the land. Beyond the customary practices of war, which sanctioned the use of captured property for military purposes, Congress had given President Lincoln the legal means to effect lasting changes in Southern landholding. The Second Confiscation Act, which permitted the government to seize real and personal property belonging to disloyal citizens and sell it to loyal ones, provided one tool, but an unwieldy one. Confiscation required formal proceedings in federal courts, which had ceased to function in the seceded states. Moreover, the President had the power to pardon individual rebels, and, at his insistence, Congress

[78] *Destruction of Slavery*, doc. 107.   [79] *Official Records*, ser. 3, vol. 2, pp. 897–912.

had adopted an "explanatory resolution" prohibiting forfeiture of land beyond the life of the offender. Like most Northerners, Lincoln had no taste for wholesale expropriation and, even in wartime, remained wary of any seizure of property by the state.[80]

The Direct Tax Act of June 1862 offered a more straightforward way to transform property holding. In order to collect in the seceded states a federal tax that had been levied upon each state in 1861, the act provided for assessments on individual parcels of land, which would be forfeited to the government if the owner failed to pay. Tax commissioners, appointed by the President for each insurrectionary state, would then assume control, with authority to rent out the property or to subdivide and sell it at auction. In contrast to transactions under the Confiscation Act, the sale of land under the Direct Tax Act would convey fee-simple title, with no restrictions whatsoever. Indeed, as its authors readily admitted, the purpose of the act was less to raise revenue than to "[divest] . . . by law, the titles of rebels to their lands." By the end of 1862, Lincoln had appointed direct-tax commissioners for South Carolina and for Florida, and the South Carolina commission was taking the steps required to put a substantial number of Sea Island plantations on the block. Commissioners were not yet appointed for the other Union-occupied states, however, and the President showed no inclination to speed proceedings.[81]

Only a tiny amount of land within Union-occupied territory had been formally alienated from its owners by the confiscation or direct-tax acts, but the army controlled large tracts by military occupation. Although they lacked authority to determine final disposition of captured

[80] *Statutes at Large*, vol. 12, pp. 589–92. On the framing and enforcement of the act, see James Garfield Randall, *The Confiscation of Property during the Civil War* (Indianapolis, Ind., 1913), chaps. 1–6, and John Syrett, "The Confiscation Acts: Efforts at Reconstruction during the Civil War" (Ph.D. diss., University of Wisconsin, 1971).

[81] For the Direct Tax Act, see *Statutes at Large*, vol. 12, pp. 422–26; for a summary of its provisions, see *Wartime Genesis: Lower South*, doc. 27n. On its authors' intent, see *Wartime Genesis: Lower South*, doc. 30. On the appointment of direct-tax commissioners, see U.S., Senate, "Letter of the Secretary of the Treasury . . . [on] the collection of direct taxes in insurrectionary districts . . . ," *Senate Executive Documents*, 38th Cong., 1st sess., No. 35.

or abandoned land, military authorities did not hesitate to use it temporarily for the benefit of the Union war effort, the former slaves under their jurisdiction, and the nation in general. In doing so, they did not lack for offers of assistance.

Ambitious men with an eye on the soaring price of cotton urged federal authorities to open the South – particularly the rich plantation lands of the Mississippi Valley and the South Carolina Sea Islands – to the invigorating influence of Northern capital. Tough-minded capitalists, they argued, could transform Southern society more effectively than abolitionist dreamers or government bureaucrats. None was more impatient to bring the plantations "within the reach of private Enterprise" than Edward S. Philbrick, who had spent 1862 as a plantation superintendent in the Sea Islands. Other Northern newcomers to the occupied Confederacy sounded similar themes. For George B. Field, a New York attorney who toured the Mississippi Valley in the early months of 1863 on behalf of Secretary of War Stanton, nothing would ensure public support for emancipation better than a demonstration that "free negro labor under good management can be made a *source* of *profit* to the *employer*." Seeing no contradiction between private gain and public good, would-be planters pledged their lives and their fortunes to recast the plantation South in the image of the North.[82]

Not all Northerners shared this confidence that the interests of private investors would benefit either former slaves or the public at large. From his perspective as superintendent of contrabands in the Department of the Tennessee, Chaplain John Eaton feared the consequences of placing the freedpeople in the hands of speculators. Eaton advocated a system of plantation labor similar to that earlier instituted on the Sea Islands, in which government-appointed superintendents, not private employers, would control agricultural operations and all other aspects of the former slaves' transition to freedom. Meanwhile, on the Sea Islands, the machinations of Philbrick and a "horde" of other Yankees who wished to purchase direct-tax land alarmed the Gideonites, their

[82] *Wartime Genesis: Lower South*, docs. 34, 76, 159, 206. On the outlook of Northern planters and would-be planters, see Powell, *New Masters*, especially chaps. 1–2.

military allies, and the former slaves. General Rufus Saxton, military governor of the islands, feared that the engrossment of land by private purchasers would put the freedpeople "at the mercy of men devoid of principle," to the detriment of "their future well being." Saxton wanted the national government to "give the negroes a right in that soil to whose wealth they are destined in the future to contribute so largely."[83]

In the end, such misgivings yielded before the promise of Northern entrepreneurs to diminish the government's expenses and increase its revenue. In the South Carolina Sea Islands, the Mississippi Valley, and southern Louisiana, Yankee capitalists gained access to some of the most productive land in the United States. Nowhere, however, did they enjoy as clear a field as they desired. In the Sea Islands, President Lincoln instructed the direct-tax commissioners to reserve a substantial portion of the forfeited land from sale. He also empowered them to bid on behalf of the government for what land was to be offered at auction. In March 1863, when the first direct-tax sales came off, Northern entrepreneurs acquired half the available land. By far the largest purchaser was a syndicate of investors organized by Philbrick.[84]

In southern Louisiana, resident planters obstructed the path of Northern businessmen. Sugar planters claiming loyalty to the federal government retained control over many of the great estates. Heartened by the region's exemption from the Emancipation Proclamation, they pressed General Nathaniel P. Banks, Butler's successor in the Department of the Gulf, to respect their right to manage their plantations and command slave labor. Banks responded by instituting a "voluntary system of labor" that, like Butler's expedient of the previous fall, required small wage payments and promised military enforcement of plantation discipline. Abandoned estates, along with those owned by planters who refused Banks's terms, fell to the department quartermaster, who was authorized to lease them out or operate them under direct government supervision. But because most loyal planters accepted the new regime, however reluctantly, relatively few estates came into government

---

[83] *Wartime Genesis: Lower South*, docs. 27, 30, 158n.
[84] *Wartime Genesis: Lower South*, docs. 27n., 30, 31.

hands. Yankee entrepreneurs leased some of them, but the others were so ravaged by the war or so vulnerable to Confederate attack as to dissuade prospective investors from risking their capital.[85]

Farther north in the Mississippi Valley, Northern planters had a freer hand. In March 1863, Secretary of War Stanton sent Adjutant General Lorenzo Thomas to the valley to inaugurate the recruitment of black soldiers. Traveling in the company of George Field, Thomas soon saw a connection between mobilizing black men, providing for their families, fostering loyalty to the Union, and reestablishing plantation agriculture. Within days of his arrival, he had appointed a commission, headed by Field, to lease plantations to Northerners. Assuming that "the employment and subsistance of negroes [was] a matter to be left to private enterprise," Thomas expected the lessees to hire the families of black soldiers and provide for at least some dependent freedpeople. The leased plantations, protected by newly organized black troops, would unite staple production and many of the relief functions previously borne by the contraband camps.[86]

In most of the Union-occupied Mississippi Valley, however, Thomas's plan could not yet be implemented. At Helena, Arkansas, for instance, where the reach of the small garrison extended barely beyond the town, thousands of former slaves languished in an overcrowded and unhealthy contraband camp for want of securely held plantations. In early 1863, the local commander began transporting them to Cairo, Illinois, and St. Louis, Missouri. Before long, a St. Louis-based network had been established to hire former slaves to midwestern farmers. By the fall of 1863, more than 1,000 had been relocated from Helena to the free states.[87] Midwesterners generally welcomed these migrants. A year earlier, proposals to move black Southerners to the North had sparked Negrophobic hysteria, but circumstances had changed. Even as the

---

[85] For the orders establishing Banks's system, see *Wartime Genesis: Lower South*, docs. 81, 84. On the estates leased out or operated by the government, see *Wartime Genesis: Lower South*, doc. 93.

[86] *Official Records*, ser. 3, vol. 3, pp. 100–101; *Wartime Genesis: Lower South*, doc. 162; *Black Military Experience*, doc. 194.

[87] On the relocation, see *Wartime Genesis: Upper South*, docs. 162–63, 165, 171; *Wartime Genesis: Lower South*, docs. 161, 167.

conscription of white men created a labor shortage in the North, emancipation and the enlistment of black soldiers engendered a new respect and sympathy for former slaves. Self-interest and sentiment jointly refuted Democratic predictions of race war.

The removal of several hundred former slaves from the Mississippi Valley to the Midwest hardly alleviated the plight of most fugitive slaves or solved the problems of military commanders. Resumption of agricultural production in the South offered the best hope of providing for the increasing number of freedpeople entering Union lines. In 1863, however, secure territory was extremely limited. Adjutant General Thomas found only one promising setting for his plantation-leasing scheme, a small area in northeastern Louisiana that was held by Northern troops operating against Vicksburg. There Thomas's commission rented at least forty plantations to Northern entrepreneurs and a few Southern loyalists. By the fall of 1863, between 3,500 and 5,300 former slaves were living on the leased plantations. Despite the small territory embraced, Thomas believed his plan would eventually "line the [Mississippi] river with a loyal population" of Yankees, emancipated slaves, and native white unionists.[88]

Lured by the prospect of bonanza profits from cotton, Northern lessees bypassed the regions of mixed farming that had also fallen under Union control. No eager capitalists challenged Charles Wilder for land and labor in tidewater Virginia. During the spring of 1863, after receiving Stanton's authorization, Wilder and his fellow superintendent of contrabands, Orlando Brown, settled freedpeople on land abandoned by disloyal owners. Residents of "government farms" literally worked for the government, which supplied rations, livestock, and farm implements and, at the end of the year, paid the laborers with a portion of the

[88] On the extent of territory and number of plantations leased in 1863 under Thomas's system, see *Wartime Genesis: Lower South*, docs. 180 (which estimates the number of leased plantations at sixty) and 189 (which puts the number at forty). The total number of residents on the leased estates has been estimated by first calculating the average number on twenty-one plantations whose residents were enumerated in October 1863 (*Wartime Genesis: Lower South*, doc. 177) and then multiplying that average (eighty-eight per plantation) by each of the two figures for the total number of leased plantations.

crop. Some months later, Colonel Elias M. Greene, chief quartermaster of the Department of Washington, instituted a similar system on several abandoned estates in northern Virginia, just across the Potomac River from the District of Columbia. However, the number of freedpeople working government-controlled land remained small. As of August 1863, only 1,600 former slaves resided on government farms in tidewater Virginia – about 6 percent of the region's black population. Fewer than 200 worked the abandoned estates near Washington.[89]

While the expansion of Union-held territory made it possible for some former slaves to return to the land, it also changed the character of military labor. The surrender of Vicksburg and Port Hudson in July 1863 gave federal forces control of the Mississippi River and set the stage for offensive operations elsewhere, notably Arkansas and middle and east Tennessee. Union armies on the move had little use for laborers to erect stationary fortifications. Instead, they needed teamsters to drive wagons, hostlers to tend the teams, drovers to herd livestock to the front lines, wood choppers to supply fuel for steamboats and locomotives, and laborers to construct and repair roads, bridges, and railbeds. Naval vessels that patrolled the Mississippi and its tributaries also required a large number of hands. Both the army and the navy needed thousands of workers to operate supply depots and maintain lines of communication. In the most active theaters, Union officers mobilized every black man within their reach. By August, the army was employing 11,000 black laborers in middle Tennessee alone.[90]

During the summer and fall of 1863, black men also enlisted in the federal army in large numbers. The opportunity to don Union blue and strike a blow at slavery drew thousands of ex-slaves and free blacks to recruiting stations in the Union-occupied South. Recruitment officers

---

[89] On the tidewater farms, see *Wartime Genesis: Upper South*, docs. 16–17, 28; *Destruction of Slavery*, doc. 13. On those near Washington, see *Wartime Genesis: Upper South*, docs. 63, 77. In the summer of 1864, with farm operations considerably larger than they had been the previous year, only 241 laborers were employed on the northern Virginia farms. (*Wartime Genesis: Upper South*, doc. 77n.)

[90] *Wartime Genesis: Upper South*, doc. 95. The 11,000 laborers represented more than one-fifth of the 51,000 black men between the ages of eighteen and forty-five who lived in the entire state of Tennessee in 1860. (*Black Military Experience*, p. 12.)

promptly sent the new volunteers into the field to enlist friends and relatives. Black soldiers also participated in raids and foraging expeditions that brought still more ex-slaves into Union ranks. By war's end, 179,000 black men – the vast majority former slaves – had served in the federal army. More than half of them originated in the Confederate states, from some of which they constituted a substantial proportion of the black men of military age. More than a fifth of such men in Arkansas and Mississippi served in the Union army, as did nearly a third of those in Louisiana and almost two-fifths in Tennessee.[91]

Black soldiers often found themselves assigned to menial labor instead of combat duties. Laborers for the quartermaster or other military departments formed the nucleus of several black regiments, which, once mustered into service, continued to work much as before. From the standpoint of their military employers, black soldiers had two advantages over civilians. First, they were subject to army regulations and could not leave their duties at will. Second, in areas where civilian workers commanded high wages, black soldiers performed the same work for lower pay. The combination was too much to resist. Although all Union soldiers performed fatigue duty, black soldiers did more than their share.[92]

Black men struggled to realize their own expectations of martial life. Upon learning that black soldiers earned less than white soldiers, less than white military laborers, and also less than many black military laborers, they often refused to enlist. In Nashville, where black quartermaster employees received $25 per month, more than double the $10

[91] On the extension of recruitment to the Union-occupied Confederacy, see *Black Military Experience*, chap. 3. For the number of black soldiers credited to each state, see Table 1 in Chapter 3, this volume.

[92] *Wartime Genesis: Upper South*, doc. 100; *Black Military Experience*, chap. 10, and docs. 42, 68, 130A, 243, 265. If black soldiers often worked as laborers, black laborers sometimes served as quasi soldiers. Even before Adjutant General Thomas inaugurated the enlistment of black men in the Mississippi Valley, armed ex-slaves were guarding contraband camps. Black civilians in the valley and elsewhere were often provided with weapons and organized to defend work parties and leased plantations, and black military laborers were liable to duty in local militias. (See, for example, *Wartime Genesis: Upper South*, docs. 28, 138; *Wartime Genesis: Lower South*, docs. 23, 160; *Official Records*, ser. 3, vol. 4, pp. 874–902.)

allotted to a black private, "no laborer with his eyes open" would join the army. When they did enlist, even the greenest recruits insisted upon being treated as soldiers rather than uniformed drudges. Before long, some of them had the opportunity to meet their old masters on the field of battle. At Port Hudson, Fort Wagner, Milliken's Bend, and dozens of lesser encounters, black men did a soldier's work.[93]

Large-scale employment of black men as soldiers and military laborers affected plans both to reorganize plantation agriculture on free-labor principles and to provide for destitute former slaves. The mobilization of adult men restricted the pool of laborers available to private planters and government superintendents. Work gangs had to be constructed around able-bodied women, assisted to varying degree by the old and the young of both sexes. Throughout the Union-occupied South, black women constituted the backbone of the agricultural labor force.[94] Although the planters would rather have had nothing to do with aged, sick, or disabled freedpeople and preferred not to hire women with numerous small children, they usually had no choice but to accept some of the dependent relatives of their workers. Former slaves spurned employment that entailed separation from their families, and military authorities forbade hiring practices that worsened the government's burden of relief. There remained, however, some dependent freedpeople who had no one to provide for them. To accommodate such unfortunates, federal officials in southern Louisiana and the Mississippi Valley reserved several plantations as "infirm farms," where unemployable former slaves received rations while contributing whatever they could to their own support.[95] The officials also abandoned all illusion that the contraband camps could function merely as receiving depots, from which fugitive-slave men would be inducted

93 *Black Military Experience*, doc. 68. In accordance with the provisions of the Militia Act of July 1862, black soldiers earned $10 per month, $7 in cash and $3 in clothing. On the combat role of black soldiers, see *Black Military Experience*, chap. 11.

94 On the character of the wartime agricultural labor force, see, for example, *Wartime Genesis: Upper South*, docs. 28, 42; *Wartime Genesis: Lower South*, docs. 36, 163, 165.

95 *Wartime Genesis: Lower South*, doc. 177; Geo. B. Field et al. to the Hon. E. M. Stanton, 16 May 1863, filed with #1315 1886, Letters Received, ser. 12, Records of the Adjutant General's Office, RG 94, NA [K-574].

into the army and virtually all others hired to plantation owners or lessees.

However genuine their acceptance of the government's responsibility for relief, military officials were overwhelmed by the thousands of slaves liberated by Union victories in 1863. Refugees who sought shelter at contraband camps faced recurrent shortages of food, clothing, housing, and medical supplies. Skyrocketing mortality – the result of wartime privation and of diseases fostered by overcrowding and unsanitary facilities – horrified sympathetic observers. In November 1863, officials of the Western Sanitary Commission ventured the bleak prediction that half the black people in the Mississippi Valley were "doomed to die in the process of freeing the rest." Much to the discomfiture of the Lincoln administration, opponents of emancipation seized upon such reports to support their contention that black people would be worse off in freedom than in slavery. General James S. Wadsworth, who investigated conditions in the Mississippi Valley, deliberately understated the extent of suffering, for fear of putting "ammunition in the hands of the copperheads."[96]

Whereas the contraband camps of the Union-occupied Lower South operated as adjuncts to the plantations, those in the Upper South played a more independent role, chiefly because federal authorities controlled so little abandoned land. In the tiny Union-held enclaves of tidewater North Carolina, where nearly all able-bodied black men had enlisted in the army, contraband camps were established at New Berne and Roanoke Island to house their families, who had no other means of support. Drawing upon government funds and private donations, Horace James, "superintendent of blacks" in North Carolina, strove to make Roanoke Island a model of life in freedom, with right-angled streets, gardens, and a hospital. Officials in the District of Columbia had similar goals in establishing "Freedman's Village" on the estate of Confederate General Robert E. Lee, across the Potomac River from

---

[96] *Wartime Genesis: Lower South*, doc. 107; James E. Yeatman et al. to His Excellency, A. Lincoln, 6 Nov. 1863, vol. R-S 1863, #342, Miscellaneous Letters Received: K Series, ser. 103, General Records of the Department of the Treasury, RG 56, NA [X-12]. See also *Destruction of Slavery*, doc. 110.

Washington. Freedman's Village became a showplace to which government officials directed foreign visitors and other dignitaries eager to witness the progress of the former slaves.[97]

In the loyal border states, where slavery remained legal and the recruitment of black soldiers had barely begun, only a few contraband camps came into existence in 1863. Because federal policy in the border states required deference to civil authority and noninterference with slavery, these camps evolved as sanctuaries not for border-state fugitive slaves but for those who had escaped from the Confederacy. Point Lookout, a military installation at the southernmost extension of Maryland's western shore, attracted black refugees from Virginia, among whom mingled a number of Maryland slaves. The post quartermaster employed many of the men and eventually inaugurated an informal contraband camp by issuing rations and tents to the women and children. In Missouri, military authorities established a sizable camp at St. Louis, but not to provide for local fugitive slaves. Instead, it was the arrival of hundreds of freedpeople from Helena, Arkansas, that forced the army to issue rations and set up quarters, first in an abandoned hotel and then at Benton Barracks, on the outskirts of the city. Similarly, the contraband camp at Columbus, on the western border of Kentucky, signaled no offer of protection to slaves from that state. Established in conjunction with the recruitment of black soldiers, the camp, like the new regiments, consisted almost entirely of fugitive slaves from Tennessee. To reduce their unsettling effect upon Kentucky slaves, military officers steadily transferred residents of the camp to nearby Island 10, Tennessee, in the middle of the Mississippi River.[98]

Throughout the Union-occupied South, the desperate poverty of most inhabitants of the contraband camps proclaimed the hollow legacy of chattel bondage. However, not all fugitive slaves traversed the ground between slavery and freedom empty-handed. A good many brought personal possessions – clothing, bedding, and cooking utensils – to

---

[97] *Wartime Genesis: Upper South*, docs. 22, 70–71; Horace James, *Annual Report of the Superintendent of Negro Affairs in North Carolina, 1864* (Boston, 1865), pp. 6–7, 21–26.

[98] *Wartime Genesis: Upper South*, docs. 133, 162–63, 165, 171–72, 205, 209.

ease the transit. Some managed to carry away tools and other productive property. A former slave with an axe, a hoe, a wagon, or the implements of a trade stood a better chance of gaining an independent livelihood than one without such tools. Possession of a horse or mule also improved the possibilities for self-employment. Procured by various means – purchased during slavery, "borrowed" from a former master, picked up as strays, or acquired with the proceeds of wartime labor – draft animals enabled some ex-slaves to set up for themselves. Former slaves with a horse or mule worked as self-employed draymen and wagoners in such cities as Nashville, Memphis, and Washington, whose wartime economies depended heavily upon the transportation of goods. In some rural areas, freedpeople who were similarly endowed bargained with landowners for rental or crop-sharing arrangements. Freedpeople who left slavery in possession of productive property had a wider range of choices than those who owned only their ability to labor.[99]

A handful of former slaves gained legal control over land in 1863. At the South Carolina direct-tax sales, freedpeople who had pooled their resources purchased as many as eight plantations in competitive bidding. In the Mississippi Valley, about fifteen black men leased land from Thomas's plantation commissioners, and an indeterminable number struck subleasing bargains with Northern planters. Although military authorities in southern Louisiana made no effort to rent land to black lessees, a few elderly and disabled former slaves who had remained on abandoned estates won informal approval to work the land for their own benefit.[100]

If only a minuscule number of former slaves enjoyed either formal or informal possession of land, their control over other productive property was not much more extensive, in part because almost everything fugitive slaves brought into Union lines was subject to expropriation. Military regulations permitted freedpeople to retain their possessions only if they could prove ownership, making it difficult for them to hold

---

[99] For examples of former slaves' ownership and use of productive property, including draft animals, see *Wartime Genesis: Upper South*, docs. 10, 96–97, 112, 116–17; *Wartime Genesis: Lower South*, docs. 51, 104, 174–75, 184.

[100] *Wartime Genesis: Lower South*, docs. 31, 91, 97, 180.

any property that was of use to the army. Even when assured that the expropriated livestock, tools, and other goods would be used in the contraband camps or on government-controlled plantations, former slaves could not help but feel a twinge of bitterness as their belongings were pressed into government service. Only rarely did their complaints receive a hearing.[101]

Former slaves were not alone in their protests. Observing that many freedpeople "use their property to make a living," General John Hawkins argued that "[t]he immediate gain to Gov,ment by the seizure is very small compared with the great loss to them." "By letting the property remain in their possession," he asserted, "they will be enabled next year to cultivate a few acres of ground and the Gov,ment be relieved of their support. By taking it away they or their families are made paupers for perhaps all time to come." But Hawkins's views were rare within Union officialdom, and his superiors rejected his appeal. Draft animals and other items brought into federal lines by former slaves remained subject to confiscation.[102]

Owning little or no productive property, former slaves were perforce dependent upon whatever compensation they could obtain by laboring for an employer. Black military laborers, soldiers, and urban and agricultural workers shared a reliance upon wage work. Accordingly, the amount and kind of compensation and the regularity of payment became important issues, at times critical ones. But in the various settings in which freedpeople became wage laborers, questions of compensation merged with other matters pertaining to control over production, especially the nature and extent of supervision and the length of the workday and workweek. The ex-slaves' experience in bondage had produced sensibilities and expectations opposed to those of former slaveholders and, in many respects, equally foreign to those of Northern planters and military officers. Struggles brought forward from slavery intertwined with those characteristic of free labor. Whereas some matters of contention – including the provision of subsistence, corporal punish-

---

[101] On military policy respecting personal property claimed by former slaves, see *Wartime Genesis: Lower South*, docs. 35, 160, 175A-B.
[102] *Wartime Genesis: Lower South*, docs. 175A-B.

ment, freedom of movement, and compensation – were common to military laborers, soldiers and sailors, and agricultural and urban workers, others depended upon the particular character of each type of work.

Of all former slaves, black military laborers were perhaps the most fully attuned to the wage relation. Unlike soldiers and plantation laborers, whose work was accompanied by the promise of subsistence for nonworking family members, military laborers usually had to feed and house their dependents from their earnings alone. The amount and frequency of pay therefore weighed heavily in their lives. Although the wages of military employees arrived with greater regularity during 1863, as the federal government's fiscal crisis receded and its bureaucracy gained experience, a substantial number of black laborers found themselves short-changed on account of irregularities or fraud. Nonpayment ranked high among the causes leading black military laborers to "desert," but it was not the only reason. Long hours of work, abusive superintendents, and substandard food, clothing, and shelter all prompted disgruntled workers to search for more attractive employment. To the consternation of military employers, black laborers learned only too well that their new status allowed them to sell their labor power wherever they wished. With the freedom to change employers, however, came the "freedom" to be discharged. Many military laborers experienced periods of unemployment or irregular employment, with the accompanying uncertainty of support for themselves and their families.[103]

Black soldiers surrendered the right to change employers, but they gained other rewards, including the respect of their comrades-in-arms and the gratitude of the nation for which they fought. Former slaves expected military service to mean, at the very least, that they would be treated the same as other soldiers, but black soldiers found themselves barred from promotion, assigned to labor gangs instead of combat, issued inferior rations and equipment, and subjected to punishments that, at times, bore uncomfortable resemblance to those meted out by

[103] *Wartime Genesis: Upper South*, docs. 16–17, 20, 22, 25, 27, 55–56, 60, 62, 70, 82, 92, 99, 102–3; *Wartime Genesis: Lower South*, docs. 31, 182; *Black Military Experience*, doc. 45.

slaveholders. Despite the fact that military discipline rested upon impersonal law rather than personal sovereignty, corporal punishment of any form infuriated men who had known the master's lash.[104]

These burdens aside, black soldiers were guaranteed rations, clothing, and a wage. To be sure, the quantity and quality of rations and clothing frequently fell short of their expectations, and black soldiers complained of the deficiency. But nothing angered them more than the government's failure to pay them at the same rate as their white comrades. Connected as it was with both their ability to support their families and their conviction that equal service merited equal recompense, their demand for equality had special resonance in the wider black community. Their families and friends – along with many Northern abolitionists – joined the soldiers in demanding justice. "We have done a Soldiers Duty," protested a black corporal to Lincoln in June 1863. "Why cant we have a Soldiers pay?"[105]

Farm and plantation workers also wished to enjoy the rights and privileges of free laborers. They especially wanted to erase the hallmarks of personal sovereignty that characterized slavery. At first, some asked little more than the prohibition of corporal punishment and a guarantee of family security. A group of former slaves in southern Louisiana assured an emissary of General Banks that they were "willing to go to work immediately . . . even without remuneration," provided that "they would not be whipped and separated from their families." Objections to the lash extended to the men who had historically wielded it. Steadfastly opposed to working under "Secesh overseers," freedpeople sometimes nominated a replacement of their own, either a fellow freedman or a Northerner who respected their determination not to be commanded by force.[106]

With plantation laborers united in opposition, planters courted rebel-

---

[104] For the experience of black soldiers, see *Black Military Experience*, especially chaps. 6–11.

[105] *Black Military Experience*, doc. 157A. The struggle for equal pay is discussed more fully in *Black Military Experience*, chap. 7.

[106] *Wartime Genesis: Lower South*, doc. 87. On the rejection of overseers, see *Wartime Genesis: Upper South*, doc. 43; *Wartime Genesis: Lower South*, docs. 34, 86, 94, 106C, 116–17, 121.

lion if they refused to accede. The consequence of trying to maintain
the old order, according to one army provost marshal, was "trouble,
immediately – and the negroes band together, and lay down their own
rules, as to when, and how long they will work &c &c. and the
Overseer loses all control over them." Occasionally, former slaves took
matters into their own hands. Armed with sticks, laborers on one
plantation drove the overseer away, declaring that "they would make
Laws for themselves."[107]

Union military authorities generally sympathized with the freedpeople's efforts to obliterate vestiges of the slave regime. Although they
stopped short of removing overseers, army officers prohibited corporal
punishment and established procedures for adjudicating disputes between employers and employees. They also required that freed laborers
be paid. In their view, prohibiting physical coercion and guaranteeing
compensation were fundamental to free labor. To some officers, the
principle of compensation mattered far more than its character or
amount. "It is free labor if but one cent a year be paid," declared the
head of General Banks's "Bureau of Negro Labor," to the ready assent of
the general himself.[108]

To the former slaves, Banks's penny represented not the certainty of
their liberation but the narrow confines of their freedom. Without
exception, military regulations prescribed low wages for plantation
hands, substantially lower than the earnings of black soldiers or military laborers. In 1863, monthly wages for the highest-rated field hands
ranged from $2 in southern Louisiana to about $6.50 in the Sea Islands
and $7 in the Mississippi Valley. The great majority of plantation
workers – women, children, and old people, all of whom were rated
below first-class hands – earned even less. Like black soldiers and military laborers, plantation laborers received rations in addition to wages
but, except in southern Louisiana, had to pay for their own clothing.
Unlike black soldiers and most military laborers, plantation laborers
also received rations for dependent family members, the value of which,

[107] *Wartime Genesis: Lower South*, docs. 90Cn., 94.
[108] *Wartime Genesis: Lower South*, doc. 110.

for some large families, may have offset the lower wage rates. Nevertheless, their cash income barely sufficed to purchase blankets, supplemental foodstuffs, medical care, and tobacco. Little or nothing remained to buy items like schoolbooks and Sunday clothes, much less to save toward future independence.[109]

Differences in the organization of work and relief gave free labor a somewhat distinctive cast in each region of the Union-occupied South. These differences derived from antebellum practices, particular military circumstances, and the policies of individual commanders. In the Sea Islands, for instance, the antebellum organization of labor by "tasks" left its mark on wartime arrangements. At least initially, military officials and civilian plantation superintendents saw task work as readily adaptable to the requirements of free wage labor, because it assigned responsibility for particular work to particular workers, facilitating both the measurement of each individual's labor and payment in proportion to work accomplished. General Saxton issued plantation regulations that organized all steps of cotton production (except harvesting) into daily tasks, each with a precise monetary payment. In effect, federal authorities transmuted antebellum task labor into piecework, expecting that some laborers would redouble their efforts and complete more than one task per day. Piecework also prevailed during harvest, with each worker paid on the basis of the amount of cotton picked. To encourage former slaves to remain at work to the end of the year, wages for planting and cultivation were set at a low level, with picking pegged at higher rates. At the heart of the new regime lay cash payment for work in cotton. With the money they earned, plantation hands were expected to purchase their clothing, whatever food they did not raise, and "luxuries" like tobacco, which in the past had often been provided by the owner. Obligatory labor on provision crops earned no wages at all.[110]

---

[109] *Wartime Genesis: Lower South*, docs. 28, 84, 162. The rate for the Sea Islands, where wages were set by the day rather than the month, is calculated on the basis of twenty-six days of work per month, at $.25 per day.

[110] For the order establishing the labor system on government plantations in the Sea Islands, see *Wartime Genesis: Lower South*, doc. 28. For elucidations of its provisions, see *Wartime Genesis: Lower South*, docs. 31–32, 36.

The reorganization of plantation labor was accompanied by new provisions for nonworkers. Except where the estates had been stripped by Union soldiers, Saxton and the plantation superintendents refused to dispense rations, on the grounds that such issues encouraged dependency and resembled the old system of "allowances" from the master. Instead, the laborers on each government plantation collectively produced food for the entire plantation population, workers and dependents alike, on land designated for that purpose. Each family also received a garden plot. Alone among the federally supervised plantation systems, that of the Sea Islands permitted the laborers some voice in decisions about what crops they would cultivate, and in what proportion. The freedpeople clearly preferred food crops. On plantations controlled by private entrepreneurs in 1863, cotton accounted for 40 percent of the cultivated acreage; on those operated under the direction of government superintendents, only 25 percent was in the staple.[111]

In most other respects, however, Saxton's regulations for the government plantations set the standard for those in private hands. In particular, the freedpeople employed by Northern planters expected prompt remuneration. One planter complained that he could induce them to cultivate cotton only "by going among them and paying on the spot." Northern entrepreneurs had little choice but to provide garden plots, because the laborers demanded them. To the extent that the planters were therefore able to reduce capital outlays in the form of rations, they found the system acceptable, though they rued the tendency of the laborers to devote their energies to food production instead of additional tasks in the cotton fields. Some laborers failed to complete even a single daily task, leaving the field at midday to work in their gardens.[112]

In another concession to the freedpeople, some Northern planters divided the fields into separate tracts, each worked collectively by the members of one or more households. Edward Philbrick, for one, favored such allocation of land because it gave the laborers "a proprietary

---

[111] Calculated from figures in *Wartime Genesis: Lower South*, doc. 36.
[112] *Wartime Genesis: Lower South*, docs. 32, 34, 40.

interest in the crop." By this arrangement, households or other self-organized work groups in effect supplanted individual task hands. These collective work units allowed the former slaves a greater measure of control over the disposition of their own labor, permitting some family members, for example, to leave the field early to perform domestic tasks, or allowing more experienced workers to assist the weaker and less experienced.[113]

In southern Louisiana and the Mississippi Valley, Union military officials devised a substantially different plan for organizing labor and relief. Both General Banks and Adjutant General Thomas retained certain formal features of the old regime. Plantation laborers continued to be organized into gangs whose composition was determined by the operator of the estate, not the workers. Despite the opposition of the freedpeople, the vast majority of planters – whether former slaveholders or Northern lessees – employed overseers. Hours and conditions of labor were left to the discretion of planters and overseers, subject only to the restraints of custom, the army's ban on corporal punishment, and a vaguely worded insistence that workers receive "proper" and "humane" treatment. The subsistence of plantation residents also remained largely the responsibility of planters, who were required to feed, clothe, and house nonworkers as well as workers. In the view of military authorities, the planters' assumption of that responsibility, together with the risks of planting in a war zone, justified low wages. For their part, former slaves were expected to devote their energy to raising staple crops, not food. Government officials, resident plantation owners, and Northern lessees were of one mind: Cotton and sugar, not corn and potatoes, promised profits for the planters and taxes for the treasury.[114]

Whatever the particular stipulations, military regulation of labor delivered a crippling blow to the master's sovereignty and limited the employer's power. No longer was the planter the court of first and last

---

[113] *Wartime Genesis: Lower South*, docs. 31, 34; see also Saville, "A Measure of Freedom," pp. 75–82.
[114] For the military regulations governing plantation labor in southern Louisiana and the Mississippi Valley, see *Wartime Genesis: Lower South*, docs. 81, 84, 162.

resort. Freedpeople recognized even the most rudimentary recourse to higher authority as a radical departure from slavery. When an employer trampled on their rights, they protested to the nearest superintendent of contrabands or provost marshal. Throughout the Union-occupied South, employers complained that their laborers appealed even "the least thing," undercutting all discipline. No matter what the decision in any given instance, intervention by federal officials signified the demise of the slaveholder's omnipotence.[115]

Union soldiers, black and white, often interposed their authority on behalf of agricultural laborers. Just as they had disseminated news of freedom, soldiers expounded the rights of free men and women, informing one group of ex-slaves, for example, that "they need never mind a driver any more, that each of them was good as a driver." Some soldiers attempted to redress forcibly the wrongs suffered by plantation workers. From the planters' perspective, black soldiers wielded especially subversive influence. Armed, mobile, and politicized, their very presence demonstrated the freedpeople's new power. Because most black soldiers had themselves toiled in the fields and often had families and friends on the plantations, they identified with those who worked the land and were determined to prevent their abuse.[116]

Plantations that had once been virtual fiefdoms, whose proprietors jealously guarded their boundaries and screened all visitors, became subject to all manner of intrusion. The separation of able-bodied men — most of whom were serving as soldiers or military laborers — from the women, children, and old people who made up the bulk of the plantation work force necessitated frequent visits, because former slaves viewed a secure family life as fundamental to freedom. Planters protested the visits as violations of their private domain, but their complaints availed little. Although military regulations generally forbade plantation laborers to leave an estate without permission, such rules were often honored only in the breach. "[W]e cannot keep our people at home," complained a Sea Island planter, who lamented the effect upon

[115] See, for example, *Wartime Genesis: Lower South*, doc. 32.
[116] See, for example, *Wartime Genesis: Lower South*, docs. 19, 74, 77, 199; *Black Military Experience*, doc. 55.

labor discipline.[117] The new permeability of plantation boundaries broke down the isolation of plantation life, permitting rural laborers to gain broader knowledge of the world and to develop solidarity with their counterparts on other estates and with black townspeople.

Within the narrow geographical bounds of Union occupation, the circumstances of plantation life forced all but the most intransigent slaveholders to accommodate the changes wrought by emancipation. Slowly and reluctantly, former masters began to come to terms with the reality of free labor. Few retired the lash voluntarily, and none welcomed the necessity of paying wages, but most planters were compelled to accept at least the rudiments of free labor in order to continue operations. Before long, they even discerned certain advantages in the new order.

Whereas former slaveholders were loath to assume the responsibilities of free labor, they eagerly jettisoned the burdens of mastership. Under the slave regime, they had been obliged to support sick, young, and elderly slaves; under free labor, they derived no benefits from doing so. Employers in the North, they pointedly insisted, bore no such responsibility. Accordingly, many erstwhile slaveholders evicted elderly and unproductive laborers with no consideration for years of service or putative bonds of affection. The wives, parents, and children of black soldiers became special targets of the planters' zeal to "sift out" unproductive former slaves, but anyone unable to contribute labor was liable to be ousted. Masters-turned-employers also refused to provide medical care, declaring that such expenses were no longer their responsibility. "When I owned niggers," announced a Louisiana planter in characteristic fashion, "I used to pay medical bills and take care of them; I do not think I shall trouble myself much now."[118]

The entry of Northerners into the plantation business and the acquiescence of former slaveholders in the requirements of free labor placed relations between planters and laborers on new ground. Even as corpo-

---

[117] *Wartime Genesis: Upper South*, doc. 21; *Wartime Genesis: Lower South*, docs. 32, 74, 79, 90B.
[118] *Wartime Genesis: Upper South*, docs. 102, 129; *Wartime Genesis: Lower South*, docs. 100–101, 106A, 108, 110, 200.

ral punishment and the employment of overseers remained live issues, the reorganization of agricultural labor inaugurated new contests over the length of the workday and the workweek. Planters struggled to exact as much labor as possible from freedpeople determined to work less than they had as slaves. In the Mississippi Valley and southern Louisiana, where gang labor predominated, planters tried to hold former slaves to the antebellum standard: dawn to dusk, six days a week, and, during harvest, additional labor at night and on Sunday. Freedpeople resisted such extensive claims on their time, often shortening both the workday and workweek, much to the disgust of former masters, Northern lessees, and federal officials. A government superintendent was chagrined to discover that the hands on one sugar estate "only work five days in the week and then very little." In the Sea Islands, where the task had defined a day's work, the contest centered on Saturday labor, with plantation superintendents and Northern planters insisting that the day belonged to the workweek and freedpeople claiming it as their own.[119]

Like employers elsewhere, planters in the Union-occupied South also wanted to pay their workers as little as possible, and at the last possible moment. Federal regulation of wages averted much potential conflict. But even the low rates set by military orders were too high for most planters, who would have preferred to compensate their workers with "a great present" at year's end – maintaining the fiction of their paternal rule and leaving to their own discretion the amount and form of payment. Meanwhile, the former slaves, confined to federally mandated wages, wanted more.

Within the possibilities permitted by military regulations, both planters and workers looked for ways to gain advantage. At times, each found reason to prefer that compensation take the form of a share of the crop rather than cash. Where planters lacked the resources with which to pay cash wages, they gladly acquiesced in laborers' demands for a share. In a good year, a postharvest share wage might return more to the laborers than monthly cash payments, although a short crop would

[119] See, for example, *Wartime Genesis: Lower South*, docs. 19, 21, 100n., 106B.

result in smaller compensation. From the standpoint of the planters, share wages offered the important benefit of holding laborers through the entire year, lest they forfeit their portion by leaving before the harvest. Federal officials also encouraged year-long commitments. In southern Louisiana, General Banks offered the option of a postharvest payment instead of monthly cash wages, setting the rate at one-twentieth of the crop, to be divided among the workers. Even when there was no explicit sanction of share wages, freedpeople and planters occasionally negotiated such arrangements on their own.[120]

Gradually former slaveholders and former slaves navigated the terrain of free labor more comfortably. Former slaveholders discovered that wage-earners expected to be paid, and paid promptly. They also came to see advantage in allowing their employees access to the resources of the plantation: the right to cultivate garden plots, to hunt or cut wood in forests and fish in streams, to keep swine and poultry. Such concessions were prized by former slaves, who saw them as a means to labor for their own benefit and to expand control over their own lives. Acceding to their wishes helped employers attract and retain a work force and, at times, permitted reductions in the amount or frequency of monetary compensation.[121] Employers learned not only to cater to the "wants" of the freedpeople, but also to turn them to their own ends. Yankee planters, familiar with the operation of a wage system, pioneered in establishing plantation stores where laborers could purchase items previously beyond their reach. Before long, Southern planters also realized that such stores could help keep their workers on the plantation and provide another source of profit.[122]

While they continued to condemn military regulation as a poor substitute for physical compulsion, planters learned to benefit from the authority of local superintendents or provost marshals. Denouncing anarchy in the quarters and presenting themselves as friends of good order, planters cultivated the goodwill of nearby army officers, who often welcomed the attention and granted them a sympathetic hearing.

---

[120] *Wartime Genesis: Upper South*, doc. 129; *Wartime Genesis: Lower South*, docs. 84, 86.
[121] See, for example, *Wartime Genesis: Lower South*, docs. 141, 171.
[122] *Wartime Genesis: Lower South*, docs. 40, 100, 108; Powell, *New Masters*, pp. 87–93.

General James Bowen, provost marshal general of the Department of the Gulf, went so far as to instruct his subordinates that "planters must be regarded as conservators of the peace" on their estates. Planters found the army particularly useful in curbing the former slaves' freedom of movement. Military restrictions against unauthorized travel dovetailed conveniently with the planters' insistence that black workers, once committed to a particular estate, not be allowed to leave except by permission.[123]

Free-labor arrangements, however circumscribed, endangered the old regime, a truth rebel leaders clearly understood. In the summer of 1863, the Confederate high command unleashed a series of raids on the plantations operated by Yankee lessees and reconstructed Southerners. The results were devastating. In the Mississippi Valley, rebel soldiers killed several lessees and hundreds of freedpeople, hundreds more of whom were captured and reenslaved. The attacks thoroughly disrupted the plantation-leasing system, sending panicked laborers and lessees to nearby army posts. Some lessees returned to their homes in the North, and many freedpeople refused to accept work in the countryside. Freedpeople in more secure areas, including the South Carolina Sea Islands and tidewater Virginia, escaped such wholesale terror, but they, too, suffered harassment by Confederate soldiers and guerrilla marauders.[124]

The Confederate raids failed to shake the federal commitment to reconstructing Southern agriculture on the basis of free labor. By the fall of 1863, many erstwhile secessionists were suing for peace. Disloyal planters, reports claimed, were "discouraged and hopeless of the rebellion, and ready to do almost anything that will keep their negroes in the fields." Such accounts were not long in reaching President Lincoln, who liked what he heard. Eager to revive Southern

[123] Bg. Genl. James Bowen to Captain Fitch, 27 Apr. [1863], vol. 296 DG, pp. 594–95, Press Copies of Letters Sent, ser. 1839, Provost Marshal, Dept. of the Gulf, Records of U.S. Army Continental Commands, RG 393 Pt. 1, NA [C-1099]. For examples of military restrictions upon the mobility of rural laborers, see *Wartime Genesis: Upper South*, doc. 21; *Wartime Genesis: Lower South*, docs. 15, 54, 109, 198.
[124] *Wartime Genesis: Lower South*, docs. 96, 168, 177, 196.

unionism, Lincoln directed his generals, particularly those in the Mississippi Valley, to encourage slaveholders to accept free labor. Adjutant General Thomas endorsed unionist associations in such former hotbeds of secession as Vicksburg and Natchez. Other federal officers courted both long-time loyalists and repentant rebels, promising them protection from Confederate raiders and assistance in marketing crops and acquiring supplies, if they agreed to compensate their laborers and abjure corporal punishment. Military commanders in Arkansas aided in the formation of a provisional unionist government, while the brightening fortunes of war invigorated antislavery unionists in Louisiana and Tennessee. Sensing the change, Lincoln urged General Banks in southern Louisiana and Military Governor Andrew Johnson in Tennessee to mobilize opponents of slavery in support of loyal state governments.[125]

As the new order spread to areas exempt from the Emancipation Proclamation, federal officials evaluated the success of the labor and welfare arrangements established during 1863. Secretary of War Stanton solicited suggestions from knowledgeable observers, and he dispatched a special emissary, General James S. Wadsworth, to the Mississippi Valley. Equally interested was Secretary of the Treasury Chase, to whose department the President had assigned control over all abandoned and captured "houses, tenements, lands, and plantations" that were not needed for military purposes. Preparing to devise new regulations for leasing plantations and organizing agricultural labor, he, too,

---

[125] *Official Records*, ser. 1, vol. 24, pt. 3, pp. 549–50. On unionist politics in the Mississippi Valley, see *Destruction of Slavery*, doc. 110; *Wartime Genesis: Lower South*, doc. 182; *Official Records*, ser. 1, vol. 24, pt. 3, pp. 549–50, 570, 578, 582–88; Lawrence N. Powell and Michael S. Wayne, "Self-Interest and the Decline of Confederate Nationalism," in *The Old South in the Crucible of War*, ed. Harry P. Owens and James J. Cooke (Jackson, Miss., 1983), pp. 29–46. On Louisiana, see LaWanda Cox, *Lincoln and Black Freedom: A Study in Presidential Leadership* (Columbia, S.C., 1981), chaps. 2–4; Peyton McCrary, *Abraham Lincoln and Reconstruction: The Louisiana Experiment* (Princeton, N.J., 1978), chaps. 5–8. On Tennessee, see *Wartime Genesis: Upper South*, doc. 101; *Black Military Experience*, docs. 64–65, 67; John Cimprich, *Slavery's End in Tennessee, 1861–1865* (University, Ala., 1985), chaps. 7–8.

sought suggestions from military and civilian authorities. Still other Northerners, stirred by the possibility of remaking the South, needed no invitation to volunteer their views.[126]

Nearly all such commentators agreed that the experience of 1863 had demonstrated the superior productivity of free over slave labor. "Every body admits that the cash System works better than the lash system," declared a treasury agent. Freed black laborers had given the lie to the proslavery dogma "that negroes are very valuable as slaves, but when free, worthless, and unable to take care of themselves." "[I]t is now generally conceded," observed Charles Wilder, "that the labor of one freeman, is worth that of two slaves." From the Sea Islands, General Saxton reported with satisfaction that the 1863 crop had proven beyond doubt "that the cotton fields of South Carolina can be successfully cultivated by free labor, that the negroes will work cheerfully and willingly with a reasonable prospect of reward." Evidence from the Mississippi Valley seemed to bear out Adjutant General Thomas's earlier prediction "that the freed negro may be profitably employed by enterprising men."[127]

And so it did. Despite unfavorable weather and Confederate raids, lessees in the Mississippi Valley had made money, some of them a good deal of it. Northern planters in the South Carolina Sea Islands had also reaped handsome profits. Even under wartime conditions, the new labor system had fulfilled the prophecy of a New England textile magnate who touted "Cheap Cotton by Free Labor." To judge from the hundreds of Northerners who sought permission to operate plantations in the occupied South for the coming year, the profitability of free labor – at least in cotton-growing regions – had been established beyond cavil. For some Northerners, that was quite enough. In granting the former slaves ownership of their own persons and transforming

---

[126] *Official Records*, ser. 3, vol. 3, pp. 872–73; *Wartime Genesis: Lower South*, docs. 185–86.

[127] Tho. Heaton to Hon. Wm. P. Mellen, 10 May 1864, Letters Received from Assistant Special Agents, Records of the General Agent, Records of the Civil War Special Agencies of the Treasury Department, RG 366, NA [Q-169]; *Wartime Genesis: Upper South*, doc. 43; *Wartime Genesis: Lower South*, docs. 36, 162, 180.

them into wage-workers, the government had done all it should to secure freedom.[128]

Others disagreed. As long as the war continued, military and political constraints precluded any thoroughgoing overhaul of Southern society, but many Northerners worried that steps taken during the conflict might foreclose options available in peacetime. They therefore viewed wartime labor arrangements with one eye on what was immediately possible and the other on what was ultimately desirable. Because acceptance of the possible did not necessarily imply concurrence on the desirable, observers divided among themselves in complex ways. Their debates focused on four related questions: the condition of black wage-workers in the Union-occupied South as compared with their Northern counterparts; the proper disposition of land controlled by the government; the ultimate political status of the former slaves; and the political status of former Confederates, particularly large property owners.

While acknowledging the productivity of black wage laborers amid the uncertainty of war, many Northerners denounced the limited prospects afforded former slaves under the new regime. Pointing to the meager pay, regimentation of labor, restriction of physical movement, and absence of written contracts and lien laws, they emphasized the extent to which freedpeople were denied rights that Northern wage-earners took for granted. General John Hawkins, whose command included almost all the Mississippi Valley plantations leased out in 1863, attacked the leasing system as a travesty of free labor. Although he expected most former slaves to remain wage laborers, at least for the immediate future, he condemned the terms under which they were working. By renting immense tracts of land to unscrupulous "adventurers" and setting low wages for laborers, the government had ceded control to "a monopoly." Hawkins urged federal authorities to subdivide the great estates into small farms and lease them to Northerners and ex-slaves, multiplying the number of agricultural units and, accordingly, the demand for hired labor. Wage

[128] For arguments that cotton and other staples could be produced more profitably with free labor than with slave labor, see *Wartime Genesis: Lower South*, docs. 7, 36, 70, 93; [Edward Atkinson], *Cheap Cotton by Free Labor: By a Cotton Manufacturer* (Boston, 1861).

rates, he argued, should be established by the market instead of the government, workers should be permitted to change employers at any time, and employers should have the right to discharge workers for any cause. Only then, Hawkins emphasized, would the labor of the former slaves become "as free as the labor of the northern white man."[129] In two influential reports prepared in late 1863, James E. Yeatman, president of the Western Sanitary Commission, disseminated Hawkins's antimonopoly views to a wider audience, adding his own unflattering judgments about the leasing system and suggestions for its reform. Yeatman thereby established himself as the leading critic of existing policy and gained the attention of Secretary of the Treasury Chase.[130]

Many Northerners concurred with Hawkins and Yeatman in their harsh assessment of free labor in the Union-occupied South. General Wadsworth, Stanton's emissary, was particularly critical of Banks's regulations because they denied what he believed to be the essential right of wage laborers: the freedom to rise to the limits of their own ability. Low wages, inadequate legal protection, and restrictions upon freedom of movement, he feared, would immobilize former slaves at the bottom of the social order, "not as freedmen, but as serfs." James McKaye, a member of the American Freedmen's Inquiry Commission, shared Wadsworth's reservations. "If the only object to be accomplished [were] simply 'to compel the negro to labor' in a condition of perpetual subordination and subjection," he argued, Banks's system would suffice. But it was unacceptable "if the object [were] to make the colored man a self-supporting and self-defending member of [the] community." The freedpeople, maintained McKaye, Wadsworth, and many others, deserved more at the hands of the government.[131]

---

[129] *Wartime Genesis: Lower South*, docs. 177, 181.

[130] Yeatman, *A Report on the Condition of the Freedmen of the Mississippi, Presented to the Western Sanitary Commission, December 17th, 1863* (St. Louis, 1864), and *Suggestions of a Plan of Organization for Freed Labor, and the Leasing of Plantations along the Mississippi River . . .* (St. Louis, 1864). For a summary of the latter, see *Wartime Genesis: Lower South*, doc. 189n. For Yeatman's influence on Chase, see *Wartime Genesis: Lower South*, doc. 186.

[131] *Wartime Genesis: Lower South*, doc. 107; J. McKaye, "The Emancipated Slave face to face with his old Master: Valley of the Lower Mississippi," [Apr.? 1864], filed with

Among the things they deserved was land to cultivate on their own account. Widespread acquisition by purchase seemed impossible, given the poverty of most former slaves, the insecurity of wartime land tenure, and the absence – except in the Sea Islands – of legal procedures for conveying forfeited property. But renting was another matter. The government had leased abandoned and confiscated land to poorly capitalized Yankees; surely those ex-slaves who had the experience and resources to work a farm might be similarly favored. The success of those few black farmers who had rented land in 1863 reinforced such reasoning. In the course of debates about the government's leasing policy for the coming year, some Northerners, including James Yeatman, advocated preferential treatment for black lessees. Influenced by their arguments, Secretary of the Treasury Chase directed his subordinates to give special consideration to former slaves who wished to rent land from the government.[132]

A handful of Northerners continued to see the war as an opportunity to endow former slaves with an independent competency. General Saxton maintained that restricting freedpeople to the status of wage laborers would lock them "in the condition of a peasantry only a little higher than chattelism . . . when so many of them had proved their fitness to be owners of the soil." McKaye argued that the interests of both former slaves and the nation would be best served by permitting them to own the land they occupied, for "you can never have in any country a democratic society, or a society substantially, practically free, where the land all belongs to a few people."[133] Asserting the connection between productive property and freedom against those who viewed self-ownership as the ultimate goal, men like Saxton and McKaye revealed the ongoing conflict within Northern society over the sources and meaning of liberty – a conflict that was fast being transferred to the former slave states.

Advocates of redistributing land gained support from the growing

O-328 1863, Letters Received, ser. 12, Records of the Adjutant General's Office, RG 94, NA [K-66].

[132] *Wartime Genesis: Upper South*, doc. 28; *Wartime Genesis: Lower South*, docs. 107, 186.

[133] *Wartime Genesis: Lower South*, docs. 57, 187.

number of Northerners who believed that loyal ex-slaves had a better claim to the land than traitorous rebels. The freedpeople's uncompensated labor during slavery and their loyalty during the war, declared one treasury agent, gave them "an equitable lien upon the lands of their masters." Arguing upon similar grounds, General Saxton declared that the freedpeople deserved their former owners' land as a matter of "simple justice." Such Northerners thought it morally wrong as well as politically naive to restore land to former slaveholders while dispossessing former slaves. Fully aware that ultimate settlement of the question would await the end of the war, proponents of a property-based freedom wished to avert wartime policies that might prejudice the outcome. Actions taken during the conflict, they feared, could leave former slaves economically dependent and politically subordinate when peace finally came.[134]

If the constraints of war limited the possibilities for transforming Southern society, those possibilities became narrower still with President Lincoln's Proclamation of Amnesty and Reconstruction, issued in December 1863. The edict offered to pardon most participants in the rebellion (excepting, most notably, high-ranking Confederate military and civil officials), on condition that they forsake the Confederacy, swear allegiance to the United States, and agree to abide by wartime laws and proclamations concerning emancipation. That done, they could again enjoy all rights of property, "except as to slaves." Moreover, the amnesty proclamation proposed a method by which the loyal people of a seceded state could form a government and seek readmission to the Union. The new state governments, Lincoln suggested, might then assume legal control over the former slaves. Although he acknowledged that he lacked constitutional power to dictate terms of reunification, the President hinted that he would welcome state legislation confirming emancipation and providing for the education of former slaves, "which may yet be consistent as a temporary arrangement with their present condition as a laboring, landless, and homeless class." In proposing his own model for reconstructing the South, Lincoln fueled the

[134] *Wartime Genesis: Lower South*, docs. 47B, 57.

ongoing debate about the character of the war, the terms of national reunification, and the future of the former slaves.[135]

Widely praised in the North as a magnanimous yet politically shrewd measure, the amnesty proclamation also received high marks from most federal officials in the South. George Field, chief plantation commissioner in the Mississippi Valley, regarded the edict as the foundation for "an enduring and mutually advantageous reconstruction of the Union." Within a month of its issue, two-thirds of the Mississippi Valley plantations leased out during 1863 were restored to their antebellum owners. Field lauded the "amicable connections" that were forming between *"loyal Northern men"* and Southern *"owners* of the soil."[136]

Others took a more skeptical view. Many Northerners feared the consequences of remanding homeless, landless freedpeople to the tender mercies of "loyal" state governments. Under such a reconstruction policy, predicted Wendell Phillips, a noted abolitionist, the restored states would render "the freedom of the negro a sham," leaving the South "with its labor and capital at war." Some Union field commanders, drawing upon firsthand experience with former slaveholders, expressed similar doubts. Disputing the notion that the occupied Confederate states were ripe for readmission, General Napoleon B. Buford, commander of the District of Eastern Arkansas, avowed that he had "not yet seen a man of fortune or standing in the South who was to be relied on as a Union man." Far from accepting the demise of slavery, "every slaveholder sticks to the institution as his only hope for fortune[,] respectability and means of liveing." Northerners in the army and out worried that the Lincoln administration was conceding too much too soon in allowing such "unionists" to reclaim both their political rights and their land.[137]

---

[135] *Statutes at Large*, vol. 13, pp. 737–39.

[136] *Wartime Genesis: Lower South*, doc. 189.

[137] Edward McPherson, *The Political History of the United States of America, during the Great Rebellion* (Washington, 1865), p. 412; Brig. Genl. [Napoleon B. Buford] to Hon. Secy. of War, 11 Dec. 1863, vol. 37 DArk, pp. 240–42, Letters Sent, ser. 4664, Dist. of Eastern AR, Records of U.S. Army Continental Commands, RG 393 Pt. 2 No. 299, NA [C-7539]. See also Berlin et al., " 'To Canvass the Nation,' " pp. 243–44.

To the extent that the President's amnesty policy promised to re-instate Southern planters, it also threatened the prospects of former slaves, who expected still more radical changes to follow wartime emancipation. Like Northern critics of federal labor policies, freedpeople objected to the low levels of compensation, restrictions upon freedom of movement, and inadequate protection against fraud or abuse. But their criticism extended beyond the details of wage labor. Freedom from a master, they believed, should mean more than the right to change masters. It implied access to those productive resources, especially land, without which freedom would be compromised.

Not even those Yankees most sympathetic with the aspirations of the former slaves viewed landownership precisely as they did. Land, ex-slaves and Northerners concurred, could provide subsistence and foster independence from former owners. But there agreement usually ended. Former slaves, like many of their contemporaries throughout the world, generally did not view land as property in the abstract or as a commodity whose worth was determined by the market. Instead, they valued it in proportion to labor expended and suffering endured. Given a choice, they preferred to own or occupy not just any plot of ground, but the land where they had been born and reared and in which they and their forebears had invested so much blood and sweat. Land was a link to generations past and future and a foundation for family and community among the living. Nor did former slaves fully subscribe to Northern concepts of absolute property. Instead, rights to particular tracts might bear little resemblance to the specifications of a deed. When left to their own devices, freedpeople often allowed for overlapping rights in any one property; conversely, an individual's use rights might encompass several parcels, not necessarily contiguous. Nonetheless, under the terms of the Yankee occupation, freedpeople desiring to obtain control over land had to comply with the incongruous conventions of the Northerners.[138]

---

[138] *Wartime Genesis: Lower South*, docs. 47A, 58; Saville, "A Measure of Freedom," pp. 59–64. See also Ira Berlin, Steven Hahn, Steven F. Miller, Joseph P. Reidy, and Leslie S. Rowland, "The Terrain of Freedom: The Struggle over the Meaning of Free Labor in the U.S. South," *History Workshop* 22 (Autumn 1986): 127–29. On North-

The most favorable wartime opportunities to acquire land were those afforded freedpeople in the Sea Islands, where absent proprietors had been dispossessed under the Direct Tax Act. Developments in the latter months of 1863 held special promise. Under instructions from President Lincoln, the direct-tax commissioners reserved certain of the forfeited estates for "charitable" purposes, to be sold in twenty-acre tracts exclusively to heads of black households. That policy, which won the favor of two of the three commissioners and several prominent military officials, spared former slaves from having to bid against Northern speculators in order to obtain any land at all. But the freedpeople and many of their advocates – including General Saxton, Mansfield French, and Abram D. Smith, the dissenting tax commissioner – felt that Lincoln's instructions did not go far enough. The total reserved acreage, they pointed out, was far too small to provide a homestead for all black residents of the Sea Islands. They wanted former slaves to enjoy preferred access to any of the forfeited land on the islands, not solely to that on the reserved estates. Hoping to circumvent the instructions, Saxton, French, and Smith encouraged would-be black landowners to settle wherever they wished and lobbied the Lincoln administration to permit the freedpeople to enter preemption claims.[139]

For a time, the strategy worked. On the last day of December 1863, Lincoln instructed the direct-tax commissioners to permit loyal residents of the Sea Islands to preempt forty-acre tracts on any government-controlled land before it was put up for auction.[140] The news seemed a vindication for the freedpeople of the Sea Islands, many of whom had already staked out a claim "on the old homestead, where they had been born, & had laborered & suffered." Former slaves on some plantations made applications "in mass . . . without the names of the negroes & without designating the particular tracts for each." But preemption evoked strong opposition from Smith's colleagues on the direct-tax commission, whose objections led in February 1864 to a reinstatement

---

ern concepts of absolute property, see Morton J. Horwitz, *The Transformation of American Law, 1780–1860* (Cambridge, Mass., 1977).

[139] *Wartime Genesis: Lower South*, docs. 39, 45.

[140] *Wartime Genesis: Lower South*, doc. 41.

of Lincoln's initial instructions. The disappointment of the freedpeople was "almost unbearable." Although a number of them eventually acquired plots on the estates earmarked for "charitable" purposes (110 families by March 1864), the undoing of preemption marked the passing of the former slaves' best wartime hope for landownership.[141]

However disappointing, the opportunities of Sea Island freedpeople to acquire land far exceeded those afforded their counterparts elsewhere in the Union-occupied South. Although the President possessed authority to appoint direct-tax commissioners for every seceded state, by the beginning of 1864 he had done so only for South Carolina, Florida, Virginia, and Tennessee.[142] Lincoln's inaction, coupled with the Proclamation of Amnesty and Reconstruction, signaled his intention to use expropriation chiefly to induce Confederates to return to their "proper allegiance," and not as a means to recast Southern society. Although his policy did not foreclose entirely the possibility of providing former slaves with homesteads from the land of disloyal owners, it established a precedent that had momentous consequences in the postwar struggle over land.

The waning possibility of acquiring land was only one source of concern to the freedpeople and their Northern allies in the spring of 1864, as Union armies once more took to the field and the new agricultural season commenced. As earlier, military considerations shaped the evolution of free labor. With the territory under federal control substantially enlarged, especially in the western theater, the army needed every black soldier it could get. Like veterans, the new recruits spent most of their time at noncombat duties, garrisoning towns, guarding railroad bridges, protecting leased plantations and contraband camps, and performing heavy fatigue labor. But increasingly large numbers of black troops traded shovels for rifles. Experienced black soldiers, some of whom had served for over a year, demanded more from military service

---

[141] *Wartime Genesis: Lower South*, docs. 39, 42, 45, 49, 62; see also Rose, *Rehearsal for Reconstruction*, chap. 10.

[142] U.S., Senate, "Letter of the Secretary of the Treasury . . . [on] the collection of direct taxes in insurrectionary districts . . . ," *Senate Executive Documents*, 38th Cong., 1st sess., No. 35.

than did raw recruits, and greater familiarity with official regulations and procedures aided their struggle against the inequities of military service. A handful of black men attained the status of commissioned officers. Of far greater significance for the common soldier, Congress abolished the difference in the pay of black and white soldiers, and Adjutant General Thomas ordered that black regiments perform no more than "their fair share of fatigue duty." Eventually Congress also guaranteed the freedom of all black soldiers' families, whatever the loyalty of their owners and even where slavery remained legal.[143]

The expansion of Union-held territory and the extension of federal supply lines also increased the need for military laborers. In the two major offensives of 1864 – the drive from Chattanooga to Atlanta in the western theater, and the campaign against Richmond and Petersburg in the east – the labor shortage was exacerbated by the scarcity of suitable black men in the contested territory. As a result, laborers and teamsters from previously occupied areas worked endlessly moving supplies and materiel from distribution points in the rear to armies in the field. Black "pioneers," many of them from Tennessee, built miles of corduroy road during the Atlanta campaign. Black men from the contraband camps and towns of tidewater Virginia and North Carolina were dispatched to the James River to dig a canal at Dutch Gap and to construct field works for the troops operating against Richmond.

At times, this heightened demand for military laborers worked to the advantage of black men. Some short-handed quartermasters, commissary officers, and engineers offered premium wages, favorable working conditions, and refuge and support for the families of their laborers. Black women benefited from the construction of general hospitals at Washington, Nashville, Louisville, and St. Louis, which provided employment for hundreds of nurses and laundresses. At the great supply depots, notably Washington and Nashville, black laborers received pay

---

[143] For the experience of black soldiers, see *Black Military Experience*, especially chap. 6 on black commissioned officers, chap. 7 on the struggle for equal pay, and chap. 10 on disproportionate assignment to fatigue duty (including Adjutant General Thomas's order, doc. 201). The families of black soldiers were freed in March 1865 by joint resolution. (*Statutes at Large*, vol. 13, p. 571.)

increases along with their white counterparts, and both were paid with greater regularity, as their employers sought to minimize discontent. The War Department eliminated another longstanding grievance when it decided to pay wages directly to black laborers whose loyal owners still claimed them as slaves.[144]

Union military authorities did not always meet their labor needs by increasing the rewards of service. Often they resorted to subterfuge and force, seizing black men without so much as first soliciting volunteers. Sometimes the superintendents of contrabands found themselves forced to do the army's dirty work. Operations against Richmond and Petersburg in mid-1864 led to the impressment of hundreds of men from contraband camps and government farms throughout tidewater Virginia and coastal North Carolina. Elsewhere, too, the opening of a new front or an impending Confederate raid occasioned mass levies that wrenched black men from their homes and sent them to distant places to labor for the army.[145]

The entry of black men into federal service, whether by their own volition or at gunpoint, placed at risk other freedpeople whose livelihood depended upon their labor. To reduce this vulnerability, some military commanders promised to provide "suitable subsistence" for the families of black soldiers. Others, particularly at garrison towns in the Mississippi Valley, tolerated (and sometimes sanctioned) the creation of "regimental villages" near the camps of black troops. In these settlements, the soldiers' kin could share the men's rations and wages and

---

[144] For examples of wage increases for military laborers, see *Wartime Genesis: Upper South*, doc. 70; *Wartime Genesis: Lower South*, doc. 122; Ass't. Qr. Mtr. General Chs. Thomas to Brig. Gen'l. M. C. Meigs, 22 Jan. 1864, vol. 74, pp. 158–60, Letters Sent, ser. 9, Central Records, Records of the Office of the Quartermaster General, RG 92, NA [Y-681]; unsigned note, [Nov. 1864], enclosed in A.A. Genl. Wm. Fowler to Bvt. Brig. Genl. G. V. Rutherford, 8 Nov. 1866, Letters Received from the Freedmen's Bureau, ser. 34, Central Records, Records of the Office of the Quartermaster General, RG 92, NA [Y-664]. For the policy respecting direct payment of wages to black laborers who, their owners claimed, were legally still slaves, see *Wartime Genesis: Upper South*, doc. 99.

[145] *Wartime Genesis: Upper South*, docs. 36, 40, 47A, 104, 113, 129, 165. In December 1864, an urgent need to repair the levees along the Mississippi River had similar effects; military authorities impressed hundreds of ex-slaves and free blacks. (*Wartime Genesis: Lower South*, docs. 131–32.)

contribute to their own support by cultivating garden patches or working for military or private employers. Such possibilities continued to attract former slaves to federal posts, despite the determined efforts of government officials to assign them to plantation labor. In the Vicksburg area, 3,700 former slaves left contraband camps for leased plantations during a single week in March 1864, yet at week's end the population of the camps had not diminished appreciably. [146]

When the recruitment of black soldiers was extended to the Upper South, contraband camps assumed an importance in both federal policy and the lives of fugitive slaves that had formerly characterized only the Lower South. Given the opportunity to gain freedom through military service, slaves left their owners and enlisted by the tens of thousands. Eventually, 57 percent of Kentucky's black men of military age served in the army, as did 39 percent of those in Missouri and in Tennessee and 28 percent of those in Maryland. [147] Slave men fled to recruiting stations in large numbers, often accompanied by their families. Black women and children also made their way to army posts when their owners, having lost the labor of the men, heaped overwork and abuse upon the remaining slaves or simply refused to support them any longer. The influx of fugitive slaves re-created in Tennessee and the border states the problems of relief that federal officials had earlier confronted in other parts of the Union-occupied Confederacy, but with the added complication that slavery was still legal. [148]

The soldiers' families and other black refugees overwhelmed the resources of established camps such as Freedman's Village and Roanoke Island. Freedman's Village became so crowded that military authorities shunted new arrivals to an employment depot on Mason's Island, in the Potomac River, which itself quickly became overcrowded and disease-

---

[146] *Wartime Genesis: Upper South*, docs. 26, 33; *Wartime Genesis: Lower South*, docs. 204n., 212; *Black Military Experience*, docs. 47A-C, 313. On the Vicksburg camps, see *Wartime Genesis: Lower South*, doc. 200.

[147] See Table 1 in Chapter 3, this volume.

[148] *Destruction of Slavery*, docs. 191–92, 237; *Wartime Genesis: Upper South*, docs. 177, 181, 225A-C, 226, 229; *Black Military Experience*, docs. 90B, 91, 106–7, 111, 294, 298, 302.

ridden.[149] In middle and east Tennessee and northern Alabama, where enlistment of black men did not begin in earnest until late 1863, contraband camps sprang up at major recruiting posts. By June 1864, some 5,500 former slaves were living at seven camps, the largest at Clarksville, Nashville, and Gallatin, in middle Tennessee, and at Decatur and Huntsville, in northern Alabama.[150]

In the border states, by contrast, the recruitment of black soldiers crippled slavery without impelling the federal government to sponsor either contraband camps or free labor. Despite the pleas of soldiers' relatives and other runaway and castaway slaves, military authorities refused to provide rations or housing: Since they were legally still slaves, their owners, not the government, were responsible for their care. Orders called upon local commanders to enlist the able-bodied men but turn away all other black refugees.[151]

Border-state black soldiers protested vehemently against such treatment of their families, and they found numerous allies among sympathetic army officers. General William A. Pile, superintendent of black recruitment in Missouri, repeatedly sought permission to transfer fugitive slaves to the contraband camp at Benton Barracks, there to be furnished both protection and rations. Loath to assume responsibility for the fugitives, Pile's superiors instead authorized another officer to remove them to the Kansas border. In central Kentucky, hundreds of black women and children gathered in and near Camp Nelson, which in mid-1864 became the state's largest center of black recruitment. But Union military authorities, from the post commander to Adjutant General Lorenzo Thomas, refused to care for the soldiers' families. Throughout the summer and fall, in a drama that became more somber with each enactment, the women and children were driven from the post, often into the clutches of owners who had received advance notice of the expulsion. A final wholesale eviction, undertaken on a freezing

[149] *Wartime Genesis: Upper South*, docs. 47A, 77, 80.
[150] On the Tennessee and Alabama camps, see *Wartime Genesis: Upper South*, docs. 108, 110, 114, 123, 129.
[151] *Destruction of Slavery*, doc. 233; *Wartime Genesis: Upper South*, docs. 167, 169, 177, 219; *Black Military Experience*, docs. 93, 102A-C, 105.

November day, caused such suffering that the ensuing publicity forced military authorities to reverse their policy. At the end of the war, the "Colored Refugee Home" at Camp Nelson sheltered about 1,000 black women and children.[152]

In addition to spawning contraband camps, military enlistment sped the disintegration of slavery, encouraged legal emancipation, and, especially in Tennessee, advanced the development of free labor. Without the direct sanction of military or treasury officials, many slaves negotiated new terms of work, either with their owners or with nonslaveholders who welcomed an opportunity to employ black laborers. Such informal accommodations, usually involving one-to-one bargaining, had appeared with increasing regularity in late 1863 as recruitment diminished the pool of young black men. Private free-labor arrangements proliferated during early 1864, as landowners rushed to secure workers for the coming year. In the Nashville basin and in parts of the border states, farmers and planters made numerous concessions in order to retain "the services of there slaves – or in other words to conciliate & prevent them from running away." Some promised cash wages; others, to match the terms offered by government employers or to pay "as much as was given to other colored persons"; still others permitted former slaves to cultivate land as renters.[153]

Based on verbal agreement, private free-labor bargains left broad latitude for conflicting interpretation, renegotiation, or abandonment by either party. Employers generally held the balance of power and seldom hesitated to use it. Many of them simply refused to pay what they had promised. Eviction might take place at any moment and for any reason. Families of black soldiers were especially liable to be driven

---

[152] *Destruction of Slavery*, doc. 191; *Wartime Genesis: Upper South*, docs. 176–77, 182, 187, 190, 219, 225–27, 230; *Black Military Experience*, docs. 94, 107, 312A-B.

[153] *Wartime Genesis: Upper South*, docs. 102, 105, 107, 113, 125, 128, 139, 188, 222; *Wartime Genesis: Lower South*, docs. 231A-B; *Black Military Experience*, docs. 95–96. In Kentucky, where slavery remained legal until the ratification of the Thirteenth Amendment in December 1865, such informal, unsanctioned, and unstable free-labor arrangements also characterized the summer and fall following the end of the war. (*Destruction of Slavery*, docs. 240–41, 245–51, 253–54; *Wartime Genesis: Upper South*, docs. 231–32, 234–36, 238–42.)

off or denied food and clothing, as was any former slave who showed "a disposition to send his children to school or to favor the *Yankees.*" Employers who had lured workers into the field with promises of a postharvest payment often reneged and, instead, drove them away "to save taking care of them during the winter."[154]

The disruptions of war and the continued legality of slavery also hindered the spread of private free-labor agreements – sometimes fatally. In many places, guerrilla bands took direct action against planters and farmers who countenanced any breach of slavery or who introduced black laborers into previously all-white communities. The guerrillas reserved especially deadly venom for the black laborers themselves. Such attacks were widespread in much of Missouri, but by no means confined there. In their struggle to contain free labor, defenders of slavery also deployed the law. Threats of prosecution under statutes that prohibited hiring a slave without the owner's consent deterred many would-be employers from dealing with "slaves" – even when the "slaves" were beyond reclamation by their "owners." Although they eventually capitulated to the new regime, slaveholders and their allies retained many weapons to obstruct its progress. Their bitter resistance prevented free labor from taking root in some areas and stunted its development in others.[155]

Free labor stood on firmer ground in those parts of the Upper South that were under the jurisdiction of federal superintendents – tidewater Virginia, coastal North Carolina, the District of Columbia, and the immediate vicinity of Union posts in middle and east Tennessee and in northern Alabama. During 1864, only a small proportion of the

---

[154] *Destruction of Slavery*, docs. 150A-B, 152, 191–92, 231, 233; *Wartime Genesis: Upper South*, docs. 114, 125, 127, 130, 139, 177n., 181, 193, 222, 226; *Black Military Experience*, doc. 298. On similar developments in the Lower South, see *Destruction of Slavery*, docs. 122–23; *Wartime Genesis: Lower South*, docs. 211, 231A-B.

[155] On guerrilla attacks, see *Destruction of Slavery*, doc. 196; *Wartime Genesis: Upper South*, docs. 141, 178, 186, 193, 195–96, 197n., 199; *Black Military Experience*, doc. 85. On prosecution under antebellum statutes, see *Destruction of Slavery*, docs. 239, 242, 246, 248–49, 252, 255; *Wartime Genesis: Upper South*, docs. 184, 189, 238–39, 241; *Black Military Experience*, doc. 112.

freedpeople in these areas lived and worked on government-controlled land. A far greater number labored under contracts with local farmers or other private employers. In Union-occupied tidewater Virginia, which had a total black population of approximately 35,000 at the end of 1863, only a few thousand ex-slaves and free blacks cultivated "government farms" as either wage laborers or renters. A similar pattern appeared in middle and east Tennessee and northern Alabama, where probably no more than 1,000 former slaves resided on estates leased out by treasury agents. The impact of federally sponsored labor arrangements extended, however, well beyond their direct partici-pants. Private employers in the vicinity generally had to meet the same standards in order to retain their laborers, and military officials sometimes supervised free-labor contracts between masters-turned-employers and slaves-turned-employees.[156]

Union officers exerted much greater control over labor and relief in the Lower South, where they continued to view the plantations as the proper place to employ and subsist most former slaves. In the cotton-growing regions along the Mississippi River, the government-supervised planta-tions stretched from Helena, Arkansas, to Natchez, Mississippi, in 1864. They included not only estates leased to Northern entrepreneurs, but also those operated by Southern planters pardoned under Lincoln's amnesty proclamation. In mid-March, an estimated 60,000 freedpeople resided on the leased plantations alone, and the number on owner-operated places probably approached the same dimensions. In southern Louisiana, where the northern boundary of federal occupation reached beyond Baton Rouge, free labor under federal auspices also became more widespread. As of the summer of 1864, 35,000 former slaves were working under formal contracts supervised by the army; about 15,000 more labored under terms similar to those mandated by military regula-tions, but without written agreements. Meanwhile, in lowcountry South Carolina, Georgia, and Florida, the extent of Union-held territory re-mained largely unchanged. Approximately 15,000 freedpeople lived

---

[156] *Wartime Genesis: Upper South*, chap. 3, and docs. 42–43, 105–6C, 109.

within federal lines, most of them on the South Carolina Sea Islands; roughly half were employed on plantations.[157]

In all parts of the Union-occupied South, the struggle between former slaves and former slaveholders involved more people and a broader range of issues than it had during the previous two years. Many of the freedpeople were fresh from bondage, having lately escaped to Union lines or fallen under the control of advancing federal armies; others had one or more years' experience in freedom. While recently liberated slaves prepared to fight the old battles, the veterans undertook new ones. More experienced freedpeople not only tutored neophytes in their rights as free men and women, but also led the way. Those who had acquired tools, agricultural implements, and work animals served as exemplars; occasionally, they even employed other ex-slaves.[158]

The interchange between veterans and neophytes proceeded among the employers as well. Planters were an even more diverse lot than plantation laborers, including among their number both newly arrived lessees and old-time proprietors, Northerners conversant with free-labor practices and Southerners entirely unfamiliar with them. North-ern entrepreneurs expounded upon the rights of employers and the myriad ways to encourage productivity without resorting to force, while Southern planters shared their technical knowledge of plantation routine and their notions about the peculiar characteristics of black workers. In many instances, exchanges between Northern and Southern planters took place within formal partnerships, in which the latter supplied the land and the former the capital and good offices necessary to resume staple production in a war zone. Like their laborers, planters entered the new crop year with more definite ideas about what they wanted, what they would accept, and what they would not tolerate.[159]

---

[157] *Wartime Genesis: Lower South*, docs. 57, 197; Chaplain Thomas W. Conway to Major General N. P. Banks, 9 Sept. 1864, C-228 1864, Letters Received, ser. 1920, Civil Affairs, Dept. of the Gulf, Records of U.S. Army Continental Commands, RG 393 Pt. 1, NA [C-732].

[158] For examples of freedpeople employing other ex-slaves, see *Wartime Genesis: Upper South*, doc. 58; *Wartime Genesis: Lower South*, docs. 177, 208–9, 216n.

[159] On relations between Southern planters and Northern planters, see Powell, *New Mas-ters*, especially chaps. 3–5. See also *Wartime Genesis: Lower South*, docs. 182, 189, 209.

Federal policy makers had also learned from experience, and they, too, acquired new responsibilities. In the Sea Islands, where the government-operated plantations passed into private hands at direct-tax sales in March 1864, General Saxton and his subordinates were reduced to the role of arbiter between private employers and contract laborers. Elsewhere in the Union-occupied Lower South, federal officials continued to supervise plantation labor on both the estates leased out by the government and those operated by antebellum owners. Early in 1864, they revised the regulations governing agricultural labor. Designed chiefly to resolve conflicts that had arisen the previous year, the new guidelines also endeavored to placate Northern critics by requiring terms of agricultural labor more like those in the free states. In the sugar- and cotton-growing regions along the Mississippi River, where labor regulations had been sketchy outlines in 1863, federal officers elaborated more fully the rights and duties of both employers and laborers. The new regulations were particularly specific about the amount and form of compensation, the days and hours of work, and the use of garden plots and work animals. They addressed, moreover, vexatious questions concerning which plantation residents were obligated to work, whether laborers or employers should pay for food, clothing, and medical care, and who should provide for nonworkers.

Both plantation laborers and planters gained from the new labor codes. For the laborers, improvements were substantial. The regulations increased minimum wages, limited daily hours of labor to ten in summer and nine in winter, and required extra pay for work on Sunday. They gave workers a lien on the crops they produced and codified their right to garden plots. In addition, military authorities urged planters to offer such incentives as compensation for extra work and "appropriation of land for share cultivation." By such means, General Banks believed, former slaves and former slaveholders could prepare themselves "for the time when [the laborer] can render so much labor for so much money, which is the great end to be attained." At the same time, Union officials recognized that wartime conditions prohibited a shift to full monetary compensation. Military orders reinforced the claim of all plantation residents – workers and nonworkers, healthy or sick – to a subsistence, by requiring the plantation owner or lessee to provide food and clothing for all former slaves on the estate.

The new regulations also strengthened the employer's hand. In the interest of maintaining plantation discipline, federal officials barred soldiers from visiting without authorization and prohibited workers from leaving the estates without permission. To secure the fidelity of laborers to year-long contracts, the regulations required monthly payment of only half wages, with the remainder withheld until after the harvest. Once a laborer had "exercised the highest right in the choice and place of employment, he must be held to the fulfillment of his engagements."[160]

Rather than resolving all differences, the new rules became objects of contention, as both planters and laborers tried to turn them to their own advantage. Workers exercised "the power to be idle" until desperate planters were willing to meet their terms. Many former slaves declined to sign contracts until early spring. In February, after Confederate raiders again terrorized leased plantations along the Mississippi River, laborers increased their demands, refusing to return to work without suitable protection and greater pay. The raids were occasional events, but the regular seasonal rhythm of agricultural production also operated both for and against the former slaves. Once workers had "laid by" the crop in the summer, they became expendable until harvest time, when the demand for hands again strengthened their bargaining position. During slack periods, they found themselves liable to dismissal, despite regulations that required planters to support their workers for the duration of the contract.[161]

Sensitive to the dynamics of the new relationship, both plantation hands and planters took care to specify their terms of agreement. Contracting time became an occasion to ventilate grievances from the past and maneuver for future advantage. Laborers took special pains to guarantee their families' subsistence by securing access to gardens, woodlots,

[160] *Wartime Genesis: Lower South*, docs. 109, 198.
[161] *Wartime Genesis: Lower South*, doc. 130. On the effects of Confederate raids in 1864, see *Wartime Genesis: Upper South*, doc. 39; *Wartime Genesis: Lower South*, docs. 196–97, 209.

and forage, and to insist upon assurances of protection from Confederate raiders. Many workers – a majority in some areas – demanded compensation in a share of the crop instead of a monthly wage. For their part, employers enumerated workers' responsibilities in greater detail, including standards of acceptable deportment. The increased length and specificity of contracts attested to the breadth of the contest.[162]

Both at contracting time and throughout the year, freedpeople sought to allocate the labor of family members at their own and not their employers' discretion. Planters – eager to compensate for the shortage of men by claiming the labor of most women and children – distinguished only between workers and nonworkers, insisting that all of the former should be in the field. The freedpeople, on the other hand, believed that their new status implied greater opportunity for wives and mothers to devote time to child care and to productive labor in house and garden. Moreover, wage scales that accorded female field hands substantially less than their male counterparts offered women scant inducement to labor for the planters. Those whose husbands were at work on the same estate were especially likely to spurn such employment. On one Louisiana plantation, the women would work only "on the patches of ground given to their husbands by the overseer"; on another, "[s]ome of the women peremptoraly refuse[d] to work in the field stating that they are ladies and as good as any white trash." The labor of children also became a matter of contest. The planters' insistence upon putting them into field gangs conflicted with the freedpeople's desire that they attend school or perform domestic chores.[163]

---

[162] For examples of crop-sharing arrangements, see *Wartime Genesis: Lower South*, docs. 192, 214n. On the prevalence of such arrangements in one Louisiana parish, see *Wartime Genesis: Lower South*, doc. 129. For examples of nonmonetary compensation for plantation work, see *Wartime Genesis: Lower South*, docs. 125–26. On plantation laborers' insistence upon physical security, see *Wartime Genesis: Lower South*, docs. 201, 209.

[163] *Wartime Genesis: Lower South*, docs. 100n., 116, 199. For examples of former slaves' desire to send their children to school, see *Wartime Genesis: Upper South*, doc. 42; *Wartime Genesis: Lower South*, docs. 21, 110, 217. On postwar struggles over family labor, which exhibit many of the same themes, see Ira Berlin, Steven F. Miller, and Leslie S. Rowland, "Afro-American Families in the Transition from Slavery to Freedom," *Radical History Review* 42 (Fall 1988): 89–121.

As the range of free-labor relations increased, the struggle between planters and laborers moved beyond matters of production to matters of consumption. During 1864, a growing number of planters established plantation stores that sold a variety of merchandise. The availability of consumer goods, they argued, would "multiply [the workers'] simple wants & stimulate industry." One plantation manager confessed that exhortations about the virtues of honest toil failed to motivate his workers as much as did their desire "to procure a coveted calico dress or straw Hat." For some Northern planters, well-developed purchasing habits and a wide array of merchandise were veritable hallmarks of civilization.[164]

Whatever their boon to civilization, plantation stores also served more immediately useful ends. The ready availability of consumer goods helped keep workers at home, and if their purchases drew them into debt, so much the better. Clever planters learned to manipulate accounts to keep their laborers in arrears. Those who thought they could get away with it set retail prices at levels above the mark-up permitted by government regulations. Some planters-turned-merchant flouted the regulations altogether and required their workers to purchase clothing or rations that were supposed to be furnished free of charge.[165]

Freedpeople appreciated the availability of goods but resented attempts to gouge them. Wherever possible, they patronized stores operated by merchants more friendly to their interests. Former slaves in the Vicksburg area took their business to a special "freedmen's store," whose proprietors were prohibited by military order from overcharging. Elsewhere in Union-occupied territory, establishments operated by Northern freedmen's aid societies gave former slaves an alternative to the plantation stores.[166]

While most former slaves struggled to earn a living wage during

---

[164] *Wartime Genesis: Lower South*, docs. 40, 216. See also Powell, *New Masters*, pp. 87–90.

[165] *Wartime Genesis: Lower South*, docs. 108, 120A-C, 227. See also Powell, *New Masters*, pp. 90–92.

[166] *Wartime Genesis: Upper South*, docs. 32, 42; *Wartime Genesis: Lower South*, docs. 47A, 225, 227.

1864, some managed to rise above the status of wage laborer. Several hundred Sea Island freedpeople entered the ranks of small landowners by purchasing plantations cooperatively or by acquiring plots earmarked for "charitable" purposes. In the Mississippi Valley, chiefly around Vicksburg and Helena, a similar number leased land from the government. Possessed of little capital, nearly all the black lessees rented small farms, not large plantations, and they generally worked the land with only the labor of their families, occasionally augmented by hired workers. On a still smaller scale and in more informal fashion, former slaves tended plots on "home farms" administered variously by the Treasury Department, military officials, and representatives of Northern benevolent associations. Such cultivators – whose ranks included some black soldiers and their families – worked tracts ranging from a few acres to a small homestead.[167]

Some black families in the Upper South also gained access to land through official channels. Superintendents of "Negro Affairs" in tidewater Virginia made about 200 parcels available to black tenants, charging them cash or a share of the crop as rent and otherwise allowing them to control their own farming operations. Similarly, treasury agents in coastal North Carolina leased small farms to former slaves, as well as rights to collect turpentine from the pine forests.[168]

In both the Upper and the Lower South, black landowners, lessees, and residents of the home farms placed greater emphasis upon subsistence than upon commercial agriculture. Seeking first of all to provide food for their own households, ex-slave farmers generally put most of their land in corn and vegetables. Any surplus could readily be sold to the residents of nearby towns and army posts. When their resources permitted, they added other marketable crops. The chief limit upon such additional production was often the number of workers in the household, a problem that some black farmers solved by hiring additional laborers.[169]

[167] *Wartime Genesis: Lower South*, docs. 49, 207–9, 217.
[168] *Wartime Genesis: Upper South*, docs. 38, 42–43.
[169] *Wartime Genesis: Upper South*, doc. 28; *Wartime Genesis: Lower South*, docs. 144, 171, 208.

In regions where cotton had been the predominant crop, some black landowners and lessees planted none at all, and those who did grow the staple generally cultivated modest amounts. Nevertheless, at stratospheric wartime prices, the proceeds of small cotton patches permitted black farmers not only to improve their families' living conditions, but also to purchase livestock, tools, and other productive property. Late in 1864, the superintendent of freedmen at Helena reported that "[a]ll of the colored lessees have made more than a living, and will be ready to begin another year with capital that will enable them to work to better advantage than in the past."[170]

In general, black lessees in tidewater Virginia and North Carolina reaped fewer material rewards than those in the Mississippi Valley. The land they farmed was depleted from years of tillage, and military superintendents lacked both the means and the will to invest in improvements and fertilizer. The only available draft animals were worn-out beasts "condemned" by the quartermaster's department. Many of the leaseholds were too small and unproductive to support the renters and their families. Often the lessees earned a subsistence by working for white farmers in the neighborhood; their share of the crop on their leaseholds thus became "profit for their seasons work." Such arrangements usually involved a division of labor whereby the father hired out for wages while the mother and children worked the rented plot. But, depending upon the number of people in the household and their age and sex, the division sometimes differed, reflecting each family's assessment of how best to preserve an independent standing. Although their choices were dictated in part by the local demand for agricultural labor, access to land, however limited, reduced their dependence upon wage employment and often permitted them to engage in such labor for only part of the year.[171]

A large number of freedpeople who had neither the means nor the opportunity to rent land found other ways of earning a living without entering into year-long contracts for agricultural labor. Fishing, oys-

[170] *Wartime Genesis: Lower South*, docs. 217, 222A.
[171] *Wartime Genesis: Upper South*, docs. 42–43.

tering, and crabbing provided a means of self-support for former slaves near the water who could afford a modest investment in nets, lines, and perhaps a small boat.[172] Wood yards that supplied fuel for steamers and locomotives offered another alternative, though seldom a means of self-sufficiency. Operated variously by government superintendents, individual landowners, and private contractors, wood yards employed thousands of freedpeople, especially along the Mississippi River and other waterways and in the vicinity of military railroads. Both men and women labored in the wood yards, the men cutting wood and the women cording it. They were paid at piecework rates that probably permitted vigorous workers to surpass the earnings of agricultural laborers. Although taxing, work in the wood yards also allowed considerable control over the hours and pace of work. That measure of self-direction made wood-yard workers reluctant to hire out for agricultural wage labor.[173]

Short-handed planters and farmers complained when former slaves were able to make a living on their own, and they begged military authorities to curtail independent employment. Their appeals met a favorable reception from those officials who viewed year-long contracts for wage labor – not subsistence cultivation or independent jobbing – as the key to social stability. A superintendent of contrabands in the Sea Islands deplored the practice of "getting a precarious livelihood by doing a little at this thing, & a little at that." To encourage *"honest steady* labor" and control "the floating Negro population," military authorities restricted physical movement and confiscated boats. In the Mississippi Valley, superintendents reduced the issue of rations to wood-yard workers as a means of inducing them to hire to planters.[174]

In Union-occupied cities and towns, too, federal regulations often undermined the ability of former slaves to support themselves. Many military officials saw unemployed or irregularly employed black people as a threat to good order. Accordingly, they adopted pass systems and

---

[172] *Wartime Genesis: Upper South*, doc. 42; *Wartime Genesis: Lower South*, docs. 53, 55.
[173] *Wartime Genesis: Upper South*, docs. 17, 115; *Wartime Genesis: Lower South*, docs. 171, 177–79, 193, 200, 210.
[174] *Wartime Genesis: Lower South*, docs. 53–55, 210n.

vagrancy regulations to "clean out" former slaves who lacked "steady" employment or independent means, thereby treating as criminals those who were self-employed or who earned a living by "chance work." In Natchez, Mississippi, orders ostensibly issued to prevent the spread of "pestilential diseases" virtually forbade any "contraband" to live or work independently of a white employer. The regulations resulted in the expulsion of numerous self-supporting freedpeople, including relatives of soldiers. Their outraged protests were seconded by agents of Northern benevolent societies, provoking a controversy that eventually reached Congress and contributed to the resignation of the general who had approved the "health" orders.[175]

In the border states, the legality of slavery obstructed the development of free labor. Consequently, border-state slaves and former slaves generally had to leave their homes in order to obtain freedom and free-labor employment. The District of Columbia remained an attractive destination for fugitive slaves from Maryland, as did nearby Northern states. Kansas, Illinois, and Iowa received refugees from Missouri, where the continued strength of slavery, guerrilla warfare in the countryside, and the refusal of military authorities to provide contraband camps or free-labor employment made it difficult for fugitive slaves to find work or protection. Meanwhile, Kentucky slaves who could successfully evade civil authorities and military pickets crossed the Ohio River into freedom, especially at Cairo, Illinois; Jeffersonville, Indiana; and Cincinnati, Ohio. Beginning in late 1863, when black recruitment opened in neighboring Tennessee, slave men from southern Kentucky fled to the Tennessee camps, often with their families in tow.[176]

On occasion, federal officials supported the efforts of freedpeople to migrate north; indeed, they attempted to remove freedpeople from "overpopulated" parts of tidewater Virginia, the District of Columbia,

---

[175] *Wartime Genesis: Lower South*, docs. 15, 89, 166, 169, 202A-B, 212.

[176] *Destruction of Slavery*, docs. 41, 44, 46, 51, 135–37, 144–45A, 190, 194–96, 213A, 219A-B, 224, 227, 228A-B, 232; *Wartime Genesis: Upper South*, docs. 132, 158B, 173, 177, 179n., 194, 224; *Black Military Experience*, docs. 72, 85, 97–98, 303.

and Missouri. Midwestern army chaplains in St. Louis relied on connections in their home states to find employment for hundreds of former slaves. Elsewhere in Missouri, the army sought less to help freedpeople find work than simply to expel them. During the spring and summer of 1864, General Egbert B. Brown ordered the removal of former slaves – chiefly women and children – from military posts in central Missouri to the Kansas border. Although they eschewed the harsh methods of General Brown, officials in tidewater Virginia and Washington also sought to reduce the number of black people under their charge. As new arrivals swelled the ranks of dependent freedpeople, superintendents of "Negro Affairs" in tidewater Virginia worked with Northern benevolent societies and "intelligence offices" (the employment agencies of the day) to transport several hundred black women and children to northeastern cities, where they were hired out as domestic servants. Military officials in Washington used similar tactics to reduce the population of former slaves dependent on the government. Yet, no matter how desperate their condition, most freedpeople refused offers to live and work among strangers in the North. As the end of the war neared, and with it the prospect of freedom on their home ground, they gave even shorter shrift to northward migration.[177]

The deterioration of slavery hastened the progress of legal emancipation. By the end of 1864, unionist governments in Arkansas and Louisiana had ended slavery, as had the new state of West Virginia and the border state of Maryland. During the early months of 1865, Missouri and Tennessee also wrote slavery out of their fundamental law. Meanwhile, congressional passage of a constitutional amendment abolishing slavery and its ratification by a number of Northern states placed further pressure on those Union-held regions of the South in which slavery remained legal. Of the areas exempted from the Emancipation Proclamation, only tidewater Virginia failed to enact emancipation before the

---

[177] *Wartime Genesis: Upper South*, docs. 34–35, 41–42, 176–77, 179n., 182, 187, 190, 194; Capt. J. M. Brown to Jos. M. Truman, Jr., 31 Dec. 1864, vol. 60, p. 39, Press Copies of Letters Sent, ser. 527, Asst. Quartermaster & Disbursing Officer, DC Asst. Commissioner, Records of the Bureau of Refugees, Freedmen, and Abandoned Lands, RG 105, NA [A-10639].

end of the war, and citizens in those few Union-controlled counties were scarcely in a position to take such action had they so desired. The loyal slave states of Kentucky and Delaware also refused to act, holding fast to the remnants of chattel bondage until the incorporation of the Thirteenth Amendment into the Constitution. Even in those places, however, slavery's supporters were on the defensive well before the end of the war.[178]

The advent of legal freedom insinuated free labor into the lives of previously unaffected Southerners. The process whereby slaves became employees and slaveholders employers repeated itself on new terrain, with many of the same false starts and dead ends that had characterized such developments earlier in the war. At the same time, increasing numbers of nonslaveholders began bidding for the labor of men and women previously beyond their reach. Eager to hire black workers, they augmented the ranks of Southern supporters of free labor.[179]

Even in the wake of formal emancipation, not everyone accepted the new order. Many erstwhile slaveholders resorted to naked force to sustain their accustomed power over black people. Others, more far-sighted, fashioned new modes of exacting labor. Often they made use of the same state authority that had recently legislated emancipation. In Maryland, former slaveholders drew upon antebellum apprenticeship statutes. Within a month of emancipation, local courts had apprenticed more than 2,500 black children and young adults, generally to their former owners. Reluctant to intervene in the affairs of a loyal state that had voluntarily abolished slavery, federal authorities in Washington overruled orders by the local military commander to "break up the practice now prevalent of apprenticing young negroes without the con-

---

[178] For the legal changes enacting emancipation, see Francis Newton Thorpe, comp., *The Federal and State Constitutions*, 7 vols. (Washington, 1909), vol. 1, pp. 288–306, vol. 3, pp. 1429–48, 1741–79, vol. 4, pp. 2191–2229, vol. 6, p. 3445; Richard O. Curry, *A House Divided: A Study of Statehood Politics and the Copperhead Movement in West Virginia* (Pittsburgh, Pa., 1964), pp. 100–130; Henry Wilson, *History of the Antislavery Measures of the Thirty-Seventh and Thirty-Eighth United-States Congresses, 1861–64* (Boston, 1864), chap. 13.

[179] See, for example, *Wartime Genesis: Upper South*, docs. 154, 159A, 196–97.

sent of their parents." Newly freed black people found themselves with little protection.[180]

If some former owners tried to maintain control over their erstwhile slaves, others used emancipation as an excuse to eliminate costly and unwanted responsibilities. Often they simply terminated customary issues of food and clothing. In many places, freedpeople were driven from their homes. In an increasingly familiar scenario, Missouri slave-holders took "unprofitable, and expensive" black women and children "within a convenient distance of some military post, and set them out with orders to never return home – telling them they are free." Freed from the former owner's support as well as his control, such slaves had little choice but to take refuge in cities, contraband camps, or garrison towns. The collapse of the old order heaved up new hardships as well as opportunities.[181]

The steady advance of Union armies accelerated that collapse. Cutting a broad swath of destruction across Georgia, General William T. Sherman and his troops arrived at Savannah in December 1864. Accompanying them were thousands of hungry, footsore slaves who, despite discouragement, had joined their fortunes to those of the Yankee invaders. Their hostile reception by Sherman's army extended in one widely reported instance to removing a pontoon bridge upon which the soldiers had crossed a swift stream; the black refugees who followed were thereby abandoned to the mercy of pursuing Confederates. Many of them drowned when they attempted to swim to safety.[182]

Concerned both about such accounts and about Sherman's long-

---

[180] On the forcible maintenance of slavery after emancipation, see, for example, *Wartime Genesis: Upper South*, docs. 122, 141, 144–45; *Wartime Genesis: Lower South*, docs. 145, 211. On apprenticeship in Maryland immediately following emancipation, see *Destruction of Slavery*, doc. 151; *Wartime Genesis: Upper South*, docs. 140–43, 146–49, 151–54, 158–60; Richard Paul Fuke, "A Reform Mentality: Federal Policy toward Black Marylanders, 1864–1868," *Civil War History* 22 (Sept. 1976): 222–24.

[181] *Destruction of Slavery*, docs. 152, 196; *Wartime Genesis: Upper South*, docs. 150, 153, 155A, 192–93, 221.

[182] Joseph T. Glatthaar, *The March to the Sea and Beyond: Sherman's Troops in the Savannah and Carolinas Campaigns* (New York, 1985), chap. 3.

standing opposition to the enlistment of black soldiers, Secretary of War Stanton journeyed to Savannah in early January. He found Sherman preparing to advance into South Carolina and searching for a way to disencumber his army of its black followers. On January 12, 1865, at Stanton's instance, he and Sherman met with local black religious leaders to ascertain their views about how former slaves could best defend and support themselves. Freedom, declared Garrison Frazier, a spokesman selected by the twenty churchmen, "is taking us from under the yoke of bondage, and placing us where we could reap the fruit of our own labor, take care of ourselves and assist the Government in maintaining our freedom." "The way we can best take care of ourselves," he advised, "is to have land, and turn it and till it by our own labor. . . . until we are able to buy it and make it our own."[183]

Within days, General Sherman responded in a way that addressed both his own pragmatic military problems and the former slaves' fondest hopes. His Special Field Order 15 "set apart" the coastal islands and mainland rice plantations between Charleston and the St. Johns River of Florida "for the settlement of the negroes now made free by the acts of war and the proclamation of the President." The order authorized families of former slaves to occupy as much as forty acres each in the reserved district, for which they would receive "possessory title." Aside from military officials, "no white person whatever" was to reside in the area. "[S]ole and exclusive management of affairs will be left to the freed people themselves, subject only to the United States military authority and the acts of Congress." As the black people who had followed his army through Georgia took up land in the Sherman reserve, thousands of other slaves and ex-slaves set out for the coast, including many lowcountry natives who had been "refugeed" inland by their owners. Their numbers further increased as Sherman's army marched northward through the Carolinas. By the time of the Confederate surrender, about 20,000 former slaves had settled on 100,000 acres in the reserved district. Understanding Sherman's grant as official recog-

---

[183] Benjamin P. Thomas and Harold M. Hyman, *Stanton: The Life and Times of Lincoln's Secretary of War* (New York, 1962), pp. 343–45. For the meeting with black churchmen, see *Wartime Genesis: Lower South*, doc. 58.

nition of their rightful claim to the land, they began to put in crops. Tens of thousands more would join them in the months to come.[184]

As former slaves in lowcountry Georgia and South Carolina took possession of land under Sherman's order, acreage in tidewater Virginia was offered for sale under the Direct Tax Act and the confiscation acts. Hoping to secure "a spot of land" for at least some of the freedpeople under his jurisdiction, Charles Wilder, the local superintendent of "Negro Affairs," joined with representatives of Northern aid societies to buy six estates. He and his partners hoped thereby not only to prevent eviction of the black people occupying the land, but also to subdivide and resell the property to them.[185] The possibility of additional purchases for the same purpose ran aground, however, when the Lincoln administration suspended further sales until deliberations about a bureau of emancipation were concluded. In March 1865, Congress established the Bureau of Refugees, Freedmen, and Abandoned Lands (Freedmen's Bureau), with a mandate to supervise the transition from slavery to freedom in the former slave states, provide for destitute freedpeople and white refugees, and administer the land that had fallen into the hands of the government by confiscation, abandonment, or military occupation.[186]

An expectation that fundamental changes would accompany the return of peace and the organization of the Freedmen's Bureau tempered plans for the new crop year. Unwilling to take steps that might only be undone, federal authorities for the most part continued extant labor arrangements. A proposal to revise labor and welfare policies in southern Louisiana and the Mississippi Valley provoked considerable debate, for it would have sharply increased the wages of plantation workers and

---

[184] For Sherman's special field order, see *Wartime Genesis: Lower South*, doc. 59. On the earliest settlement of freedpeople under its provisions, see Bvt. Maj. Genl. R. Saxton to Maj. Genl. M. C. Meigs, 6 Apr. 1865, "Negroes," Consolidated Correspondence File, ser. 225, Central Records, Records of the Office of the Quartermaster General, RG 92, NA [Y-211].

[185] Proceedings of general court-martial in the case of Captain Charles B. Wilder, 1–16 May 1865, MM-2065, Court-Martial Case Files, ser. 15, Records of the Office of the Judge Advocate General, RG 153, NA [H-54]; Adjutant General L. Thomas to Hon. Edwin M. Stanton, 5 June 1865, filed as A-1411 1865, Letters Received, ser. 12, Records of the Adjutant General's Office, RG 94, NA [K-223].

[186] *Statutes at Large*, vol. 13, pp. 507–9.

made them responsible for their own food and clothing. But, in the
end, superiors of the treasury agent who drafted the new rules, including President Lincoln himself, refused to sanction them. Agricultural
operations in 1865 therefore commenced under regulations little different from those of the previous year. Throughout the Union-occupied
South, nearly everyone – Northerners and Southerners, black people
and white – expected the end of the war to bring a full reconsideration
of the terms of free labor.[187]

By the spring of 1865, at least 474,000 former slaves and free blacks
had taken part in some form of federally sponsored free labor in the
Union-occupied South – as soldiers, military laborers, residents of contraband camps, urban workers, or agricultural laborers on government-
supervised plantations and farms.[188] In addition, an indeterminable
number had negotiated private free-labor bargains with their former
owners or other employers.[189] Still other former slaves, whose numbers

[187] *Wartime Genesis: Lower South*, docs. 119, 135, 137, 222A-B. An attempt to revamp
the system of relief in the District of Columbia was squelched by Quartermaster
General Meigs. (*Wartime Genesis: Upper South*, doc. 77.)

[188] The number of black people who experienced some form of federally sponsored free
labor can be estimated only roughly. Because many slaves were "refugeed" away
from areas that came under Union control and others fled to Union lines from
Confederate-held territory, the wartime black population of Union-occupied counties cannot be derived from the slave and free-black populations of 1860. Official
estimates – ranging from systematic censuses to barely educated guesses – exist for
some regions. When such figures seem reliable, the editors have used them; when
contemporary evidence is lacking or seems unreliable, they have tried to arrive at an
estimate by other means.
  Louis S. Gerteis has estimated that 237,800 black people were "organized by
freedmen superintendents during the war," a category that overlaps, but is not
identical to, the one used here. For example, the regional figures that make up his
total do not consistently incorporate black soldiers. His geographical focus is also
different. While his estimate accounts for most Union-occupied parts of the Confederacy, it does not include such territory in Alabama, Florida, Georgia, and middle
and east Tennessee; in addition, it omits the District of Columbia and the border
states. (*From Contraband to Freedman*, pp. 193–94.)

[189] To the private free-labor arrangements that were individually negotiated throughout the Union-occupied South might be added the more generalized labor systems
that began to take shape in Maryland, Missouri, and Tennessee during the final
months of the war, following the abolition of slavery by state action.

are also impossible to estimate, had left the South to become free workers in the North, some of them under the auspices of official relocation and employment programs, others on their own or with the assistance of individual army officers.

Of the black people who worked under officially sanctioned free-labor arrangements, about 271,000 lived in the plantation regions of the Lower South that came under Union control. Some 125,000 were in the Mississippi Valley.[190] Those in southern Louisiana numbered about 98,000.[191] Another 48,000 experienced wartime free labor in the South Carolina Sea Islands or elsewhere along the south Atlantic coast; two-fifths of these were latecomers who took up land in the Sherman reserve.[192]

[190] The figure is derived from a report in July 1864 by Colonel John Eaton, which noted that 113,650 former slaves (including soldiers) were engaged in free labor under his jurisdiction. Assuming that new arrivals from Confederate territory increased that number by 10 percent before the end of the war, the total becomes 125,015. (Eaton, *Grant, Lincoln and the Freedmen: Reminiscences of the Civil War* [1907; reprint ed., New York, 1969], pp. 133–34.)

[191] According to an official estimate, 80,000 black people (apparently not including soldiers) were living under free-labor arrangements in southern Louisiana in September 1864: 50,000 in the countryside and 30,000 in New Orleans. There is no reason to assume any significant change during the remaining months of the war. Adding to that number the black soldiers recruited in the region (perhaps three-fourths of those credited to Louisiana, or 18,039 men), the total reaches 98,039. (Chaplain Thomas W. Conway to Major General N. P. Banks, 9 Sept. 1864, C-228 1864, Letters Received, ser. 1920, Civil Affairs, Dept. of the Gulf, Records of U.S. Army Continental Commands, RG 393 Pt. 1, NA [C-732]; Table 1 in Chapter 3, this volume.)

[192] Estimates of the number of former slaves who lived and worked under federal supervision in the South Carolina Sea Islands include 16,000 in early 1862 (before the opening of black recruitment) and 15,000, exclusive of soldiers, in 1863. The latter number probably did not increase by more than 10 percent (to about 16,500) during 1864; many of the new arrivals were refugees from points in Florida and Georgia that were held for a time by Northern troops but subsequently abandoned. Perhaps 1,200 additional freedpeople could be found at Fernandina, Florida, and the handful of other coastal outposts that remained continuously in federal hands. Nearly 10,000 black soldiers were credited to South Carolina (5,462), Georgia (3,486), and Florida (1,044); they bring the total to 27,692. Finally, some 20,000 former slaves had been settled in the Sherman reserve by mid-April 1865, making a grand total of 47,692. (*Wartime Genesis: Lower South*, docs. 29n., 36; *Official Records*, ser. 3, vol. 4, pp. 118–19; Table 1 in Chapter 3, this volume; Bvt. Maj. Genl. R. Saxton to Maj. Genl. M. C. Meigs, 6 Apr. 1865, "Negroes," Consolidated Correspondence File, ser. 225, Central Records, Records of the Office of the Quartermaster General, RG 92, NA [Y-211].)

In the Upper South, some 203,000 former slaves and free blacks lived and worked under federal auspices. About 74,000 could be found in tidewater North Carolina and Virginia.[193] Perhaps 37,000 were in middle and east Tennessee or northern Alabama.[194] Another 40,000 lived in the District of Columbia, in Alexandria, Virginia, and in the contraband camps on the Virginia side of the Potomac River.[195] In all

[193] The figure for tidewater North Carolina is derived from a census conducted in January 1865, which counted 17,307 black people (evidently excluding soldiers) in the territory under Union control. Adding the 5,035 black soldiers credited to the state brings the total to 22,342. (James, *Annual Report*, p. 4; Table 1 in Chapter 3, this volume.) The total for tidewater Virginia (52,004) has been reached by adding figures from censuses taken in late 1864, which enumerated 24,850 black people south of the James River (including more than 4,000 soldiers) and 13,305 north of the James (excluding soldiers), plus an estimated 1,000 soldiers in the latter district, plus 12,849 former slaves and free blacks on the eastern shore (the black population of Accomac and Northampton counties in 1860). (*Wartime Genesis: Upper South*, docs. 42–43; U.S., Census Office, 8th Census, *Population of the United States in 1860* [Washington, 1864], pp. 504–13.)

[194] Rough estimates can be obtained by beginning with the number of black soldiers recruited in the three regions and assuming a relationship between that figure and the number of other former slaves and free blacks who lived in contraband camps, performed military labor, or worked as agricultural laborers under military supervision. About 18,400 black soldiers enlisted from these areas (assuming that middle and east Tennessee contributed two-thirds of Tennessee's total, and northern Alabama all the soldiers from that state). (See Table 1 in Chapter 3, this volume.) If it is assumed that an equal number of black people participated in other free-labor arrangements, the total becomes 36,800. (The ratio of only one civilian to each soldier is employed because middle and east Tennessee and northern Alabama had relatively few contraband camps – all established late in the war – and very limited government-sponsored agricultural operations; the number of black civilians in federally supervised labor settings was therefore much smaller in proportion to black soldiers than was the case in tidewater Virginia and North Carolina or the occupied regions of the Lower South, where, for every one soldier, between two and nine civilians participated in Union-sponsored free labor.)

[195] Estimates for the District of Columbia, Alexandria, and the contraband camps across the Potomac from Washington, D.C., involve consideration of several different sets of figures, as well as an element of conjecture. According to the 1860 census, 3,185 slaves and 11,131 free blacks lived in the District, virtually all of whom presumably had free-labor experience during the war, as did untold thousands of fugitive slaves from Virginia and Maryland. A military census of March 1865, which was almost certainly marred by undercounting, enumerated 16,092 black refugees (excluding quartermaster employees living in government housing, and house servants) in the District, Alexandria, Freedman's Village, and Mason's Island; other estimates of the number of wartime black migrants to Washington and its vicinity run as high as 40,000. Probably the most useful figures come from

the border states combined, probably no more than 52,000 black people took part in Union-sponsored free labor.[196]

Former slaves in the Union-occupied South worked in a wide variety of free-labor settings. Most of the men – about 101,000 in the seceded states and 47,000 in the border states and the District of Columbia – served as soldiers or sailors.[197] Many of them had previously worked as military laborers, along with tens of thousands of men who never entered the armed service. A few thousand women also worked for military employers. Most ex-slave women in Union-held territory, and a sizable proportion of the men, toiled as agricultural laborers on plantations and farms supervised by federal officials. A similar number – mainly women, children, and elderly people – lived in contraband camps, infirm farms, or "regimental villages," where they received rations and occasionally performed remunerative labor. Significant numbers of black men and women found free-labor employment that was not directly sponsored by Union authorities. Most civilian workers in towns and cities did so, and an indeterminable number of rural ex-slaves negotiated new terms of labor on their own. The experiences of soldiers, military laborers, residents of contraband camps, and agricultural and

a census taken in 1867, which placed the black population of the District alone at 31,937, of whom 22,747 had been resident since at least 1864. Beginning with the latter figure, and then assuming that 17,000 other black people experienced free labor in Alexandria and the northern Virginia camps during the war or else had lived and worked in the District during the war but were gone by 1867, results in a total of 39,747 for the nation's capital and nearby northern Virginia. (*Population of the United States in 1860*, p. 588; *Wartime Genesis: Upper South*, doc. 86; Green, *Secret City*, p. 62; Allan John Johnston, "Surviving Freedom: The Black Community of Washington, D.C., 1860–1880" [Ph.D. diss., Duke University, 1980], pp. 162–66.)

[196] Estimates of the extent of federally sponsored free labor in the border states, excepting that for soldiers, are highly conjectural. Although a sizable proportion of border-state black men served in the Union army, few other forms of free-labor employment were available: Military labor was limited in scope, contraband camps few in number, and government-sponsored agricultural operations almost nonexistent. More than 42,000 black soldiers and sailors were credited to the states of Missouri, Kentucky, and Maryland (see Table 1 and note 38 in Chapter 3, this volume); perhaps an additional 10,000 black people worked in other federally sponsored free-labor settings.

[197] See Table 1 (soldiers) and note 38 (sailors) in Chapter 3, this volume.

urban workers provided somewhat different perspectives on freedom. These variations were compounded by differences in antebellum status, the character of federal occupation, and the policies of particular Union commanders.

Yet a common thread ran through the diverse experiences. Only a tiny minority of black people in Union-held territory attained the status of independent proprietor or tenant; the overwhelming majority provided for themselves through some form of wage labor. In escaping slavery they had relinquished any claim upon their owners for subsistence, protection, or provision for old age, youth, and illness. Their survival now depended, not upon their place in a system of hierarchical personal relations, but upon the sale of their labor power in an impersonal market. Granted self-ownership but no productive property, former slaves were simultaneously permitted and compelled to work for wages.

Although wartime wage labor did not satisfy the aspirations of former slaves to become freeholders, it broke decisively and irrevocably with slavery. Freedpeople gained proprietorship over their own persons. The new conditions of labor generally prohibited physical punishment, encouraged independent family, religious, and social life, and required compensation. Ex-slave laborers gained rudimentary legal protection, backed by the force of federal arms. They made the most of whatever opportunities the war created. Except for the youngest, oldest, and most infirm, nearly all black people within the Union-occupied Confederacy were self-supporting at the time of Appomattox.[198]

Even in territory still controlled by Confederate forces, particularly those areas adjacent to Union lines, the proximity of free labor and the prospect of universal freedom eroded slave discipline. With freedom within reach, some slaves demanded new terms of labor – an end to corporal punishment, the elimination of overseers, more time to work garden plots, payment in cash or in kind. To slaveholders, such notions smacked of rebellion, to be answered by the lash, sale, or removal to the

---

[198] For assessments of the extent of self-support in one region, see *Wartime Genesis: Upper South*, docs. 42–43.

interior. But as Confederate military hopes dimmed, slaveholders found themselves increasingly unable to wield the old authority. Free labor in the Union-occupied South helped subvert slavery far beyond federal lines.[199]

The advance of free labor within Union-occupied territory and the disintegration of slavery within the Confederacy seemed to vindicate Northerners' faith in the superiority of free over slave labor. Having planted the seeds of free labor in the South, however, federal officials disagreed about how they should be nurtured. Some, like Colonel Samuel Thomas, superintendent of freedmen in the District of Vicksburg, believed the government had done enough. Its job was simply to put the former slave's "labor on an equal footing with white labor . . . [g]uard him against imposition, give him his just dues at the end of each month, . . . and let him work his way up." "Capital does now, and will for some time to come carry on great enterprises," Thomas affirmed, "and a large portion of the human family, both white and black, must labor for this capital at regulated wages, without any direct interest in the result of the enterprise." Arguing that "[o]ur country has enough to bear without undertaking the enormous task of starting out each freedman with a competency," he considered the opportunity for individual self-improvement to be the true boon of freedom.[200]

Others believed that meddling Northerners had already done too much. Colonel Frank J. White, superintendent of "Negro Affairs" on Virginia's eastern shore, condemned benevolent associations and "enthusiasts" in the army for having made the former slave "dependent upon a bounty that can not last [and] would enevitably render him helpless in the future." White also rejected "communistic" plans to settle freedpeople on abandoned or captured land, on the grounds that they would "[divide], instead of [unite] the interests of the two classes" − former slaves and their former owners − whose futures were necessarily intertwined.[201]

Still others were convinced that not enough had been done to aid the

[199] *Destruction of Slavery*, pp. 40−43, and chap. 9, especially docs. 327−31.
[200] *Wartime Genesis: Lower South*, doc. 209.
[201] *Wartime Genesis: Upper South*, doc. 46.

emancipated slaves. Reporting upon conditions in Tennessee shortly after the war, Captain Richard J. Hinton, an officer of a black regiment from Kansas, urged the government to allot land to the freedpeople. "Nothing," he argued, "not even the bestowal of suffrage, will so materially aid [in] destroying the effects of Slavery [as] the creation of a self-reliant independent yeomanry out of the former slaves." Hinton feared that black people would be subject to "the serfdom of capital" if the nation were merely to grant "personal freedom, secure no political or civil rights, and leave the freed class to struggle out of the slough the best way they can with the narrow plank of free labor."[202]

No one knew better than the freedpeople just how deep the slough and narrow the plank. Resolutely determined never again to be slaves, they were nevertheless ambivalent about their wartime encounter with free labor. If the "freedom" of wage work marked their long-awaited liberation from the personal dependency of the past, it also fell far short of the independence to which they aspired. The imminence of Northern victory and the final destruction of slavery therefore encouraged them to become increasingly active in pursuit of their own interests. In so doing, they confounded those federal officials who viewed them as mere objects of policies or a "problem" to be solved. Pointing to their vital contribution to the Union cause, as soldiers and as civilians, former slaves established their claims upon the government that had granted them liberty and in many instances was also their employer. Although frequently couched in the language of supplication, their communications to federal authorities – from local commanders to the President himself – asserted their rights as free citizens and the nation's obligations to them. A group of black men in coastal North Carolina took such ground in a protest against impressment, declaring it inconsistent with "there cause as Freemen and the Rights of their families."[203]

As black people began to assert the prerogatives of citizenship, they assumed a more visible place in public affairs. Throughout the Union-

---

[202] Captain Richard J. Hinton to Captain T. W. Clarke, 31 July 1865, H-47 1865, Registered Letters Received, ser. 3379, TN Asst. Commissioner, Records of the Bureau of Refugees, Freedmen, and Abandoned Lands, RG 105, NA [A-6135].
[203] *Wartime Genesis: Upper South*, doc. 25.

occupied South, former slaves and free blacks formed political and quasi-political associations. Such organizations were particularly active in New Orleans, Nashville, and Washington, where federal control dated from early in the war and large antebellum free-black communities were ready to take the lead; but they also appeared elsewhere, especially in localities where black soldiers were stationed. These associations became vehicles by which black people sought to elevate their political status, demanding the right to testify in court, to sit on juries, and to vote. As the movement to reconstruct the South gained momentum, they became an active, though not yet fully sanctioned, force in local politics.[204]

The divisions among federal officials and the burgeoning political presence of black people revealed that if the Civil War had destroyed slavery, the meaning of freedom was no more certain than before the first shots at Fort Sumter. Wartime labor and welfare policies had necessarily rested more upon military exigencies than upon considered decisions about the future of the former slaves. Restricted to the narrow confines of securely held territory and subordinate at all times to the demands of waging war, they bore little resemblance to the requirements of ordinary times. Almost everyone – North and South, black and white – saw peace as an opportunity to begin afresh.

Yet wartime experience did not count for nothing. As the victorious North set about reconstructing Southern society, the labor and relief programs established within Union lines became points of reference for postwar plans. In the course of the debate, both those who equated freedom with independent proprietorship and those who understood it as the unfettered right to sell one's labor power cited wartime developments to bolster their positions. For their part, the former slaves and free blacks who had lived and worked in Union-occupied territory entered the contest with a confidence born of the pivotal role they had played in the Union's triumph and their wartime initiation into the practices of free labor. As freedom burst the bounds of its wartime

[204] See, for example, *Wartime Genesis: Upper South*, docs. 84–85; *Wartime Genesis: Lower South*, doc. 139; *Black Military Experience*, doc. 362.

limitations and advanced into the entire South, more than three and a half million newly liberated slaves joined the half-million who had experienced free labor amid civil war. Their abrupt passage into the American working class as propertyless, unenfranchised free laborers raised fundamental questions about the nation's "new birth of freedom."[205] The answers would affect all Americans.

[205] The phrase appears in the Gettysburg Address. (Lincoln, *Collected Works*, vol. 7, pp. 22–23.)

3

The Black Military
Experience 1861–1867

FREEDOM CAME to most American slaves only through force of arms. The growing Northern commitment to emancipation availed nothing without victory on the battlefield. But once federal policy makers had committed the Union to abolishing slavery, the Northern armies that eroded Confederate territory simultaneously expanded the domain of freedom. The Union army perforce became an army of liberation, and as it did, both the Northern public and the freed slaves themselves demanded that the direct beneficiaries of freedom join the battle against the slaveholders' rebellion. The incorporation of black soldiers into Union ranks at once turned to Northern advantage a vast source of manpower that the Confederacy proved incapable of tapping and enhanced the antislavery character of the war. The liberating force of black enlistments weakened slavery in the loyal border states and the Union-occupied South no less than in the Confederacy, thereby extending the nation's commitment to freedom beyond the limits of the Emancipation Proclamation. Black enlistees in the border states received their freedom, and, eventually, their enlistment also guaranteed the liberty of their immediate families. Throughout the slave states, black enlistment and slave emancipation advanced together and, indeed, became inseparable.

Black men coveted the liberator's role, but soldiering remained a complex, ambiguous experience. If most free blacks and slaves rushed to join the Union army, others entered federal service only at the point of a bayonet. Once enlisted, ex-slaves who yearned to confront their former masters on terms of equality found themselves enmeshed in another white-dominated hierarchy, which, like the one they had escaped, assumed their inferiority. Organized into separate black regiments, paid at a lower rate than white soldiers, denied the opportunity to become commissioned officers, often ill-used by commanders whose mode of discipline resembled that of slave masters, and frequently assigned to menial duties rather than combat, black soldiers learned forcefully of the continued inequities of American life. Nonetheless, the war left black soldiers with far more than their freedom. They gained new skills in regimental schools and a wider knowledge of the world in army service. Fighting and dying for the Union advanced the claims of black men and women to the rights and privileges of full citizenship. Victory over those who had previously dominated their lives bred a confidence that soldiers proudly carried into freedom and that permeated the entire black community. The successes of black soldiers in their war against discrimination within the army, however limited, politicized them and their families, preparing all black people for the larger struggle they would face at war's end.[1]

At the beginning of the war, few Union policy makers foresaw a military role for either black freemen or bondsmen. Southern leaders and Northern abolitionists may have placed slavery at the cornerstone of the Confederacy, but Northern policy makers minimized the connection between secession and chattel bondage. In the eyes of Northern leaders and most Northern whites, the conflict would be a war for Union – not against slavery – fought by the white men of each section. Most Union army commanders followed the same line of reasoning, even after local

[1] This essay, like the others in this volume, is based primarily upon documents published in *Freedom: A Documentary History of Emancipation* and other documents from the National Archives of the United States. For a valuable collection of primary sources, see "The Negro in the Military Service of the United States, 1639–1886," which was compiled by the Adjutant General's Office between 1885 and 1888; it is available as a National Archives microfilm publication. Equally indispensable are the annual reports of the Bureau of Colored Troops published in series 3 of *Official Records* (vol. 3, pp. 1111–15; vol. 4, pp. 788–90; vol. 5, pp. 137–40, 1029–31). The final report of the Provost Marshal General's Bureau summarizes the laws and orders affecting the military service of black soldiers (*Official Records*, ser. 3, vol. 5, pp. 654–62). Important secondary studies of the black military experience include Dudley Taylor Cornish, *The Sable Arm: Negro Troops in the Union Army, 1861–1865* (New York, 1956); Joseph T. Glatthaar, *Forged in Battle: The Civil War Alliance of Black Soldiers and White Officers* (New York, 1990); Mary Frances Berry, *Military Necessity and Civil Rights Policy: Black Citizenship and the Constitution, 1861–1868* (Port Washington, N.Y., 1977). See, in addition, the general sources on the Civil War and emancipation cited in note 1 of Chapter 1, this volume. Also of use are three important nineteenth-century studies by, respectively, a prominent black abolitionist and two black Civil War veterans: William Wells Brown, *The Negro in the American Rebellion* (Boston, 1867); George W. Williams, *A History of the Negro Troops in the War of the Rebellion, 1861–1865* (New York, 1888); Joseph T. Wilson, *The Black Phalanx: A History of the Negro Soldiers of the United States in the Wars of 1775–1812 and 1861–65* (Hartford, Conn., 1888).

authorities in some parts of the South mustered a few free men of color into Native Guard units.[2] But as the Northern army confronted its enemy in the field, the indispensability of slavery to the Confederate war effort soon became evident. Southern armies depended heavily on the labor of slaves and free blacks to construct fortifications, transport materiel, tend cavalry horses, and perform camp services for both officers and enlisted men. Meanwhile, slaves on the home front raised the commercial staples necessary for foreign credit, labored in armories, shipyards, and ironworks to manufacture the weapons of war, and grew the food that fed both the army and the civilian population. Slave labor thus undergirded Confederate ability to wage war, while freeing Southern white men for battlefield service.[3] Indeed, as Union generals probed their adversary, they found that Confederate spokesmen had made no idle boast: Slavery stood at the center of Southern economy and society. The revelation gave new standing to abolitionists and their demand for emancipation. Slowly Union field commanders and then desk-bound policy makers came to see that preserving the Union required an assault upon chattel bondage.

General Benjamin F. Butler, a pugnacious politician with no previous military experience, first made the connection. Commanding the Union beachhead at Fortress Monroe in tidewater Virginia in the spring of 1861, Butler gave asylum to several runaway slaves, and, when their masters tried to reclaim the fugitive property, he sent the slaveholders packing. Initially, Butler acted out of an almost instinctive reluctance to aid the enemy. But, in a manner that came to characterize his command throughout the war, he quickly transformed his instincts into matters of high principle that flamboyantly redounded to his own and the North's benefit. Contending that slave property, like other private property, might rightfully be appropriated by the army upon

[2] On the free-black units, see *Black Military Experience*, docs. 11, 127; *Official Records*, ser. 4, vol. 1, pp. 1087–88, and vol. 2, pp. 197, 941; Mary F. Berry, "Negro Troops in Blue and Gray: The Louisiana Native Guards, 1861–1863," *Louisiana History* 8 (Spring 1967): 165–90; Charles H. Wesley, "The Employment of Negroes as Soldiers in the Confederate Army," *Journal of Negro History* 4 (July 1919): 239–53.

[3] On the Confederacy's dependence upon slave labor, see *Destruction of Slavery*, chap. 9.

grounds of military necessity, especially when such property was being employed in the enemy's cause, Butler put the fugitives to work in his quartermaster's department. Shall the rebels "be allowed the use of this property against the United States," Butler asked rhetorically, "and we not be allowed its use in aid of the United States?"[4] Thus Butler established a rationale for refusing to return fugitive slaves and for turning their labor to Union advantage, while at the same time evading the question of emancipation. Without challenging their status as property, pragmatic federal commanders could remove escaped or captured slaves from Confederate strength and add them to the Union side. The issue was captured property used by the enemy to wage war – "contraband of war" – not freedom.[5]

Northerners reveled in Butler's stroke, and the label "contrabands" adhered firmly to fugitive slaves. Other Union commanders hastened to follow Butler's lead. They increasingly perceived the value of black labor to their forces and also welcomed a solution to the problems posed by the escalating influx of fugitives into their lines. In August 1861, Congress – pressed by an upsurge in emancipationist sentiment in the North – gave legal standing to Butler's logic. The First Confiscation Act provided that a master who permitted his slave to labor in any Confederate service forfeited his claim to the slave.[6] However, as so often proved true during the war, events rapidly outran this legal position. With every advance of Union forces, slaves fled bondage and sought refuge with the Northern armies. With little regard for whether the fugitives had actually served the Confederacy, federal commanders turned the potential burden of civilian refugees into an asset by putting them to work on fortifications, on supply lines, and in personal service. Furthermore, as the war moved into its second year, support swelled for vigorous punishment of secessionists. Depriving rebels of their slaves appealed to Northerners frustrated by military stalemate and all too many defeats. Mindful of the apocalyptic vision of a vengeful God,

---

4   *Destruction of Slavery*, docs. 1A-B.
5   For the contraband-of-war argument as used by another Union commander, see
    Destruction of Slavery, doc. 42.
6   *Statutes at Large*, vol. 12, p. 319.

some Northerners came to believe that their ultimate success hinged on elevating their struggle with the South to the level of high principle, demonstrating to themselves and to the world that they fought for right and justice and not for mere political or economic power. If the demands of the war sensitized Northerners to the moral necessity of freedom, the growing recognition of the evil of slavery awakened them to the South's dependence upon black laborers. Indeed, as the war dragged on, the various rationales for emancipation became increasingly detached from the motives of their advocates. Abolitionists touted the military advantages of emancipation, and generals denounced the immorality of slavery. The argument that each captured or fugitive slave put to work within federal lines would be, in effect, a net gain of two – one added to the Union, one lost to the Confederacy – grew in power. Increasing numbers of Northerners concluded that military as well as moral necessity demanded an end to slavery.[7]

Emancipation inched forward during the first half of 1862. Congress legislated compensated emancipation in the District of Columbia and prohibited slavery in the territories. President Abraham Lincoln – unsuccessfully – urged the slave states still in the Union to consider gradual, compensated emancipation.[8] Then, in July 1862, the Second Confiscation Act and the Militia Act formally adopted emancipation and the military employment of fugitive slaves as weapons of war. These acts declared "forever free" all captured and fugitive slaves owned by rebels and authorized the mobilization of "persons of African descent" in "any military or naval service for which they may be found competent."[9] If Lincoln's preliminary Emancipation Proclamation of September 1862 and the final proclamation of January 1, 1863, in

---

7 On the development of federal policy and Northern public opinion concerning fugitive slaves, see *Destruction of Slavery*. On the employment of fugitive slaves as military laborers, see *Wartime Genesis: Upper South*; *Wartime Genesis: Lower South*.

8 For the congressional legislation, see *Statutes at Large*, vol. 12, pp. 376–78, 432. On emancipation in the District of Columbia, see *Destruction of Slavery*, chap. 3. For the President's advocacy of gradual emancipation, see Abraham Lincoln, *Collected Works*, ed. Roy P. Basler, Marion D. Pratt, and Lloyd A. Dunlap, 9 vols. (New Brunswick, N.J., 1953–55), vol. 5, pp. 144–46, 160–61, 317–19, 324–25, 503–4, 529–34.

9 *Statutes at Large*, vol. 12, pp. 589–92, 597–600.

effect freed no more slaves than had the Second Confiscation Act, they captured the imagination of the Northern public and elevated the Union's commitment to emancipation far beyond the level of mere expediency by adding moral weight to the Union cause. They also pledged the federal government to the full exploitation of black labor in defeating the Confederacy.[10]

Only a short step separated arguments about the value of black labor in support of the Union army and navy to proposals that black men be used even more directly against the Confederacy. The same military and moral necessity that enlarged Northern support for emancipation pushed the question of enlisting black soldiers to the fore, and indeed, the two issues became increasingly intertwined. Once emancipation found a place on the Union escutcheon, many white Northerners demanded that the blood of black men as well as white be shed to purchase the slaves' freedom, some for obviously self-serving motives, others believing that the participation of black people in the Union's victory would render the commitment to emancipation irreversible.[11]

Still, policy makers hesitated. The prospect of arming slaves or even free blacks raised fundamental questions about the place of black people in American society, questions that went far beyond the immediate demands of the war. After emancipating their slaves in the Revolutionary era, the Northern states had consigned them to the margins of society. White Northerners alternately exploited free-black men and women as cheap, menial laborers and urged their deportation from the United States, depriving them all the while of rights equated with freedom. Most Northern states denied black men the right to vote or to sit on juries, and several states prohibited black witnesses from testifying against whites. White Americans deemed bearing arms in defense of the Republic an essential element of citizenship, and federal legislation dating from 1792 restricted militia enrollment

[10] *Statutes at Large*, vol. 12, pp. 1267–69; John Hope Franklin, *The Emancipation Proclamation* (Garden City, N.Y., 1963).
[11] For examples of various arguments, see *Wartime Genesis: Lower South*, docs. 159–60; *Black Military Experience*, docs. 21, 24–25.

to white men.[12] As recently as 1859, Massachusetts Governor Nathaniel P. Banks had vetoed a law that would have incorporated black men into the state forces.[13] Black people and their abolitionist allies challenged these proscriptions as denials of both the fundamental rights of man and the rights of citizens, and they protested racial discrimination. Thus, enlisting black men into the Union army not only would suggest a measure of equality most Northerners refused to concede, but also would enlarge the claims of black people to full citizenship. For these reasons, black enlistment raised questions few Northern leaders willingly confronted. Both Congress and the Lincoln administration moved cautiously.

If Union policy makers dreaded the implications of black enlistment, black Northerners and other abolitionists welcomed them. From the beginning of the war, Northern black men pressed for the opportunity to serve in the army.[14] They were joined by abolitionists, free-soilers, and a few career military officers of antislavery persuasion who also saw black enlistment as a lever against slavery and racial discrimination. John A. Andrew, governor of Massachusetts, stood at the front of this group. Conscious of both the vital need for manpower and the ideological implications of arming black men, in 1862 he began peppering the War Department with requests for permission to raise a free-black regiment within his state's volunteer organization. Simultaneously, James H. Lane, veteran of the Kansas border wars and now a U.S. senator from that state, pressed for and eventually assumed similar authority.[15] Two career army officers also lent early support to black enlistment: General John W. Phelps, a Vermont abolitionist serving in the Department of the Gulf, and General David Hunter, commander of

[12] Leon F. Litwack, *North of Slavery: The Negro in the Free States, 1790–1860* (Chicago, 1961).

[13] Francis W. Bird, *Review of Governor Banks' Veto of the Revised Code, on Account of Its Authorizing the Enrollment of Colored Citizens in the Militia* (Boston, 1860); Adjutant General's Office, "Negro in the Military Service," pp. 946–50.

[14] See, for example, *Black Military Experience*, docs. 17–23; Cornish, *Sable Arm*, pp. 1–7; James M. McPherson, *The Negro's Civil War: How American Negroes Felt and Acted during the War for the Union* (New York, 1965), chap. 2.

[15] On Andrew, see *Black Military Experience*, pp. 75–76, and doc. 26. On Lane, see *Black Military Experience*, pp. 44–45, and docs. 12–15; Cornish, *Sable Arm*, chap. 4.

Union forces along the coast of South Carolina, Georgia, and Florida. Although the military command structure circumscribed Phelps and Hunter in ways that hardly affected Andrew or Lane, the strategic positions of the two generals and their explicit advocacy of slave – as well as free-black – recruitment strengthened the bond between enlistment and emancipation.

In the summer of 1862, Phelps and Hunter, acting independently and on their own authority, armed fugitive-slave men and pressed for War Department recognition of their troops. Both soon ran afoul of their superiors. Phelps tangled with Butler – now in command of the Department of the Gulf – and was quickly mastered by the practiced politician. Hunter, who also barged ahead without War Department approval, had to disband his slave regiment when it failed to receive official sanction and thus could be neither uniformed nor paid. But, although Phelps and Hunter received public reprimands and reversals, events moved so quickly that their previously unacceptable policies soon won official blessing. Butler, after forcing Phelps's resignation, not only armed black men – free rather than slave – but also shamelessly claimed credit for initiating black enlistment. Similarly, within weeks of the dissolution of Hunter's regiment, Secretary of War Edwin M. Stanton authorized Hunter's subordinate, General Rufus Saxton, to raise several regiments among contrabands on the South Carolina Sea Islands.[16]

Yet the War Department's expectations in sanctioning the employment of black soldiers were different from those of Phelps or Hunter. The two generals had hoped to field a slave army of liberation; the department saw the enlistment of black men as a stopgap measure to ease manpower shortages in a few military theaters. The War Department neither proposed large-scale black enlistment nor connected black enlistment to the emerging national emancipation policy. But, if fed-

[16] On Phelps's recruitment, see *Black Military Experience*, pp. 41–44, and docs. 9–10. On his conflict with Butler, which involved differences regarding emancipation policy as well as recruitment, see also *Destruction of Slavery*, pp. 192–96, and docs. 59, 61–63, 67A; Cornish, *Sable Arm*, pp. 56–65. On the recruitment of Hunter's regiment and its effects, see *Wartime Genesis: Lower South*, docs. 20–21; *Black Military Experience*, pp. 37–41, and docs. 1–4; Cornish, *Sable Arm*, pp. 33–55. For the order authorizing Saxton to enlist black men, see *Wartime Genesis: Lower South*, doc. 36.

eral policy makers were not yet fully committed to a black soldiery, the organization of a few black regiments in Louisiana, South Carolina, and Kansas provided early opportunities for black men to demonstrate their eagerness to enlist and their potential as soldiers, important precedents upon which the proponents of enlistment could draw.

Military setbacks in the summer and fall of 1862 reoriented Union priorities. Just as military necessity prompted Congress and President Lincoln to make emancipation the centerpiece of federal war policy, so the course of the war eroded the obstacles to full-scale enlistment of black men. Differences between the preliminary Emancipation Proclamation of September 1862 and the final proclamation of January 1863 suggest changes in Lincoln's thinking even over the brief three-month period. Whereas the former made no mention of arming emancipated slaves, the latter expressed an intention to receive slaves freed by the proclamation into military service to garrison forts and other military installations.[17] After the new year, Secretary of War Stanton also showed greater awareness of the military advantages of arming large numbers of contrabands, as well as the need to find employment for the thousands of fugitives thronging army camps. In March 1863, he created the American Freedmen's Inquiry Commission to investigate the condition of refugee slaves and report "what measures will best contribute to their protection and improvement, so that they may defend and support themselves; and also, how they can be most usefully employed in the service of the Government for the suppression of the rebellion."[18] Thus, by early 1863 the Lincoln administration had tied the question of slavery to the larger issues of the nature of the war, the impact of emancipation on American society, and the role of black people in the war effort. These issues could not easily be separated, and the insatiable demand for soldiers forced the question of black enlist-

[17] *Statutes at Large*, vol. 12, pp. 1267–69. The final proclamation also declared that slaves emancipated by its provisions would be received into armed service on navy vessels. Congress had laid the legal foundations for black military service in the Second Confiscation Act and the Militia Act.

[18] *Official Records*, ser. 3, vol. 3, p. 73. For the commission's reports, see *Official Records*, ser. 3, vol. 3, pp. 430–54, and ser. 3, vol. 4, pp. 289–382.

ment to the fore. The previously inconceivable idea of large-scale enlistment of black men appeared increasingly to be common sense.

Union manpower needs gave new leverage to the proponents of enlistment. Protracted warfare overwhelmed the War Department's initial plan to supplement the small regular army with a volunteer force. Men who had entered the army enthusiastically under Lincoln's early calls for volunteers, and who had reenlisted for additional terms of service, grew impatient with the bloody stalemate, as families suffered during their absence and the death toll mounted. The number of new volunteers plummeted, worsening the army's already serious manpower shortage. Scrambling to fill depleted Union ranks, Congress in March 1863 required systematic enrollment of all male citizens aged twenty through forty-five and provided for conscription by lottery from the enrollment lists.[19] The legislation flouted popular opposition, forced military service upon the unwilling, and fueled resistance to both the draft and the war itself. The increasing manpower demands inexorably shifted Northern perceptions of the utility of enlisting black men, especially when combined with the belief that, since black people would clearly benefit from Union victory, white soldiers should not bear the entire burden of battle. The white potential draftee looked with increasing favor upon the idea of filling Union ranks with black men, even if he cared little about emancipation or disdained black people altogether. And the same manpower needs that compelled Congress to draft white men hastened a War Department commitment to enlist black men.[20]

---

[19] *Statutes at Large*, vol. 12, pp. 731–37. On the enrollment and conscription system and popular resistance to it, see James W. Geary, *We Need Men: The Union Draft in the Civil War* (DeKalb, Ill., 1991); Eugene Converse Murdock, *Patriotism Limited, 1862–1865: The Civil War Draft and the Bounty System* (Kent, Ohio, 1967), and *One Million Men: The Civil War Draft in the North* (Madison, Wisc., 1971); Fred A. Shannon, *The Organization and Administration of the Union Army, 1861–1863* (Cleveland, Ohio, 1928), vol. 1, pp. 295–323, and vol. 2, pp. 11–243. See also Grace Palladino, *Another Civil War: Labor, Capital, and the State in the Anthracite Regions of Pennsylvania, 1840–68* (Urbana, Ill., 1990), chap. 5.

[20] On the connection between the draft and growing support for black enlistment, see *Wartime Genesis: Upper South*, doc. 223; *Black Military Experience*, docs. 29–30, 33–34, 76, 100.

With Governor Andrew and others pressing the case and with black regiments already established in Louisiana, in South Carolina, and – under something less than official sanction – in Kansas, the Lincoln administration slowly, grudgingly, but irrevocably, turned to black men to offset the shortage of white soldiers. Early in 1863, Secretary of War Stanton authorized the governors of Rhode Island, Massachusetts, and Connecticut to organize black regiments. But, as if to emphasize the tentative nature of the commitment, he balked when Ohio Governor David Tod asked for similar authority. Black volunteers from Ohio and the other Northern states would have to enlist in the New England regiments.[21]

Stanton's restriction scarcely hindered the abolitionists. Before long, Andrew and others had commissioned antislavery radical George L. Stearns to recruit black men throughout the free states. Stearns, in turn, organized citizens' committees, raised money, and hired black recruiting agents to scour the North. With long years of experience in the abolition movement and deep roots in Northern black communities, men like Martin R. Delany, O. S. B. Wall, John Mercer Langston, and John Jones had no trouble locating recruits and forwarding them to the regimental rendezvous in New England.[22] Their efforts benefited from the public support of nearly all Northern black leaders. In July, a convention of black men from across the state of New York resolved that the disease of rebellion "having proved to be incurable by ordinary means, such as Reason, Justice, [and] Patriotism . . . [,] more effective remedies ought now to be *thoroughly* tried, in the shape of warm lead and cold steel, duly administered by two hundred thousand black doctors."[23] That same summer, as the Massachusetts, Rhode Island, and Connecticut regiments filled, Stanton authorized other Northern governors to initiate black recruitment in their own states. Since black

---

[21] *Black Military Experience*, pp. 75–76, and docs. 28, 31–33, 38A.
[22] *Black Military Experience*, docs. 30–32, 34–37, 142, 144; Cornish, *Sable Arm*, pp. 106–11.
[23] *Record of Action of the Convention Held at Poughkeepsie, N.Y., July 15th and 16th, 1863, for the Purpose of Facilitating the Introduction of Colored Troops into the Service of the United States* (New York, 1863). Quotation on p. 8.

volunteers counted toward state draft quotas, most of the governors happily complied.[24]

While authorizing the enlistment of free-black men in the North, Stanton also moved to expand recruitment of slave men in the Union-occupied South. He dispatched General Daniel Ullmann to southern Louisiana, assigned General Edward A. Wild to North Carolina, and sent Adjutant General Lorenzo Thomas to the Mississippi Valley to give slave enlistments full official sanction. Stanton charged Ullmann with raising a black brigade in the Gulf region, a task for which Ullmann had been preparing in New York since the new year. Pushed by Massachusetts Governor Andrew, Stanton authorized Wild to inaugurate recruitment in the Union's tidewater North Carolina foothold, and he headed south to organize what became known as Wild's African Brigade. As befitted his rank, Thomas shouldered weightier responsibilities. In addition to raising black troops, he would coordinate contraband policy with the Treasury Department and convince white soldiers of the virtues of black enlistment.[25]

Adjutant General Thomas's appointment, embodying a shift from haphazard recruitment of black men by interested parties and independent commanders to a systematic, centrally coordinated recruitment policy, confirmed the change in the War Department's approach. Thomas found skeptics aplenty within the commands of Generals Ulysses S. Grant and William T. Sherman; Sherman, among others, would never be fully convinced.[26] But the Union had made a commitment to arming black men, and growing manpower demands only deepened it. In May 1863, the War Department established the Bureau of Colored Troops to regulate and supervise the enlistment of black soldiers and

---

[24] *Black Military Experience*, docs. 33–35. The grudging compliance of the Democratic governor of New York, Horatio Seymour, was an exception to the rule. (*Black Military Experience*, docs. 38A-C.)

[25] On the extension of recruitment to the occupied South, see *Black Military Experience*, chap. 3. On Adjutant General Thomas's activities, see *Destruction of Slavery*, doc. 110; *Wartime Genesis: Lower South*, chap. 3; *Black Military Experience*, docs. 62, 194; Cornish, *Sable Arm*, chap. 7.

[26] For examples of hostility to black enlistment on the part of federal military officers, see *Black Military Experience*, docs. 39B, 50–51.

the selection of officers to command black regiments.[27] From the spring of 1863 to the end of the war, the federal government labored consistently to maximize the number of black soldiers.

During the summer of 1863, events at home and on the battlefield enlarged the government's commitment to the recruitment of black men. On the war front, Northern military victories at Gettysburg and Vicksburg arrested the Confederate offensive in the North and divided the Confederacy. The Union army's southward march – especially in the Mississippi Valley – stretched supply lines, brought thousands of defenseless ex-slaves under Union protection, and exposed large expanses of occupied territory to Confederate raiders, further multiplying the army's demand for soldiers. On the home front, these new demands sparked violent opposition to federal manpower policies. The Enrollment Act of March 1863 allowed wealthy conscripts to buy their way out of military service by either paying a $300 commutation fee or employing a substitute. Others received hardship exemptions as specified in the act, though political influence rather than genuine need too often determined an applicant's success. Those without money or political influence found the draft especially burdensome.[28] In July, hundreds of New Yorkers, many of them Irish immigrants, angered by the inequities of the draft, lashed out at the most visible and vulnerable symbols of the war: their black neighbors.[29] The riot raised serious questions about the enrollment system and sent Northern politicians scurrying for an alternative to conscription. To even the most politically naive Northerners, the enlistment of black men provided a means to defuse draft resistance at a time when the federal army's need for soldiers was increasing. At the same time, well-publicized battle achievements by black regiments at Port Hudson and Milliken's Bend, Louisiana, and at Fort Wagner, South Carolina, eased popular fears that black men could not fight, mitigated white opposition within

---

[27] *Official Records*, ser. 3, vol. 3, pp. 215–16.   [28] See above, note 19.

[29] Iver Bernstein, *The New York City Draft Riots: Their Significance for American Society and Politics in the Age of the Civil War* (New York, 1990), especially pt. 1; Adrian Cook, *The Armies of the Streets: The New York Draft Riots of 1863* (Lexington, Ky., 1974).

army ranks, and stoked the enthusiasm of both recruiters and black volunteers.

However firm, official commitment to black enlistment did not of itself put black men into uniform. In the Northern free states, where recruiters had full access to the black population, the number of potential recruits was small. According to an estimate by the superintendent of the census, only 46,000 black men of military age resided in those states (see Table 1), so that Northern free blacks alone could not hope to meet the Union's manpower requirements. The largest number of black men within reach of army recruiters resided in the border slave states that had remained in the Union (Maryland, Delaware, Missouri, and Kentucky) and in those parts of the Confederate states occupied by federal forces before the end of 1862 (especially Tennessee and southern Louisiana). But in these areas, which were unaffected by the Emancipation Proclamation or specifically exempted from it, white unionists – many of them slaveholders – raised powerful objections to the recruitment of black men. Fearful for their property, they alternately threatened to desert the Union and claimed unflinching devotion to it in order to prevent the enlistment of slaves, or even free blacks.[30] At first Union policy makers respected such claims, especially while Confederate forces still contended for military control of the states in question. But although the Lincoln administration sought to avoid alienating loyal masters, many of whom carried considerable political weight, it still desperately desired to tap these vast reserves of potential soldiers.

In each border state, and in Tennessee and Louisiana as well, the administration weighed the value of slaveholder unionism against the army's manpower needs. The reading of the scale varied from place to place and time to time depending upon the course of the war, the nature of white unionism, and the viability of slavery. But everywhere slaves, fleeing to Union lines to offer military service in exchange for freedom, shifted the balance against their owners. Often they did so at consider-

---

[30] For examples of objections by unionists, see *Destruction of Slavery*, doc. 168; *Black Military Experience*, docs. 75, 84, 97–98. On the border states, see *Black Military Experience*, chap. 4.

Table 1. *Black Soldiers in the Union Army and Black Male Population of Military Age in 1860, by State*

State	Black male population, ages 18 to 45			Black soldiers	
	Free	Slave	Total	Number credited to the state	Percentage of black men ages 18 to 45
Northern free states					
Maine	272	–	272	104	
New Hampshire	103	–	103	125	
Vermont	140	–	140	120	
Massachusetts	1,973	–	1,973	3,966	
Connecticut	1,760	–	1,760	1,764	
Rhode Island	809	–	809	1,837	
New York	10,208	–	10,208	4,125	
New Jersey	4,866	–	4,866	1,185	
Pennsylvania	10,844	–	10,844	8,612	
District of Columbia[a]	1,823	–	1,823	3,269	
Ohio	7,161	–	7,161	5,092	
Indiana	2,219	–	2,219	1,537	
Illinois	1,622	–	1,622	1,811	
Michigan	1,622	–	1,622	1,387	
Wisconsin	292	–	292	165	
Minnesota	61	–	61	104	
Iowa	249	–	249	440	
Kansas	126	–	126	2,080	
Subtotal				37,723	
Black soldiers recruited in Confederate states but credited to Northern free states[b]				(5,052)	
Total	46,150	–	46,150	32,671	71
Union slave states					
Delaware	3,597	289	3,886	954	25
Maryland	15,149	16,108	31,257	8,718	28
Missouri	701	20,466	21,167	8,344	39
Kentucky	1,650	40,285	41,935	23,703	57
Total	21,097	77,148	98,245	41,719	42
Confederate slave states					
Virginia	9,309	92,119	101,428	5,919[c]	6
North Carolina	5,150	55,020	60,170	5,035	8
South Carolina	1,522	70,798	72,320	5,462	8
Florida	131	12,028	12,159	1,044	9
Georgia	583	83,819	84,402	3,486	4
Alabama	391	83,945	84,336	4,969	6
Mississippi	130	85,777	85,907	17,869	21
Louisiana	3,205	75,548	78,753	24,052	31
Texas	62	36,140	36,202	47	<1
Arkansas	22	23,088	23,110	5,526	24
Tennessee	1,162	50,047	51,209	20,133	39
Subtotal				93,542	
Black soldiers recruited in Confederate states but credited to Northern free states[b]				5,052	
Total	21,667	668,996	689,996	98,594	14
Other areas	2,041[d]	–	2,041	5,991[e]	
Total for all areas	90,955	745,477	836,432	178,975	21

Note: The percentage of each state's black military-age population that entered the army is merely an approximation; fugitive slaves frequently enlisted in regiments outside their home states (the number of black soldiers credited to Kansas and the District of Columbia, for example, was notably swelled by such enlistments), and other population movements make the 1860 census figures somewhat inadequate for comparison with enlistment statistics. Because the early Massachusetts, Connecticut, and Rhode Island black regiments recruited throughout the North, state-by-state computation of population percentages for the free states would be misleading; hence, only a regional percentage is given.

[a] Congress had already ended slavery in the District of Columbia at the time these population figures were compiled.
[b] Enlisted under the act of July 4, 1864, that permitted Northern state agents to recruit black men in the Confederate states. See *Official Records*, ser. 3, vol. 5, p. 662.
[c] Virginia, 5,723; West Virginia, 196.
[d] California, 1,918; Oregon, 38; Colorado, 5; Nebraska, 15; Nevada, 27; New Mexico, 16; Utah, 5; Washington, 17.
[e] Colorado Territory, 95; state or territory unknown, 5,896.
Source: Population figures come from a report by the superintendent of the census, based upon the 1860 census (see *Black Military Experience*, doc. 27); the number of black soldiers credited to each state is given in the 1865 report of the Bureau of Colored Troops (*Official Records*, ser. 3, vol. 5, p. 138).

able risk, for many "loyal" slaveholders would rather have seen their slaves in a shroud than in a uniform. Everywhere slaveholders tried to discourage enlistment by threatening to abuse or sell the families of black volunteers, and then, when that strategy failed, frequently made good the threats.[31] The willingness of slaves to venture all for freedom intertwined the politics of enlistment with the politics of emancipation, and, when military necessity triumphed over political expediency, enlistment effected black freedom in those areas of the South untouched by the liberating provisions of the Emancipation Proclamation.

Military need for laborers also confounded the recruitment of black soldiers. Quartermasters and engineers increasingly depended on black teamsters, dockhands, and laborers to supply Union forces and construct fortifications. The opportunity to remain near family and friends and, frequently, to earn higher and more regular pay made such employment more attractive than uniformed service to many black men. Thus, as the number of available black men shrank, competition between quartermasters and recruiters intensified. Although the War Department resolved the problem differently at different times, this competition shaped black enlistment throughout the war.[32]

As early as the beginning of 1864, enlistment had so undermined slavery in some places that slaveholders who wished to retain a labor force were often compelled to acknowledge the freedom of their slaves in practice, if not in principle. To prevent slave men from running away and joining the Union army, they offered wages and other accouterments of freedom.[33] In such cases, freedom lost its power as an incentive for enlistment, and the slaves' enthusiasm for military service

---

[31] On measures taken to deter border-state black men from enlisting and to punish the families of those who nevertheless did so, see *Destruction of Slavery*, docs. 146, 188, 190–93, 231, 233, 235, 237; *Wartime Genesis: Upper South*, docs. 181, 225A-C, 226, 229; *Black Military Experience*, docs. 74, 88, 90–94, 100–101, 103, 105–7, 294, 296–98, 302–4, 312B.

[32] On federal employment of black military laborers, see *Wartime Genesis: Upper South*; *Wartime Genesis: Lower South*. On the government's "competing with itself" for the labor of black men, see *Wartime Genesis: Upper South*, docs. 217n., 223; *Black Military Experience*, docs. 45–46.

[33] See, for example, *Wartime Genesis: Upper South*, docs. 105, 107, 125, 188, 222; *Black Military Experience*, doc. 96.

waned. Moreover, as the war dragged on, black men, like white, learned that military service entailed considerable suffering, not only for themselves but also for their families. Many who had managed to carve out freedom and earn a living outside the army saw little reason to enlist. When the stream of black volunteers slowed, the army frequently resorted to impressment. Press gangs – sometimes composed of black soldiers – rode roughshod over potential recruits, and conscription often became indistinguishable from kidnapping. Wartime freedom thus acquainted black people with new forms of compulsion.[34]

Black men resisted impressment as they had resisted slavery and often forced Union commanders to modify coercive recruitment practices. Federal policy makers searched for more legitimate means to fill depleted military ranks. In February 1864, Congress revised the much-abused Enrollment Act, eliminating many of its inequities and also making all black men in the Union states – slaves included – subject to the formal procedures of enrollment and conscription.[35] The revised Enrollment Act threatened white Northerners with a draft that could no longer be evaded by paying a commutation fee, even as substitutes were becoming increasingly difficult and expensive to obtain. Citizens' committees and local and state governments offered new and larger bounties to volunteers – white or black – who would fill draft quotas. The Northern states also sought permission to recruit black men in the Confederate states, counting such recruits toward Northern state quotas and paying them sizable bounties. Congress complied in July 1864, and Northern agents spread across the Union-occupied South, indiscriminately enlisting and impressing black men. Many of the new recruits were already in Union employ, and their enlistment infuriated military employers and their superiors.[36] In March 1865, Congress

---

34 On the impressment of black soldiers, see *Wartime Genesis: Upper South*, docs. 75, 79, 106B, 129; *Wartime Genesis: Lower South*, docs. 57, 163, 165, 193; *Black Military Experience*, docs. 6A-B, 47A-C, 52–54C, 56–58, 81–82, 84, 170A-B.
35 *Statutes at Large*, vol. 13, pp. 6–11.
36 For one Northern request to recruit black men in the South, see *Black Military Experience*, doc. 39A. For the legislation authorizing such recruitment, see *Statutes at Large*, vol. 13, pp. 379–80; on recruitment under its provisions, see *Black Military Experience*, pp. 76–78, and doc. 39B.

repealed the enabling legislation,[37] but the problem of impressment remained, and abusive conscription continued to the end of the war.

By the spring of 1865, voluntary enlistment and conscription had placed 179,000 black men in the Union army, forming, together with those black men who served in the navy, nearly 10 percent of those who served in the Northern armed forces.[38] Of this number, approximately 33,000 enlisted in the free states. The border states of Delaware, Maryland, Missouri, and Kentucky accounted for a total of nearly 42,000, more than half from Kentucky. Tennessee contributed 20,000; Louisiana, 24,000; Mississippi, nearly 18,000; and the remaining states of the Confederacy accounted for approximately 37,000 (Table 1).

The participation of black men in the Union army varied from place to place. In some areas nearly every man of military age served, in others hardly any. Everywhere freedom provided the most powerful stimulus to enlistment. In the border states, where slavery remained legal through most of the war (and, in Kentucky and Delaware, even after it ended), a large proportion of black men joined the army. Missouri's share of the Union's black soldiers, for example, was nearly twice the state's proportion of the nation's black men, even without counting fugitive slaves from Missouri who joined the army in neighboring Kansas. In Kentucky, where, beginning in early March 1865, slave volunteers could free not only themselves but also their families,[39] army

---

[37] *Statutes at Large*, vol. 13, p. 491.

[38] According to the most thorough study of the subject, 9,596 black men served in the Union navy during the Civil War, of whom 1,081 came from foreign countries; 3,838 from the free states (including the District of Columbia after 1862); 2,379 from the border slave states (including the District of Columbia in 1861–1862); and 2,298 from the Confederate slave states. Of the border-state black sailors, roughly three-quarters were from Maryland; and of the black sailors from the Confederate states, half came from Virginia. These figures are calculated from David Lawrence Valuska, "The Negro in the Union Navy: 1861–1865" (Ph.D. diss., Lehigh University, 1973), pp. 31, 56–57, 73–74, 83–84, 91–92, 126. For different figures, see Herbert Aptheker, "The Negro in the Union Navy," *Journal of Negro History* 32 (Apr. 1947): 169–200.

[39] On March 3, 1865, by joint resolution, Congress provided for the freedom of the wives and children of all men serving in, or subsequently mustered into, army or navy service. (*Statutes at Large*, vol. 13, p. 571.) For instances of soldiers' relatives claiming freedom under the resolution, see *Destruction of Slavery*, docs. 239, 243; *Wartime Genesis: Upper South*, docs. 222, 237, 240–41; *Black Military Experience*,

service claimed nearly three-fifths of the black men of military age. Only 5 percent of the nation's black men resided in Kentucky at the start of the Civil War, and many had fled to enlist in Northern and Tennessee regiments before recruitment was finally permitted in their home state, yet the black soldiers credited to Kentucky constituted more than 13 percent of the total. However, in areas where the Union army arrived late in the war and freedom derived from the Emancipation Proclamation, few black men enlisted. Although Alabama and Georgia together contained 20 percent of all black men aged eighteen to forty-five, only 5 percent of all black troops enlisted from those states. In Texas, where federal operations began even later and involved only a small part of the state, a token forty-seven black soldiers saw Union service, from a population of more than 36,000 black men of military age. This variety in the black military experience affected the struggle for freedom both during the war and in the years that followed.

Enlistment not only strengthened the bondsman's claim to freedom; it also enhanced the freeman's claim to equality. As free blacks and their abolitionist allies had argued from the beginning of the war, Northern black men welcomed the chance to strike at slavery as a means of acquiring all the rights of citizens. Although the figures do not allow precise calculation, it appears that in many areas of the North proportionately more black men served in the Union army than white men. The Census Office estimated in 1863 that fewer than 10,000 black soldiers would be obtained from the free states if black men enlisted in the same proportion as white men had; yet more than three times that number served in Northern black regiments, an impressive showing even after discounting for the enlistment of some Southern fugitives and Canadian émigrés in the Northern units.[40]

docs. 110, 112. The Militia Act of July 1862 had declared "forever free" the mothers, wives, and children of black men who had belonged to disloyal masters and then rendered service to the United States, but only if the family members were also owned by disloyal masters – a qualification that excluded the families of most border-state black soldiers. (*Statutes at Large*, vol. 12, p. 599.) Both Maryland and Missouri abolished slavery by state action before the March 1865 joint resolution.

[40] See *Black Military Experience*, doc. 27, for the Census Office estimate. An additional 3,800 Northern black men enlisted in the Union navy. (See above, note 38.)

As the North debated the question of enlisting black men in the Union army, a similar discussion took shape in the Southern states. Measured by letters and memorials to the Confederate Secretary of War and other Southern officials, it followed the outline of the Northern debate. Like white Northerners, white Southerners – many of them slaveholders – argued that a "nigger" could stop a bullet as well as a white man; black enlistment would save white lives. Confident of the loyalty of their slaves, some slave owners itched to array slave men against the arrogant Yankees and thus authenticate the South's beneficent view of slavery. Others initially recoiled from the prospect of arming slaves, but their reluctance diminished once the North began recruiting black men. An enemy that stooped to such barbarism, they argued, deserved retaliation in kind. As in the North, wartime necessity added urgency to these arguments, and the call for slave enlistment grew more insistent as Confederate military fortunes deteriorated.

Yet in some important respects, the Southern debate differed sharply from the Northern one. Only a handful of free people of color and virtually no slaves pleaded for a chance to fight for Southern nationality and black bondage. Moreover, the South's decision to arm slaves lagged well behind the North's. Whereas Union officials accepted some slave soldiers in 1862 and began large-scale recruitment in early 1863, Confederate authorities inaugurated slave enlistment only in the desperate spring of 1865, when the war was already lost. Northern and Southern understandings of the implications of black armed service contrasted most dramatically in the combatants' respective positions about enlisting slaves and enlisting free blacks. Although the South countenanced free-black military service long before the North contemplated such a move, the Confederate government's reluctance to interfere with slavery prohibited Southern consideration of arming slaves until long after the North could expediently do so and, indeed, until the whole question had become moot.[41]

---

[41] On the Confederate debate over enlisting black soldiers, see *Black Military Experience*, chap. 5; Robert F. Durden, *The Gray and the Black: The Confederate Debate on Emancipation* (Baton Rouge, La., 1972). On those few free-black soldiers who served the Confederacy early in the war, see the sources cited above, in note 2.

Once enlisted, black soldiers had much in common with Billy Yank or even Johnny Reb. They experienced the same desperate loneliness of men fearful for their lives and separated from family and friends. The same reveille blasted them from their bunks in the morning, and the same tattoo put them to bed at night; the same mosquitoes invaded their tents in the summer, and the same wind whistled through their barracks in the winter. Like white soldiers, they enlisted expecting the glory of great battles but often found themselves wielding shovels rather than rifles. They too grumbled about long hours on the drill-field, complained about overbearing officers, and bemoaned the quality of army rations. And, like soldiers everywhere, they found relief in the camaraderie of the campfire.[42]

Yet, if military life created countless similarities, the seemingly insoluble distinctions between slave and free, black and white nevertheless remained. A white Northern private might boast of fighting for the Union and $13 a month, just as a Southern one might claim he battled for Bobby Lee and his homeland, but few black soldiers could see the war in such narrow terms. Many owed their liberty to military enlistment, and most understood that the freedom of all black people depended upon Union victory. Across the field, behind the hedge, Johnny Reb might spy a money-grubbing Yankee, just as Billy Yank might see a sotted aristocrat, but black soldiers confronted men who had sold their parents, put their sisters in the field, and scarred them with the lash, and who would gladly clap them back into bondage. Knowledge that their own freedom and that of their posterity hung in the balance made black soldiers Union patriots.[43]

The timing and circumstance of their enlistment deepened the black soldiers' commitment to the Union and magnified their expectations

---

[42] On the motivations and experiences of common soldiers during the Civil War, see Bell Irvin Wiley, *The Life of Billy Yank: The Common Soldier of the Union* (Indianapolis, Ind., 1951), and *The Life of Johnny Reb: The Common Soldier of the Confederacy* (Indianapolis, Ind., 1943); Reid Mitchell, *Civil War Soldiers* (New York, 1988); James I. Robertson, Jr., *Soldiers Blue and Gray* (Columbia, S.C., 1988). On camp life among black soldiers, see *Black Military Experience*, chap. 13.

[43] See, for example, *Black Military Experience*, docs. 22, 54D, 207, 218, 299A-B, 300–301.

about the rewards of military service. Entering the war at the Union's ebb, black soldiers came to believe that they had shifted the balance from the Confederate to the Union side. In return, they hoped that their participation would infuse federal emancipation policy with a commitment to equality. Whereas many contemporaries – Southern as well as Northern – shared this understanding of the importance of the entry of black soldiers into the war, only a handful of white Northerners believed that black military service implied a commitment to equality, and then, perhaps, only equality before the law. So if black men celebrated their acceptance into the ranks as a sign of a dramatic alteration of their place in American society, they soon learned that the changes they envisioned came slowly if at all. In fact, instead of speeding black people down the road to equality, federal officials frequently formulated policies that confirmed the established pattern of invidious racial distinctions.

Union policies at all levels shaped the distinctive nature of the black military experience. Many of them sprang effortlessly from the historical legacy of slavery and discrimination. For example, although a few light-skinned black men passed silently into white regiments,[44] no one ever gave serious consideration to placing white and black soldiers in the

[44] One such free-black soldier was Private Charles R. Pratt, a member of the 11th Ohio Infantry. In August 1864, while stationed near Atlanta, Pratt applied for transfer to the black 55th Massachusetts Infantry on the following grounds: "I am a colored man, and my position as private in a white Regiment is very unpleasant. My feelings are constantly outraged by the conduct of those who have no respect for my race." A company commander in another Ohio white regiment, also stationed near Atlanta, petitioned in September 1864 for the transfer of four men of mixed racial origins ("one of them very dark") from his company to an Ohio black regiment. While assuring the Secretary of War that he favored the use of black troops, he contended that "the presence of these men cause great dissatisfaction among the white soldiers and occasion myself a great deal of trouble to keep order and quiet in the company and is I think an injustice both to myself and the men to have them where they now are." The War Department readily complied with both requests. (Priv. Charles R. Pratt to Brig. Genl. L. Thomas, 3 Aug. 1864, P-276 1864, and Lieut. Henry C. Reppert to Hon. E. M. Stanton, 17 Sept. 1864, R-314 1864, both in Letters Received, ser. 360, Colored Troops Division, Records of the Adjutant General's Office, RG 94 [B-55, B-58].) (A bracketed number at the end of a citation is the document's control number in the files of the Freedmen and Southern Society Project.)

same units.[45] More commonly, federal policy respecting black soldiers evolved slowly and painfully against the backdrop of the war's changing fortunes, congressional and administrative politics, and Northern popular opinion. Whatever their origin, these policies touched all aspects of the lives of black soldiers, from their diet to their duties, from their relations with their officers to their relations with their families. But two Union policies proved particularly significant in giving form to the black military experience: excluding black men from commissioned office and paying black soldiers less than their white counterparts. While not necessarily more blatant in intent or effect than other discriminatory actions, these two policies fully revealed the racial inequities of federal military service. They provoked massive protests by black soldiers and their abolitionist allies and captured the attention of the general public. The questions of commissions and pay thus not only set black soldiers apart from white ones, but also encouraged black soldiers to make common cause among themselves. Although they wore the same uniform as white soldiers, observed the same articles of war, answered to the same system of military justice, and confronted the same enemy, black soldiers fought a different war. Because they struggled to end inequality as well as to save the Union, they faced enemies on two fronts, battling against the blue as well as the gray to achieve freedom and equality.

When black soldiers first entered the Union army, the assurances of federal officials – from Secretary of War Stanton to local recruiters – that those who fought under the American flag would enjoy its full protection and benefits blinded all but the most prescient to the question of treatment after enlistment.[46] Thus, the first black soldiers

---

[45] In the Union navy, by contrast, black sailors served on the same ships with white sailors, probably as a result of longstanding seafaring custom. Like their counterparts in the army, however, black sailors filled the lowest ranks. (See Valuska, "Negro in the Union Navy.")

[46] For assurances of equal treatment and protection, see *Wartime Genesis: Lower South*, doc. 57; *Black Military Experience*, docs. 28, 31, 37, 148, 151, 154, 156A-C, 157B, 158A, 158D, 158F, 159–60D, 161, 202, 291. For examples of early doubts of black Northerners about equal treatment within the army, see *The Christian Recorder*, 26 July 1862, 14 Feb. 1863.

recruited in the Sea Islands of South Carolina and the sugar parishes of Louisiana expected to be treated like other soldiers, and at first it appeared they would be. The appointment of black officers did not appear to be an issue in the Sea Islands, where General David Hunter organized the first slave regiment, but the free colored Louisiana Native Guard units, mustered into service by General Benjamin F. Butler, served from the start under officers of their own color. These black officers, almost all free by birth, worldly, and well-educated, had so impressed Butler that he readily offered them commissions in Union ranks. Recognizing the close bonds between the officers and the enlisted men, and anticipating the importance of black commissioned officers for future Union recruitment, Butler also organized a second Louisiana Native Guard regiment, with many black officers selected from men of the first regiment, and had begun recruiting a third, consisting partly of escaped slaves as well as free men of color, when his tenure as department commander ended late in 1862. As manpower shortages and the impressive performance of the Native Guard dispelled Butler's initial skepticism about the military aptitude of black men, his confidence in the ability of black officers grew.[47]

However, Butler's successor, General Nathaniel P. Banks, considered the black officers unfit for command and determined to eliminate them from the service and replace them with white men. Banks devised a variety of stratagems, ranging from formal boards of examination to outright deception, to purge the black commissioned officers. Though a few remained in the three Louisiana Native Guard regiments until mid-1864, Banks's action confirmed War Department skepticism about the advisability of commissioning black officers.[48]

Black Northerners and antislavery proponents of black enlistment like Governor Andrew in Massachusetts and Senator Lane in Kansas also

[47] *Black Military Experience*, p. 305, and doc. 127; Manoj K. Joshi and Joseph P. Reidy, " 'To Come Forward and Aid in Putting Down This Unholy Rebellion': The Officers of Louisiana's Free Black Native Guard during the Civil War Era," *Southern Studies* 21 (Fall 1982): 326–42. On black officers more generally, see *Black Military Experience*, chap. 6.

[48] *Black Military Experience*, pp. 305–7, and docs. 128–32.

assumed that commissioned offices would follow logically upon the admission of black men to armed service. During the summer of 1862, Lane had gone so far as to sign commissions for several black recruiters of his 1st Kansas Colored Volunteers. The War Department, however, silently refused to recognize their validity, reducing Lane's commissions to a hollow promise. Skeptical of the ability of black men to lead and fearful of the reaction of white soldiers to the appointment of black men to superior office, Secretary of War Stanton refused to commission black line officers throughout 1863 and 1864. During this period, black men attained commissioned office only as chaplains and surgeons – positions with the rank of major but outside the chain of command. Even these appointments came grudgingly and were accompanied by a hail of abusive complaints from white officers and enlisted men.[49]

Black people vehemently protested the War Department's exclusionary policies. The free colored former officers of the Louisiana Native Guard spearheaded the protest. They were soon joined by Northern free blacks and their white allies, who believed the appointment of black officers would give talented black men an opportunity to demonstrate the full capabilities of their race.[50] Soldiers in the 54th and 55th Massachusetts Infantry regiments pressed both their officers and Governor Andrew for promotion, and early in 1864 Andrew tested the War Department's determination to exclude black officers. Exercising a governor's authority over troops raised in his state, Andrew offered a lieutenancy to Sergeant Stephen A. Swails, an educated, light-skinned freeman who had compiled an exemplary military record. When the War Department blocked Andrew's action, Swails and others barraged federal authorities with demands for a favorable ruling. As the protest mounted, the battlefield valor of black soldiers, especially noncommissioned officers, steadily eroded the department's position. The combined pressure of black soldiers and Northern abolitionists weakened

---

[49] On Andrew and Lane, see *Black Military Experience*, pp. 44–45, 304–5, and docs. 14–15, 134–36, 161. On black chaplains and surgeons, see *Black Military Experience*, pp. 309–10, and docs. 144–47; Edwin S. Redkey, "Black Chaplains in the Union Army," *Civil War History* 33 (Dec. 1987): 331–50.

[50] *Black Military Experience*, docs. 129–32, 134A-B, 139–40.

the opposition to black officers. When a long list of prominent Republican politicians added their approval early in 1865, the War Department agreed to commission Swails.[51] Yet, even with the end of the war in sight, the department resisted wholesale appointment of black officers and succeeded in confining their number to a mere handful and restricting their service to a few – mostly Northern – regiments. Indeed, most black officers received their commissions after the cessation of hostilities and served as officers only briefly before their regiments were mustered out.[52]

The pay they received also distinguished black soldiers from their white counterparts.[53] Believing the assurances of the early army recruiters and recruitment broadsides, black enlistees assumed that they would receive the same remuneration as white soldiers. But the War Department ruled that the legal basis for black military service lay in the 1862 Militia Act and paid all black soldiers according to its provisions: $10 per month, minus $3 for clothing, rather than the $13 per month, plus clothing, that white privates received. Even black commissioned and noncommissioned officers received the same $7 monthly pay, so that the highest-ranking black officer earned barely half the compensation of the lowest-ranking white enlisted man.[54]

Unequal pay angered black soldiers as perhaps no other Union policy did. The reduced income imposed a severe strain on families dependent upon black soldiers for their support, but the principle mattered at least as much. Black men in the army, those recruiting soldiers, and those contemplating enlistment, as well as their advocates in the antislavery movement, attacked the discriminatory pay policy as yet another vestige of second-class citizenship. Led by black soldiers recruited

[51] *Black Military Experience*, docs. 141A-C.
[52] *Black Military Experience*, pp. 308, 310–12.
[53] On federal pay policies and the struggle of black soldiers for equal pay, see *Black Military Experience*, chap. 7, and docs. 199, 202; Herman Belz, "Law, Politics, and Race in the Struggle for Equal Pay during the Civil War," *Civil War History* 22 (Sept. 1976): 197–222; Cornish, *Sable Arm*, pp. 181–96; McPherson, *Negro's Civil War*, chap. 14.
[54] For the pay provisions of the Militia Act, see *Statutes at Large*, vol. 12, p. 599. For the pay allotted white soldiers of various ranks, see U.S. War Department, *Revised United States Army Regulations* (Washington, 1863), pp. 358–63.

in the free states and encouraged by sympathetic white officers, several regiments refused to accept the $7 monthly pittance, regarding it as an affront to their dignity as American soldiers. Rather than submit to inferior treatment some went more than a year without pay. The 54th and 55th Massachusetts regiments even refused Governor Andrew's offer to use state funds to increase their compensation to the amount white privates received. In the meantime, they fought and died, dug fortifications and fell ill, and fumed at the progressive impoverishment of their families.[55] In late 1863, the protest boiled over in open revolt. Black soldiers in the 3rd South Carolina Infantry, led by Sergeant William Walker, stacked their arms and refused to perform duty until the army granted equal pay. Walker's superiors charged him with mutiny and executed him as an example to other black protesters.[56] But Walker's death did not stem the protest. Instead, black soldiers stationed in other parts of the South began to agitate for change. Many teetered on the brink of mutiny until Congress passed an act equalizing the pay of black and white soldiers in June 1864.[57]

The War Department's inability to sustain its guarantees of equal treatment provoked no less fury than its overtly discriminatory practices. Confederate refusal to accord captured black soldiers the rights due prisoners of war demanded that Union policy makers ensure black soldiers the protection of the flag. Although numerous Union commanders, from regimental officers to President Lincoln, declared their readiness to retaliate in kind if the Confederates acted on their threat to hang or enslave black prisoners, enforcing federal policy proved difficult. Even the most unambiguous evidence – such as the Confederate slaughter of black soldiers after the surrender of Fort Pillow, Tennessee – never seemed proof enough for most Union officials. The reluctance, if not refusal, of federal officers to make good their promise of retaliation meant that black soldiers faced dangers white ones seldom encountered. This special vulnerability of black soldiers marked another distinctive aspect of the black military experience. Knowing

---

[55] *Black Military Experience*, pp. 364–67, and docs. 153–58A, 159–60.
[56] *Black Military Experience*, docs. 158A-F.
[57] For the law, see *Statutes at Large*, vol. 13, pp. 129–30.

that death or enslavement might follow capture, they fought all the more desperately for the Union. Knowing that the federal government offered them less protection than their white comrades, they remained alienated from the Union for which they fought and pressed for equal protection.[58]

Other distinguishing features of black military life arose from neither explicit policy decisions nor their haphazard enforcement but from the unspoken assumptions of American race relations. Dealings between black soldiers and their officers generally followed the familiar pattern of white superiors and black subordinates and thus carried all the historic burdens of white-black relationships in the United States. But the diverse expectations both black soldiers and white officers brought to soldiering complicated the traditional pattern of American race relations still further. As committed abolitionists, some white officers volunteered to lead black troops as a means of demolishing racial stereotypes and fulfilling their own egalitarian vision. Glorying in the epithet "nigger officers," they befriended their men and promoted their cause. Other white officers accepted positions in black regiments only in quest of rapid advancement. They cared nothing for the cause of freedom or racial equality and despised their men all the more because of the stigma attached to serving with black soldiers.[59]

Few white officers of black regiments exhibited all the characteristics of either the abolitionist or the careerist; instead they combined attitudes derived from the two seemingly contradictory positions. At each extreme, white officers exercised command in a variety of ways. Moreover, since black soldiers responded to their officers with similar diversity, the relationship between white officers and black soldiers defies easy categorization. If some black soldiers found support and comfort serving under men of antislavery conviction, others found the well-

---

[58] On black prisoners of war, see *Black Military Experience*, chap. 12; Cornish, *Sable Arm*, chap. 9. On the Fort Pillow massacre, see *Black Military Experience*, docs. 214A-C; John Cimprich and Robert C. Mainfort, Jr., eds., "Fort Pillow Revisited: New Evidence about an Old Controversy," *Civil War History* 28 (Dec. 1982): 293–306.

[59] On the white officers of black regiments, see *Black Military Experience*, chap. 8; Cornish, *Sable Arm*, chap. 11; Glatthaar, *Forged in Battle*, especially chaps. 2–3.

meaning paternalism of abolitionist officers more distasteful than the simple contempt of racist commanders. Black soldiers resented being treated like children no less than being treated like chattel. But whatever the specific pattern of relationships, the fact that the line of command within black regiments generally coincided with the color line added still another distinguishing element to black military life.[60]

The complex pattern of Union policies, their irregular enforcement, and the unspoken assumptions that stood behind them touched all aspects of black military life. In addition to influencing relations between enlisted men and their officers, the treatment they could expect if captured, the pay they received, and their prospects for promotion from the ranks, federal policies affected the nature of military justice and discipline, the care afforded sick and wounded soldiers, and the food, clothing, and equipment issued to healthy ones. Taken together, the policies of the federal government sensitized black soldiers to any act that might be deemed discriminatory. In such a context, racially innocent actions inexorably acquired racial meaning. The harsh discipline white officers meted out to black subordinates may in many instances have differed little from their punishment of white inferiors. In the eyes of former slaves, however, a white man striking or publicly humiliating a black man conveyed an unambiguous image of slavery. Just as white officers instituted policies based upon their understanding of racial differences, black soldiers protested perceived abuses.[61]

The timing of their entry into the Union army, like their antebellum experience and their subjection to discriminatory Union policies, guaranteed that black soldiers would view the war differently than white soldiers. By the middle of 1863, when a significant number of black troops took the field for the first time, white soldiers had been battling the rebels for more than two years. Many of them had grown disenchanted with a war that seemed to have no end, and a considerable

---

[60] On relations between black soldiers and their officers, see *Black Military Experience*, chaps. 8–9, and docs. 176, 178, 181–83, 187, 199, 240; Glatthaar, *Forged in Battle*, especially chaps. 4–6.

[61] On military discipline and punishment, see *Black Military Experience*, chap. 9, and docs. 336, 341; Glatthaar, *Forged in Battle*, chap. 6.

number evinced little sympathy for changing Union war aims –
particularly emancipation. Black soldiers rarely shared this estrange-
ment, however disillusioned they might have been by some aspects of
federal policy. Having struggled for the right to bear arms in defense of
their country, they were eager to strike a blow against the slaveholding
South. Whereas many white soldiers wearied as the war dragged on,
the enthusiasm of black soldiers grew with the Union's commitment to
freedom and to the effort – however feeble and reluctant – to eliminate
the most glaring racial inequities from military life.

The timing of their entry into the army affected black soldiers in other
ways as well. The war made different demands on Union soldiers after
1863 than before. By the time black soldiers took the field, Confederate
forces had been swept from the Mississippi Valley and parts of the
Atlantic seaboard. With their removal, the Union army required large
bodies of troops to secure the vast expanse of the occupied South and to
protect its lengthening supply lines. No matter who composed the federal army after 1863, thousands of Union soldiers would be guarding
railroad bridges and telegraph lines, manning artillery stations, constructing fortifications, and protecting contraband camps. That black
men entered the war just at the moment Union manpower needs took a
new form determined much of the course of black military service.

Could they fight? The question haunted the debate over black enlistment and followed black soldiers into the army. Black soldiers longed
for the opportunity to test their mettle on the field of battle and thus
resolve lingering doubts about their manhood and demonstrate their
worthiness for full citizenship. However, the Union army needed large
numbers of soldiers to do everything but fight. That need comple-
mented the widespread belief that black men could handle shovels
better than guns and that, as the Emancipation Proclamation suggested, black soldiers should serve mainly to relieve white ones for
front-line duty. In many instances, black soldiers found themselves
serving as nothing more than uniformed laborers.[62]

---

[62] On black soldiers and fatigue duty, see *Black Military Experience*, chap. 10. See also
Wartime Genesis: Upper South, docs. 100, 218, 223, 230; *Black Military Experience*,
docs. 62, 154, 265, 294, 314E.

Heavy fatigue duty wore out clothing as quickly as it wore down bodies. When black soldiers exhausted their $3 monthly clothing allowance, quartermasters deducted the cost of additional clothing from their $7 monthly pay, thus salting the wound of discriminatory pay. Long days of fatigue duty strung end to end sapped the morale of black soldiers, and insufficient drill compromised their military efficiency. Both they and their officers, including many antislavery champions of black enlistment, protested discriminatory labor assignments that neither military strategy nor the dignity of Union service seemed to warrant. But if they protested, they could lift but an enfeebled voice in search of public sympathy, and if black soldiers threatened mutiny, they were often too tired even to stack their arms, let alone raise them. Finally, in the face of overwhelming evidence of injustice, the most damning of which was the disproportionately high morbidity afflicting black soldiers, in June 1864 Adjutant General Thomas banned excessive fatigue duty for black troops and required that their assignments to labor details be proportionate to those of their white comrades. Many commanders ignored the order and continued to work black soldiers more like beasts of burden than national defenders, but eventually General Thomas's order established a norm.[63]

Just as Union policies and the course of the war distinguished the lives of black soldiers from those of white ones, so they fractured the black military experience in a variety of ways. Black soldiers brought diverse experiences and expectations to soldiering. Some had grown up in cities, attended schools taught by prominent clergymen, traveled widely, and enjoyed freedom for generations. Others had come from the insular, tightly circumscribed world of the plantation and knew little of life beyond the slave quarter. Some entered military service as young men, hardly more than children; others joined the army late in life and had children of their own. Whether black soldiers had been free men or slaves, Northerners or Southerners, artisans or field hands, whether they had been raised among the black majority of the Carolina lowcountry or

---

[63] For protests by black soldiers and their officers against excessive and disproportionate fatigue duty, see *Black Military Experience*, docs. 198–200, 202, 204–5B, 205D-E, 206. For Thomas's order, see *Black Military Experience*, doc. 201.

the white majority of the Northern states – all these circumstances in some measure influenced the course of black military life. Such diversity shaped the reactions of black soldiers to Union policies and affected their implementation. Free blacks, who were generally better educated and more cosmopolitan than slaves, marched into military service with different hopes and aspirations. Although black soldiers who had just escaped bondage may well have seen military service as payment for their freedom – as many Union officials suggested – those who had been free before the war saw little personal gain in the reward of liberty. The inequities of black military life thus seemed particularly galling to those black soldiers who had been free. Not surprisingly, they led demands for commissioned office and monopolized those ranks after Union policy changed. Brandishing a protest tradition generations in the making and mobilizing their connections with white antislavery advocates, they initiated complaints about federal pay policies and other inequities within the army. Although soldiers who had been slaves joined these protests and initiated still others, the free-black regiments generally took the lead. However, regiments composed of former slaves appear to have resorted to direct action – Sergeant Walker's mutiny, for example – more often than did the former freemen, perhaps because former slaves enjoyed less complete mastery of the mechanism of formal petitioning or less confidence in its efficacy.

Differences among black soldiers extended beyond the mechanics of protest to the sources of grievance. Lack of sensitivity to distinctions among black men frequently left white officers mystified at the variety of reactions to the same policies. When commissary officers altered the diet of black soldiers to include more pork and corn bread, Southern-born soldiers welcomed the change, but their Northern-born comrades, accustomed to beef and wheat bread, complained bitterly.[64] In ways similar if not as dramatic, cultural differences between those who practiced skilled trades and enjoyed literacy and those who lacked skills or education affected the deployment of black soldiers and their relations with their officers and their fellow soldiers. Even within slave regi-

[64] *Black Military Experience*, docs. 263, 267, 273.

ments, artisans, house servants, and other privileged bondsmen provided the bulk of the noncommissioned officers. The structure of the black community shaped the structure of black military life. Occasionally, physiological differences supplemented cultural ones. Like white men, black men raised in different disease environments had developed different immunities, so that for some black soldiers assignment to subtropical regions confirmed commonplace stereotypes about the ability of black people to survive in such areas, whereas for others it inevitably spelled disaster.[65]

Although the changing nature of the war consigned many black soldiers to labor and support duties, it sent others into fierce confrontations with the enemy. Again, the time and place of enlistment, the skills and knowledge black men brought to soldiering, the personal temperament and political influence of particular commanders, and the Union army's need for front-line troops all helped determine who would fight and how they would fight. From the moment black soldiers entered the war, politically potent abolitionist proponents of black enlistment pressed the War Department and army field officers to send black soldiers against the enemy to demonstrate that black men could and would stand up to the master class. At Port Hudson, Milliken's Bend, and Fort Wagner, black soldiers quickly proved that battlefield heroics knew no color line. But even after they had established their martial credentials, black soldiers did not all enjoy the same opportunity to confront Confederate forces. Because of their earlier entry into the war and their abolitionist connections, units composed disproportionately of Louisiana and Northern freemen played a large role in the early battles, as did the first slave soldiers recruited in South Carolina and Louisiana. In the years that followed, the considerable reputations of these first regiments, as well as their strategic locations, continued to thrust them into combat. Other black regiments, organized later and in different political and military circumstances, rarely engaged the enemy. In the Mississippi Valley, for example, most black soldiers saw little fighting, in some measure because Union troops had already se-

---

[65] On the health of black soldiers, see *Black Military Experience*, chap. 15, and doc. 205F.

cured the region but also because many of the region's commanders remained skeptical of the military abilities of black men.

Nonetheless, the changing course of the war could deprive even skeptical commanders of the luxury of excluding black men from battle and could put black soldiers face to face with the enemy. In the final grueling operations of the eastern theater, General Ulysses S. Grant summoned every available Union soldier to assault the Confederate strongholds in Virginia. Grant's armies included the largest concentration of black troops engaged at any time during the war, most of them eventually organized into the Union army's only all-black army corps. In the trenches before Richmond and Petersburg, black soldiers, like white ones, dug earthworks, held the Union lines, pressed the rebel defenses, and at long last participated in the triumphant march into the capital of the vanquished Confederacy. Thus by war's end nearly all black soldiers had received a taste of combat, though even then the course of the war continued to determine how they fought.[66]

For the men who fought, the Civil War was a momentous event that molded their lives and those of their descendants in countless ways. It elevated some to new heights of glory and power, propelling them into political and entrepreneurial careers. It shattered others. The thousands of limbless men found in all corners of America long after the shooting stopped provided grim reminders of the war's continuing impact. For generations after the war ended, the outcome of the struggle determined the social relations, economic standing, and political allegiance of millions of Americans. That emancipation accompanied enlistment for most black soldiers heightened the impact of military service on black life. Because so many black soldiers simultaneously achieved freedom and reached maturity, the military experience took on an even larger meaning for the men, their families, their communities, and, ultimately, the entire society.

[66] On the combat experience of black soldiers, see *Black Military Experience*, chap. 11, and docs. 163, 276B; Cornish, *Sable Arm*, chaps. 8, 13, and pp. 240–43, 258–60; Glatthaar, *Forged in Battle*, chaps. 7–8.

Soldiering provided black men with more than legal freedom. In dramatic and undeniable ways military service countered the degradation that had undermined black self-esteem during the antebellum years. Battlefield confrontations with the slaveholding enemy exhilarated black soldiers by demonstrating in the most elemental manner the essential equality of men. But nothing more fully reveals the revolutionary impact of soldiering on black life than the transit of black men from slaves to liberators. In smashing the manacles that bound their people, black soldiers elevated themselves and transformed their own consciousness. In their own eyes, in the eyes of the black community, and, however reluctantly, in the eyes of the nation, black men gained a new standing by donning the Union blue and participating in the nation's great triumph.[67]

A good deal of the liberating force of the black military experience derived not from monumental battles or stark confrontation with bondage but from military routine. Black soldiers savored the dignity of standing picket, with the power to challenge all trespassers, whatever their race or rank. As participants in foraging parties, they witnessed the futile anger of former masters who lost their slaves, their crops, their livestock, and even their homes to the claims of "military necessity." They gained a new sense of their own place in society while guarding captured Confederate soldiers, whose dejected demeanor and powerless situation contrasted markedly with former boasts of racial superiority and military invincibility. Even the most mundane activities — the mastery of the manual of arms, the deployment of large, complicated weapons, and the execution of complex evolutions — provided new sources of pride and accomplishment.

Beyond the battlefield and the drillfield, military service transformed the lives of black soldiers. As slaves or even freemen, black men had generally viewed the world through a narrow lens. As soldiers, they traveled broadly, met a wider variety of people, and expanded their range of experience. More important, black soldiers had occasion to see

---

[67] On the postbellum significance of wartime military service, see *Black Military Experience*, chaps. 17–18; *Destruction of Slavery*, doc. 244.

the world from positions of dominance as well as subordination. Although they continued to answer to higher authority, black soldiers frequently found themselves in circumstances where they alone commanded the field. Their new knowledge and authority burst the bonds of subservience bred by slavery and second-class citizenship. Soldiering thus granted black men far greater control over their own destiny and fostered a new self-confidence.

Skills and knowledge gained in military service enlarged this new self-confidence. Army schools offered black soldiers access to the printed word, an opportunity legally denied slaves and even some black freemen before the war. Black soldiers, like freedpeople generally, rushed to take advantage of book learning. Literacy not only allowed black soldiers to communicate with their families and advance into the noncommissioned ranks, but also provided the means to petition against injustice and to articulate their vision of the new world of freedom. Education in the army advanced along other lines as well. Regimental chaplains tutored black soldiers in a variety of subjects, practical as well as moral. Although many chaplains filtered their message through a brand of religious paternalism that the soldiers found unpalatable, lectures on everything from sanitary procedures to the Constitution of the United States enlarged the world of men long kept ignorant of such subjects and encouraged them to widen their intellectual horizons. In many regiments, black soldiers joined together to build schools, to hire teachers, and to form literary and debating societies.[68]

The struggle for equality within the Union army also taught important lessons. Not only did congressional provision of equal pay and the War Department's tardy acquiescence on the question of commissioning black officers stir optimism about eventual equality, but the struggle itself awakened men previously excluded from the political process to the possibilities of redressing their grievances, informed them of the

---

[68] *Black Military Experience*, chap. 14, and docs. 145A, 169, 274, 334, 342; John W. Blassingame, "The Union Army as an Educational Institution for Negroes, 1862–1865," *Journal of Negro Education* 34 (Spring 1965): 152–59; Dudley Taylor Cornish, "The Union Army as a School for Negroes," *Journal of Negro History* 37 (Oct. 1952): 368–82.

means by which their goals might be achieved, and identified the federal government as a forum for obtaining justice. Northern free blacks had a long tradition of political protest, and they drew on it freely. But the tactics pioneered by Northern freemen passed quickly to slave soldiers, most of whom had no formal political experience. Before long, regiments composed of newly liberated slaves petitioned and protested with all the skill and tenacity of those whose members were freeborn, demanding that the government they fought to preserve accord them and their families the dignity and protection due to all its citizens. In so doing, former slaves learned something about the system of government under which Americans lived. They came to understand that justice depended not on the favor of a single powerful individual, but on impersonal rules and regulations that governed all citizens. Even though some army officers played the petty tyrant and others willingly countenanced such autocratic behavior, behind their arbitrary actions stood a forest of regulations that ruled military life. In learning how to deal with abstract law as well as personal authority, previously enslaved black soldiers took their first steps as free men. And in the process, they not only asserted their claim to citizenship, but also broke down the barriers that distinguished freemen and bondsmen and thereby unified the black community as never before.[69]

Military service also offered some black soldiers opportunities for advancement that far exceeded those available during the antebellum years. Although the War Department balked at commissioning black officers until late in the war, it had no objection to the appointment of black men to the noncommissioned ranks. Indeed, the difficulties inherent in balancing the often antagonistic interests of officers and enlisted men in a highly charged racial atmosphere encouraged Union officials to turn this task over to selected black soldiers. Standing between the largely white officer corps and the black privates, black sergeants and corporals played a role similar to that of a factory foreman or even an antebellum slave driver. Although they enjoyed a considerable measure

---

[69] On black soldiers' experience with military law and justice, see *Black Military Experience*, chap. 9.

of power, their authority was never large enough to satisfy either those below or those above them in rank. Their responsibilities for assignment and discipline frequently alienated black enlisted men without gaining the approbation of white officers. But because black noncommissioned officers camped with the other enlisted men and shared their daily routine, as well as so many other common experiences, they generally gained the trust of the men they led. Black soldiers frequently took their problems and grievances to their sergeants and corporals, who in turn presented them to higher authorities. Advocacy of this kind exacted a toll, as rebuffs brought reduction in rank or other punishments. But black noncommissioned officers – along with the few commissioned ones – generally gained in stature from their wartime service and transferred their positions of leadership to civilian life when the war ended.[70]

The black military experience affected many black people who never wore the Union uniform. From the moment of enlistment, military service altered the lives of black soldiers' families. In some places, enlistment ensured their safety and secured their freedom. In the border states, where slavery was unimpeached by the Emancipation Proclamation, the enlistment of husbands and fathers established the only claim to liberty for many soldiers' families. Elsewhere, black soldiers guarded contraband camps and Union-held plantations to prevent Confederate raiders from recapturing and reenslaving loved ones. But the same act of enlistment that provided protection for some black families encouraged the abuse and confinement of others. Angry masters who vowed to take revenge upon women and children whose husbands, sons, and fathers dared to enlist had little compunction about making good their threats.[71]

[70] For examples of black noncommissioned officers serving as advocates for lower-ranking enlisted men, see *Black Military Experience*, docs. 153–54, 157A, 158C-D, 175, 180, 189, 190A, 248, 268.

[71] On black soldiers' families, see in particular *Black Military Experience*, chap. 16. For claims to freedom based upon the enlistment of husbands, sons, and fathers, see, for example, *Destruction of Slavery*, docs. 239, 243; *Wartime Genesis: Upper South*, docs. 222, 237, 240–41; *Black Military Experience*, docs. 110, 112. On the abuse of family members, see the sources cited above, in note 31.

After enlistment, the experience of black soldiers continued to shape the lives of those who remained behind. The questions of equal pay and protection, which appeared in the guise of abstract justice to interested white people, touched the wives and children of black soldiers in a direct and immediate manner. After all, the treatment accorded black prisoners was a matter of life and death, and the difference between $7 and $13 per month was the difference between subsistence and starvation for many black families. By the same token, the impoverished condition of families left at home or liable to abuse by Confederate guerrillas or former masters influenced the conduct of black soldiers. Nothing more surely moved them to protest than news of the material hardship or physical suffering of their families.[72]

Because black men served as soldiers and black women did not, military service created important differences in the way they experienced the war and emancipation. Army life exposed black men to the rigors of the march and the perils of battle, but it also incorporated them into an institution whose power and sovereignty dramatically superseded that of the slaveholders. When black women met the slaveholding enemy, they only occasionally did so under direct military auspices; as, for example, when General Edward A. Wild handed three slave women a whip and invited them to settle scores with their master. If armed service, in all its various aspects, helped liberate black men from the narrow confines of bondage and second-class citizenship, black women enjoyed no comparable experience. Whatever changes the war brought to women's lives, they rarely equaled the dramatic elevation in status that accompanied military duty. At the heart of that elevated status, moreover, lay a portrayal of black men as the liberators and defenders of their people. One recruitment order particularly solicited "[m]en of family" because, in protecting contraband camps, "they will, as soldiers, be guarding their own firesides." As mothers, wives, sisters, and sweethearts of men who fought for the Union and as the

---

[72] On the poverty endured by soldiers' families, much of it resulting from the paucity and irregularity of military pay, see *Black Military Experience*, docs. 154–55, 156C, 157A, 158B, 160A, 160E, 170A, 271, 290–94, 314D-E, 315A-B, 338–39, 341. See also *Destruction of Slavery*, doc. 231.

beneficiaries of their military triumph, black women identified fully with the contributions of black soldiers to the struggle for freedom. Yet that very identification – the celebration of black soldiers as liberators – widened the social distance between men and women.[73]

The accomplishments of black soldiers reverberated beyond the family circle. Black soldiers eagerly bore the news of emancipation. In carrying freedom's sword, they demonstrated that liberty was as much the product of the black man's valor as it was the white man's gift. Slaves understood this, and they welcomed black soldiers with special enthusiasm. Fugitives followed the soldiers' line of march, bondsmen and women fearful of their owners' wrath sought refuge with black regiments, and everywhere crowds of black men, women, and children lined the roads to cheer. Besides bearing the message of liberty, black soldiers also aided the passage of black people from slavery to freedom in countless practical ways. They informed freedpeople of their newly won rights, tutored them in the nuances of federal policy, and elaborated on the opportunities that liberty offered. Although the message they carried – like the rumored possibility of land – often proved to be an empty promise, it encouraged freedpeople to press their former owners and, indeed, their new Yankee rulers in ways that expanded freedom.[74]

Black people everywhere rallied to the support of their sable arm. Associations to aid sick and wounded soldiers and to provide for the widows and orphans of the fallen sprang up throughout the North and liberated South.[75] Whether formerly enslaved or freeborn, black civilians welcomed black soldiers into their homes and onto the podium at

[73] For the episode in which Wild invited the slave women to whip their master, see *Destruction of Slavery*, doc. 16. For the recruitment order, see *Wartime Genesis: Upper South*, doc. 205n.

[74] See, for example, *Black Military Experience*, docs. 316–18, 324–25.

[75] Louisville, Kentucky, had at least three such associations: the Louisville Colored Ladies' Soldiers Aid Society, apparently affiliated with the Methodist church; the Colored Soldiers Aid Society of the Fifth Street Baptist Church; and the Soldiers Aid Society of the Green Street Baptist Church. See *Louisville Daily Union Press*, 7, 9, 17, and 30 Jan. 1865. For a similar association in Washington, D.C., see *Second Annual Report, of the Freedmen and Soldiers' Relief Association . . .* (Washington, 1864).

public meetings and celebrations. They took pride in the martial accomplishments of black soldiers and shared the indignities they suffered at the hands of federal policy makers. The black and abolitionist press provided an important link between soldiers and the larger community. Reports from black soldiers, mostly chaplains and noncommissioned officers, filled newspaper columns in the free states and the occupied South. They not only provided news of the whereabouts of black units for concerned families and friends, but also told tales of black soldiers in mortal combat with the slaveholding enemy, thereby allowing the larger black community to share in the destruction of slavery. The press publicized and criticized discriminatory Union policies, bringing to the home front the issues of unequal pay, the refusal to commission black officers, and the abuse of black prisoners of war.[76] By counterposing black soldiers' battlefield heroics to the inequities of military life, black leaders put soldiering to work in the struggle for equal rights. After 1863, calls for the end of discrimination rarely failed to mention the importance of black soldiers in defending the Union. Thus for practical as well as emotional reasons, the military experience drew the black community together. Along with emancipation itself, victories on the issues of equal pay and black officers fueled the optimism and sharpened the political consciousness of all black people. Although most black men would not be enfranchised until several years after the war ended, their participation in the politics of reconstruction began with enlistment in the Union army.[77]

The black military experience imparted more than unalloyed optimism. Heroism and self-sacrifice inspired some black soldiers, but the appalling carnage, the inequities of military life, and the equivocal commitment of federal officials to black advancement left others disillu-

[76] See, for example, *The Christian Recorder*, New York *Anglo-African*, *Douglass' Monthly*, New Orleans *Tribune*, Beaufort *Free South*, *National Anti-Slavery Standard*, and *The Liberator*. See also James Henry Gooding, *On the Altar of Freedom: A Black Soldier's Civil War Letters from the Front*, ed. Virginia Matzke Adams (Amherst, Mass., 1991); R. J. M. Blackett, ed., *Thomas Morris Chester, Black Civil War Correspondent: His Dispatches from the Virginia Front* (Baton Rouge, La., 1989).

[77] *Black Military Experience*, docs. 362–63, 367; McPherson, *Negro's Civil War*, chaps. 18–19.

sioned. The experience of black soldiers warned black people that, at best, the Yankees were unreliable allies whose interests only occasionally coincided with those of the black community. The frequent failure of army officers to correct transparent injustices and their willingness to reject the most heart-rending protests on the cold ground of military necessity left black soldiers and civilians alike more distrustful than confident about the white man's army and the white man's government. While this disillusionment estranged some from the political process, it hardened others to the struggle still ahead and deepened their determination to press on. In either case, such attitudes reflected a new sophistication, an understanding that, as in slave times, black people would have to keep their own counsel, that even in the moment of triumph nothing would come easily, and that political victories often cost as much as military ones.

The influence of soldiering on black life did not end when the shooting stopped. If anything, its importance grew. Many black soldiers remained in uniform as part of the Union army of occupation, and they continued to advise freedpeople on the new demands of freedom and the workings of the world beyond the plantation. Their presence, especially when commanded by sympathetic white officers, helped to limit violence against freedpeople and to prevent newly returned Confederate veterans from riding roughshod over defenseless former slaves. Military service also provided a steppingstone to leadership in the black community. With wartime responsibilities behind them, black soldiers often became deeply involved in the black communities where they were stationed. Some took wives from among the local population and fully entered local community life, thereby fusing the experience of the liberator and the liberated. Drawing on their martial experience and the confidence it engendered, black soldiers framed the aspirations of many of the newly freed and also helped reconstruct the black community's institutions to meet the demands of freedom. They frequently took the lead in establishing schools, building churches, and founding fraternal societies. In the first political conventions held by black people following the war, soldiers played a prominent part. By standing armed and ready to aid black people, and by bringing knowledge and confidence to their communities, black soldiers remained significant figures after emancipation.[78]

In much the same way that the liberating impact of the black military experience radiated from black soldiers and their families into the larger black community, so it spread into white society as well. Abolitionist officers, many of whom had led the fight for black enlistment, provided the most important agents of the dissemination of a new racial liberality. Standing with black soldiers through the war and, in some quarters, suffering from identification with black troops, their commitment to equality inside the army deepened their commitment to equality in American society generally. Many remained in the South as Freedmen's Bureau agents, Republican politicians, and schoolteachers. Others who returned to the North joined with black men, including many who had served under their command, to form a nub of consistent support for racial equality within the Republican party. They attacked second-class citizenship within American society just as they had attacked it in the army. Pointing to the contribution of black soldiers in preserving the Union, they helped roll back the color line in the Northern states and urged a radical reconstruction of the defeated Confederacy.[79]

White Northerners in growing numbers became convinced that the service of black soldiers on behalf of the Union entitled them to partici-

---

[78] On black soldiers in the postwar army of occupation, see *Black Military Experience*, chap. 17; Glatthaar, *Forged in Battle*, chap. 10. On their participation in post-emancipation political meetings, which routinely insisted that the wartime service of black soldiers entitled black men to full political rights, see Philip S. Foner and George E. Walker, eds., *Proceedings of the Black State Conventions, 1840–1865*, 2 vols. (Philadelphia, 1979–80), vol. 2, pp. 242–304, and virtually all the meetings included in Philip S. Foner and George E. Walker, eds., *Proceedings of the Black National and State Conventions, 1865–1900*, 1 vol. to date (Philadelphia, 1986-), vol. 1. On the role of black veterans in postbellum politics more generally, see Eric Foner, *Reconstruction: America's Unfinished Revolution* (New York, 1988), pp. 9–10, 112–19; Glatthaar, *Forged in Battle*, pp. 248–51; Leon F. Litwack, *Been in the Storm So Long: The Aftermath of Slavery* (New York, 1979), chap. 10.

[79] See, for example, the postwar writings of two white officers of black regiments: Norwood P. Hallowell, *The Meaning of Memorial Day* (Boston, 1896); Thomas J. Morgan, *The Negro in America and the Ideal American Republic* (Philadelphia, 1898). See also Glatthaar, *Forged in Battle*, pp. 257–60.

pate formally in governing the reconstructed Confederate states. In the spring of 1864, while nudging conservative Louisiana unionists into a position more consonant with changing congressional sentiment, President Lincoln singled out former soldiers as one category of black men who might be granted the suffrage. In the years that followed, others — whether resisting more extensive changes in the racial status quo or urging still greater ones — drew upon the wartime service of black men to make similar arguments. The black military experience thus expanded and deepened the nation's commitment to equal rights.[80]

Perhaps no one more fully understood the role black soldiers played in inflating the aspirations and enlarging the opportunities of black people than did members of the old master class. Even when they admitted that black soldiers acquitted themselves in an impeccable manner, former slaveholders complained bitterly about the unsettling influence of black troops on the old pattern of subordination. Once freedpeople came in contact with black troops, they deferred less readily and labored less willingly. By their presence as well as their words and actions, black soldiers convinced former slaves and former masters alike that the old world was gone forever.[81]

As black soldiers and civilians gloried in the world turned upside down, former slaveholders detested the revolution and despised black soldiers as symbols of the new state of affairs. They pleaded for the removal of black soldiers from the South, complaining not only of the arrogance or misconduct of the soldiers themselves but also of the social disruption that would certainly follow from the provocative nature of a black military presence. Such appeals, especially when filtered through white unionists, had a powerful influence on federal officials and sped the demobilization of many black units and the relegation of others to distant corners of the South. Where black troops remained in service,

[80] Lincoln, *Collected Works*, vol. 7, p. 243; Berry, *Military Necessity*, chap. 7; McPherson, *Negro's Civil War*, chap. 19.

[81] *Black Military Experience*, docs. 316–17, 319, 321, 324–25, 328, 330B-C; Litwack, *Been in the Storm So Long*, pp. 267–74. The presence of black soldiers had had similarly disruptive effects in Union-occupied parts of the Confederacy during the war, most notably in southern Louisiana. See, for example, *Destruction of Slavery*, docs. 69–70, 72; *Wartime Genesis: Lower South*, docs. 74, 77, 83.

white Southerners did not accept their presence easily, and violence between black soldiers and white civilians became commonplace.[82]

While in the ranks of the Union army, black soldiers had protection enough. But once mustered out of service, much of that protection vanished. Black veterans became fair game for white regulators and terrorists, and, when they eluded such gangs, their families frequently became the victims of violent abuse. In some areas of the South, attacks on black soldiers and their families approached full-scale pogroms.[83]

Such assaults only confirmed the importance of the black military experience. Brutal attacks on black soldiers reemphasized their centrality in breaking the bonds of servitude and paving the way for freedom. The image of long lines of black soldiers marching through the South with slaveholders fleeing at their approach spurred black people – freeborn and former-slave – to seek a fuller freedom and sustained them in the face of continued adversity. Throughout the postwar years, the contributions of black men to Union victory provided a firm basis for claims to equality, and black veterans continued to play a central role in black communities, North and South. The skills and experience black men gained during the war not only propelled many of them into positions of leadership and sustained the prominence of others, but also shaped the expectations and aspirations of all black people. The achievements and pride engendered by military service helped to make a new world of freedom.

---

[82] For white civilians' objections to and attacks on black soldiers in the postwar army of occupation, see *Black Military Experience*, docs. 316–17, 321–22, 324–25, 327–28, 330A-C.

[83] For examples of attacks on and harassment of black veterans and their families, see *Black Military Experience*, docs. 331, 352–61. For an attempt by one group of veterans to form a militia for self-protection, see *Black Military Experience*, doc. 364.

Index

Abolitionists, 9–11, 29–30, 43, 46–47, 95–98, 190, 195, 213–14; as officers in black regiments, 47, 216–17, 231

Adjutant General's Office, U.S. *See* Bureau of Colored Troops; Thomas, Lorenzo

Agricultural labor, 38, 99–100, 161–70; composition of work force, 131, 138, 167, 170; contracts, 166–67; discipline of, 57–58, 141–43, 145–46, 166, 171; evaluations of federal policy on, 147–52; federal policy on, 122–23, 177–78; hours of work, 144, 165; and law of slavery, 63, 162; military policy on, 36, 59–60, 101, 126–29, 138–42, 144–46, 165–66, 171; organization of, 139–41, 169–70; privately negotiated arrangements, 58–59, 67, 72, 108, 161–62, 204; wages of, 138–39, 144–45, 161, 165–67; *see also* Agricultural laborers; Overseers; Planters; Slavery

Agricultural laborers, 99–100, 161–70, 178–81; attacked by Confederate soldiers, 146; attacked by guerrillas, 162; evicted by employers, 161–62, 166; medical care of, 143; mobility of, 142–43; and overseers, 137–38; and planters, 137–46, 166–68; and Union soldiers, 142; women and children as, 131, 167–68; *see also* Agricultural labor; Slaves

Alabama, 13, 93n., 180; agricultural labor in, 162–63; black soldiers, 207; contraband camps in, 160; reenslavement of former slaves in, 48–49; Union occupation of, 35–36, 101–2

Alexandria VA, 180–81; military laborers, 117

American Freedmen's Inquiry Commission, 53, 122, 150, 197

Andrew, John A., 212–13, 215; advocates enlistment of black soldiers, 51, 121, 195–96, 199–200; opposes relocation of former slaves, 114–15

Antietam MD, battle at, 42

Apprenticeship, 174–75

Arkansas: black soldiers in, 130; emancipation in, by state constitution, 69, 173; emancipation politics in, 60; reconstruction politics in, 60, 147; Union occupation of, 34, 129, 101–2; *see also* Helena AR; Mississippi Valley

Arlington VA, contraband camp at, 132–33, 159, 180–81n.

Army, U.S. *See* Black officers; Black soldiers; Conscription; Enlistment of black soldiers; Volunteers, U.S.; War Department; *name of particular officer*

Article of War (1862), 30, 36, 40

Atlanta GA, 69, 157; Union occupation of, 67

Baltimore MD, 62

Banks, Nathaniel P., 147, 150, 195; forces resignation of black officers, 212; policy on agricultural labor, 59–60, 126–27, 141, 145

Baton Rouge LA, 163

Benevolent societies. *See* Freedmen's aid societies; Mutual-aid societies

Benton Barracks MO, contraband camp at, 160

Black officers, 211–14, 225–26; military policy on, 211–14, 225

Black sailors, 206n.; number enlisted, 52

Black soldiers, 136–37, 156–57, 178–81, 189–90; and agricultural laborers, 142; attacked by white civilians, 73, 233; camp life of, 209; in combat, 52, 69, 131, 213, 218, 221–22; diet of, 220; discipline and punishment of, 217; education of, 224; federal policy on, 210–16; and former slaveholders, 232–33; guard contraband camps, 54, 226; health of, 219, 221; as laborers, 130, 218–19; as liberators, 47–48, 51–

235

Index

Index

Officers, black. *See* Black officers
Ohio, enlistment of black soldiers in, 199
Overseers, 137–38, 141

Palmer, John M., 73
Patterson, Robert, slavery policy of, 17
Pea Ridge AR, battle at, 34
Petersburg VA, 69, 158, 222
Phelps, John W.: policy on enlisting black
    soldiers, 195–96; policy on fugitive slaves,
    38; slavery policy of, 36, 38
Philadelphia PA, 99
Philbrick, Edward S., 125–26, 140–41
Phillips, Wendell, criticizes Lincoln's recon-
    struction policy, 153
Pierce, Edward L., 99
Pile, William A., 160
Planters, 126–27, 141–46, 164–68, 171;
    and agricultural laborers, 137–46, 166–
    68; Northern, 140–41, 145, 148–50,
    164; and Union soldiers, 145–46; *see also*
    Slaveholders
Point Lookout MD, contraband camp at, 133
Politics. *See* Emancipation politics; Reconstruc-
    tion politics
Pope, John, 34
Port Hudson LA: battle at, 52, 131, 201,
    221; Union occupation of, 129
Port Royal SC, Union occupation of, 25–26,
    93–94
Pratt, Charles R., 210n.
President, C.S.A. *See* Davis, Jefferson
President, U.S. *See* Lincoln, Abraham
Proclamation of Amnesty and Reconstruction
    (1863), 152–54
Property (personal): military policy on, 109,
    134–35; ownership of, by former slaves,
    133–35, 164; ownership of, by slaves, 68,
    87; seized by Union soldiers, 68, 134–35
Property (real). *See* Land

Quartermaster General's Office. *See* Meigs,
    Montgomery C.

Reconstruction politics, 60, 69–70, 146–47,
    152–54, 229–33; and free labor, 183–86;
    participation of black soldiers in, 230–31;
    participation of former slaves in, 184–86
Refugeeing, 15, 20, 37, 48, 56–57, 74; re-
    sisted by slaves, 56–57, 68
Relief, 131–33; in antebellum North, 84–85;
    military policy on, 45, 94–95, 112, 115–
    17, 131–32, 160; presidential policy on,

123; *see also* Contraband camps; Freedmen's
    aid societies; Mutual-aid societies
Religion, 111, 119
Relocation of former slaves, 45, 114–15,
    127–28, 133, 160, 172–73, 178–79; *see
    also* Colonization; Migration; Mobility;
    Refugeeing
Republican party, 11
Rhode Island, enlistment of black soldiers in,
    199–200
Richmond VA, 69, 158, 222
Roanoke Island NC: contraband camp on,
    132, 159; Union occupation of, 100

Sailors, black. *See* Black sailors
St. Louis MO, 22, 62, 157; contraband camp
    in, 133; relocation of former slaves from,
    127, 173; relocation of former slaves to,
    127, 133
Savannah GA, 68, 175–76; black leaders
    meet with Sherman and Stanton at, 176;
    Union occupation of, 67
Saxton, Rufus, 126, 148, 155, 165, 196;
    criticizes federal land policy, 151–52; pol-
    icy on agricultural labor, 139–40
Scott, Winfield, 21
Sea Islands (*region*). *See* Georgia; South Caro-
    lina
Seddon, James A., policy on impressing
    slaves, 54
Senate, U.S. *See* Congress, U.S.
Seymour, Horatio, 200n.
Sherman, Thomas W., 25–26; policy on mili-
    tary labor, 95; relief policy of, 95
Sherman, William T., 67–69, 175; land pol-
    icy of, 68, 176–77; meets with black lead-
    ers, 176; opposes enlistment of black sol-
    diers, 200; policy on fugitive slaves, 23;
    policy on military labor, 43
Ship Island MS, 36
Slaveholders, 6–7, 9–15; abuse families of
    black soldiers, 65–66, 73, 159, 204, 226;
    evict former slaves, 175; and former slaves,
    71–72; free blacks as, 8; and fugitive
    slaves, 48; oppose enlistment of black sol-
    diers, 48, 64–65, 202, 204; oppose im-
    pressment of slaves, 55–56; pursue fugitive
    slaves, 18, 24; refuse to accept emancipa-
    tion, 71, 73–74, 174; and Union soldiers,
    18–19, 24; unionist, 22, 35–38, 61–64,
    74–75, 92, 101, 202; *see also* Planters;
    Refugeeing; Slavery

241